FIGHT BACK!

FIGHT BACK!

and Don't Get Ripped Off

DAVID HOROWITZ

Published in San Francisco by
HARPER & ROW, PUBLISHERS
New York   Hagerstown   San Francisco   London

FIRST EDITION

Designed by Patricia Girvin Dunbar

Library of Congress Cataloging in Publication Data

Horowitz, David, C. 1937–
    Fight Back! And Don't Get Ripped Off
      1. Consumer protection—United States. I. Title.
HC110.C63H67 1979   381'.3   78–19498
ISBN 0–06–250390–1

---

79 80 81 82 83   10 9 8 7 6 5 4 3 2 1'

To my wife Suzanne
for her love, support
and help.

And to people everywhere
who want to fight back
and not get ripped-off.

With special thanks to Chris Barnett Godchaux
whose collaboration on the research and
writing of this book has been invaluable.

And thanks also to Erik Godchaux, Edda Shurman
Witt, Gloria Drexler, Dora Lippman Horowitz,
Amanda Leigh Horowitz, Victoria Ann Horowitz,
and Phyllis Meadows.

Contents

Introduction

I want to give it to you straight—right off the bat.

This book isn't going to make you an instant millionaire. It won't melt away 30 pounds in two weeks. It won't make you beautiful, witty, charming, or worldly in 30 days or less. In fact, it won't do all of the things that clever advertising and subtle, subliminal salesmanship promise you every day of your life.

What it will do—and this is the sole reason I'm writing this book —is make you feel like the kind of person no one will push around in the marketplace. No longer will you be easy to embarrass, easy to intimidate, easy to bluff, or easy to con when it comes to your money.

I've found during a 20-year career, first as a foreign correspondent, then as a political analyst, educational affairs reporter and, for the last six years, investigative consumer reporter for the National Broadcasting Company, that you need three basic weapons to survive in the marketplace: awareness, information, and guts.

You know it and I know it. The world is changing so damn fast it's almost impossible to keep pace. We're being sold by computers, processed like punch cards and herded through life like sheep.

But if you read this book closely, absorb the advice, and make a firm personal commitment to let it change your life, you'll separate yourself from the herd.

What's more, with this book, you write your own warranty. The facts here are good as long as you live. There are no parts to be fixed, no commissions to pay, and no costly service calls. I've even eliminated the fine print. I wanted this book to be big, bold, and uncomplicated so there could be no misunderstanding. Read it and you'll gain a confidence you'll carry with you the rest of your life.

I've seen it happen in thousands of consumer complaints I've tackled on television. People were ripped off, not because of stupidity; they just were not aware. They swallowed the hype, the salesperson's spiel, the seductive advertisement, or the blatant misrepresentation—without a question. Yet once they see firsthand how you can fight back, even after you have been fleeced, a new sense of pride emerges. Inner resolve springs forth. You've known too long what it feels like to be financially reamed. Now, suddenly, you discover you can protect yourself in almost every transaction.

That's the secret to fighting back. You don't have to be a seasoned financier to survive today. You don't have to be an obnoxious attorney to negotiate. You don't have to be a cunning manipulator to come out on top. And you don't have to be a chronic complainer, a foaming, screaming hysterical human being to make yourself heard.

In a single word, you've got to be *savvy*.

In researching this book I searched my mind and files, confronted corporate decision makers, and drew on the resources of government regulatory and consumer action agencies to give you concrete examples of how to get your money's worth every time. How I do it. How others do it. How you can rise up, reach out, and achieve a sense of self-confidence and personal satisfaction that will change your life.

Now you may be saying to yourself: David, you're psyching me up like a football coach. And you know, you're absolutely right. But it takes far more than will to win. You have to know the game plan, the smartest strategies, how to sidestep the flim-flammers and read their signals when they're about to blitz you.

Starting with Chapter 1, you're going into training; you're going to toughen yourself up mentally and physically so you can fight back in that jam-packed arena of life I call "the marketplace."

Sounds a bit theatrical, but life *is* a drama. For when you're spending your own money—whether it's a dime, a dollar, or ten thousand dollars—you're playing in the financial superbowl every time and you can't afford to lose.

FIGHT BACK!

Frustrations, Anxieties and Turmoil: How Do We Make It Through the Day?

1

Stop and think hard for a minute: How often do you allow yourself to be shoved around on an average day? How many times during your waking hours are you intimidated, bamboozled, and cheated in the marketplace by insensitive people, shoddy service, and faulty products? You probably can't count the number of times.

But you sure know what it *feels* like to be had. You get flushed, irritated, angry, even boiling mad.

Yet what do you do about it? Probably nothing. You just take the abuse over and over again. You let yourself be victimized and you don't even put up a fight.

Those day-to-day petty annoyances and outright rip-offs are really damaging—and not just to your wallet. But to your personal self-esteem. You may not consciously think about it, but when you've been suckered you feel instantly powerless and you tend to punish yourself and the people close to you. You yell or you sulk or you simply don't communicate and you hurt other people— your family, friends, co-workers—the people who are really important to you every day of the year.

1

And here's the real crime: Today you're victimized from the minute you wake up.

The alarm in your new AM-FM digital clock radio failed to go off again and you're an hour late for work. Boy, that makes you mad. But not half as mad as your boss gets. Your job starts at 8 AM sharp; he wants you there and he hates excuses.

You jump into the shower and wash your hair but that new $4-a-tube natural herbal shampoo doesn't lather half as much as that 79¢ balsam you've been using for three years. Hell, it doesn't foam at all like it did on the television commercial that persuaded you to try it. That's four bucks down the drain.

You dry off and plug in your blow dryer. It's 1200 watts but this morning it seems like it's putting out only 50 watts. The hair dryer's been working flawlessly for three months, so wouldn't you know that it conks out on the ninetieth day—just when the guarantee runs out. You want to smash it against the sink.

You reach into your dresser. The elastic band in your underwear has given out after the first washing. Damn it! You look out the door and the newspaper isn't there. Now maybe somebody snatched it this morning or maybe the deliveryperson just forgot your house. It's happened before and it always gives you fits, but you've never taken the time to call up and complain.

You're late for work but starved for breakfast, so you reach in the refrigerator for that new pound of bacon. You can almost smell it frying when you open the package—and retch. There's furry green mold growing over half the slices you couldn't see when you bought it. Your appetite's gone. And you slam the refrigerator door.

You back out of the driveway, step on the brakes, and your car swerves to the left, running over your freshly planted geraniums. You're enraged. The flowers are squashed, sure, but you just spent $184 to reline your brakes and turn your drums. Your brake problems should be over for another 30,000 miles. *Now* what's wrong?

Time is tight but you swing by your dry cleaners. You're still steamed that your clothes weren't ready by five last night after they promised you one-day service. This morning your clothes are ready, but there's a button missing off your jacket and when you complain to the counter clerk, she just jerks her thumb toward a sign over the cash register that reads: "Not responsible for buttons."

Now you're really frustrated. You throw down your money, pay the bill and walk out vowing to yourself that you'll drive ten miles out of your way to find another dry cleaner before you'll give those deadbeats another nickel's worth of business.

You get to work—late—and you stick a quarter in the coffee machine. It gobbles your 25¢ and spits out an empty cup: no coffee. You pound on the machine and the coffee comes out all right—all over your new shoes.

No sooner do you sit down when the telephone rings. Not the boss, thank God. Worse—the television repairman. And he's got some news for you, good and bad. First, the good news: The picture tube wasn't blown after all. It was only a special color rectifier tube. Now the bad news: There's not another color rectifier tube that fits your model in stock in the entire country. He's going to have to order one directly from Japan.

You're flabbergasted, but when he reminds you that you bought a year-old discontinued model just to save $50 you want to kick yourself that much harder. You'll have the part in a month, he says. Of course, you can always pay $55 extra and have it air-freighted from Tokyo in 48 hours. Take your choice—cough up the extra cash and you won't miss a single episode of Laverne and Shirley; otherwise, you've got a dead screen for a month. What a bummer. That damn television's programmed to break. You're convinced of it.

Nearly noon already and you almost forgot your luncheon date. Good thing you reserved a table a couple days ago. But uh-oh. You spent all your money at the cleaners. You better go to the bank first. No problem, you think to yourself; the bank is right around the corner from the restaurant.

You've got an hour for lunch so you get to the bank promptly at noon but, wouldn't you know it! There are only two tellers available to handle ten people in line. That always burns you up. If the bank wants your business why don't they treat you better? Ten minutes go by and you're one step away from the window when the teller waves you over to the next line and announces she's going to lunch.

You're just about to explode when another teller opens up but this wiry little old lady slithers in front of you and dumps out a purseful of rolled coins. The bank, naturally, wants to break open the rolls and count the coins. Another exasperating delay. You want to choke that grandmotherly little old lady.

You get to the window and write out your check, but sorry, the bank's computer is temporarily "down" and there's no way to verify your balance. "Can you step aside for ten minutes?" the teller asks. The computer should be repaired in a jiffy and then they'll be glad to cash your check.

By the time you get to the restaurant, you're in a rotten mood and your stomach's in a knot. You're nervous and uptight watching your lunch hour tick away.

Your luncheon guest is patiently waiting for you in the bar, but despite the fact you had reservations, the hostess says it will be "just a few minutes" before they seat you at a table. You aren't really in the mood for a drink, but then you don't want to stand around in the chairless foyer so you herd yourself in and order a cocktail; your friend orders a lemon lime. The tab comes to $2.50. You feel robbed paying $1.25 for a soft drink, but you only make a meek comment to the waitress who tells you, rather icily, that soft drinks are only 50¢ on the restaurant side. You resent her condescending tone and want to tell her so but you bite your tongue instead.

Your lunch hour is half over before you get a table. The waiter though is prompt with the menus, and while you don't want the second round of drinks he's pushing, you discover you're out of cigarettes and order a pack. He wants the dollar in advance and returns, three minutes later, with the cigarettes and a dime on his change tray. *Ninety cents for cigarettes?* That's stiff, you think to yourself. Then he wants to get his tray back and you leave the dime on it so you don't look cheap. But inside you're burned up that you didn't get your own smokes and save yourself a quarter.

You order spaghetti and fresh clam sauce and your friend orders fresh scallops. A problem. The waiter says the head chef is ill today and he forgot to order clams for the sauce. How about eggplant parmesan?

Sure enough, the eggplant is only fair and you're ticked off that you allowed yourself to order it. And the scallops just don't taste fresh, according to your friend, who had truly fresh scallops in a seafood restaurant several weeks ago. But you swallow your disappointment rather than send it back. After all, you're going to be late getting back from lunch as it is. And you don't have time for them to substitute another dish.

You're gulping down your coffee when you notice the cream tastes funny. You ask the waiter about it, and he confesses it's a non-dairy coffee lightener without an ounce of cream in it. Too late now to complain, you think. You just want to get out as quickly as possible.

Somehow you get the less-than-subtle impression that the waiter can't wait for you to leave either. Since bringing you the check he's been practically circling the table, one eye nervously on the front door searching for new customers. The bill is $15.50 although you know it wasn't worth it, but you clench your teeth and add on a $2.50 tip anyway because you don't have the nerve to leave anything less.

You feel angry and depressed by what should have been an enjoyable, uplifting experience. But you'll get back at them, in your own way. As you quietly confide to your friend, "Don't worry, we'll *never* come back to this place. Never."

All the frustrations and tensions you've endured so far have given you a splitting headache, and even the exotic, heavily advertised painkiller doesn't help. You have this long-standing doctor's appointment this afternoon, so maybe he'll give you something to calm you down. You're not going to the doctor for tension alone, but to get rid of that annoying rash that's been on your leg for three weeks. You thought it would be gone by now—after two earlier office calls, at $25 a visit.

You get to his office, on time, and his waiting room is packed, probably with people who have a later appointment than yours. Wrong. "They're all ahead of you," explains the nurse. The doctor is just running late.

Twenty-five minutes later and patients are stacked up like planes over an airport on a holiday weekend. He's gaining patients and you're losing your patience. You can just feel your own temperature rising. Why in the hell does he book so many for the same time if he has to keep them waiting. You're trying to get up enough nerve to cancel the appointment when the nurse calls your name and ushers you into an examination room. Actually, it's just another waiting room because you're still waiting.

After drumming your fingers on the cold examination table for another 15 minutes, you've just about decided to storm out. Waiting 45 minutes past your scheduled appointment is enough to drive you nuts. Finally he walks in, with not even an apology. He glances at the rash, asks if it still itches, and just as you start to explain that there's been no improvement in two weeks, he scratches out a prescription and dispenses some advice: "Try this three times a day for the next four days—and see me next Tuesday." You look up and he's gone. Houdini couldn't have escaped more quickly. Total examination time: five-and-a-half minutes. Cost: $25.

As if that weren't enough, his nurse took the liberty of calling your prescription into the pharmacy downstairs. Since 20 doctors in the building are phoning in prescriptions, naturally it's crowded, too. But worse than that: its prices are twice as high as the discount drugstore around the corner from your house. Next time you'll speak out before you get screwed over.

Meanwhile, you've got some friends and neighbors coming over for dinner and you haven't done your shopping yet. Originally you were going to whip up a simple casserole, but you really want to impress your guests with rare roast beef.

You pull into the supermarket parking lot and it's choked with cars and stray shopping carts. The store itself is jammed with people. You grab the first shopping cart and the wheels are stuck. The second one is filthy. Finally, you corral a clean cart that rolls straight and you head for the meat department.

There's no rolled sirloin roast in the meat case so you push the service button, only to be told by a butcher that he doesn't have the time to cut one because the other butcher is on his dinner hour. Then, of course, *he* takes *his* dinner break. "Come back in two hours," he says, slamming the glass window.

Naturally you can't come back in two hours so you settle for a triangle tip roast rather than demand that he take care of you—the customer. You wheel off muttering how you'd like to carve him up and might even report him to the store supervisor. But you won't.

Instead, you walk past the potato chip rack and load up on family snack packs even though you know they don't have an ounce of nutritional value in them. You just don't want to look like a cheap host. There are, of course, plenty of crackers and chips at the end of every aisle, but your favorite brand of cream cheese, dinner rolls, and canned fruit salad are all "out of stock." The clerks tell you there is no more in the backroom, although you are secretly convinced they're just too lazy to walk back and look.

To make matters worse, the produce department looks like it's been hit by a drought. The fresh vegetables have been picked over, but since you have to make a salad, you settle for brown-tinged lettuce and overripe tomatoes. You know you're buying leftovers but you don't have the time to race around to other markets.

You fight your way through a tangle of shopping carts, but when you get to the checkstands only four of the ten are operating and each has a long snaking line. You ask a checker to call another clerk and she snaps your head off and tells you all available checkers are busy, on breaks, on their dinner hours.

Naturally, the line you think is moving the fastest turns out to be the slowest and you're silently berating yourself for putting up with this kind of service. It also has the grouchiest checker—she nails you with an incensed look when you ask her to double-check the price of those eggs.

But that is only a minor annoyance. Her mood really sours when you hit her with a fistful of cents-off coupons you've been saving for at least three months. Gotcha, you say in a triumphal moment. But she beats you two out of three when she audits the expiration date and finds that ten of the twelve coupons have expired. That whole eyeball-to-eyeball confrontation nets you a grand 13¢, when you thought for sure you'd finally tap the supermarket for at least $2, maybe more.

Out in the parking lot, as you struggle to put the bags in the trunk of your car, one splits a seam and your groceries spill out on the asphalt, the eggs splattering, the tomatoes rolling just out of reach under the next car. The boxboy has not only forgotten to give you a double bag, he has loaded that single shopping bag to the breaking point. You are absolutely fit to be tied, crawling around on all fours retrieving lettuce and rolling cans.

At home you unload the groceries and collect your mail. At last, your famed Swedish weight-reducing plan with the secret Scandinavian diet has arrived. You thought it was a real bargain at $12.95. But you quickly discover it's nothing more than a booklet of common sense dieting guidelines—tips that are free from any doctor or health food store.

You're so infuriated you tear the booklet into pieces and throw it in the garbage. How could you have been such a patsy? Only then does it dawn on you that the booklet had a full money-back guarantee on the last page.

The mailman also delivered your banana trees. The last seedlings you bought from the mail-order nursery are just now starting to sprout, but they certainly haven't grown ten feet in six months as the advertisement claimed.

The new banana seedlings are as dry as tumbleweeds, hardly worth the $29.95 you sent them six months ago. But what's really maddening is the fact that your next-door neighbor predicted you'd be ripped off by those "magic trees." He's going to be over for dinner tonight—now, what are you going to tell him? Admit that you've been duped?

The frustrations don't end when the sun goes down.

You can forget using your new food processor to help you prepare dinner tonight. It broke down two weeks ago and the only way you can get it fixed is to box it up and mail it back to the manufacturer in Connecticut. The problem is that you threw away the original carton.

And you can't play any records for your guests either. The stereo amplifier is on the fritz. Sometimes you get music, sometimes you get static. Even though it's under warranty, you've got to take the whole system—the amplifier, turntable, and speakers—to the nearest factory-authorized repair station, which is on the other side of town. Stereo stores don't make housecalls and you can forget pickup and delivery service.

Amazingly enough, your dinner is a success. Your guests enjoy themselves and go home early. You've suddenly got a second burst of energy, and since your television is in the shop, why not take in a movie?

You scan the movie ads in the newspaper and then call the number listed at the theater. A busy signal. Keep dialing. Another busy signal. Finally, the phone is automatically answered and you're put on hold awaiting a recorded message. Your happy disposition is starting to turn sour again. This is worse than the damn airline reservations system.

Ten minutes later, a recorded announcement tells you what's playing at what time for Cinemas I, II, and III. All you wanted to know is what time the movie starts in Cinema IV. Finally, it imparts that nugget of information.

When you get to the theater, you discover that the automatic recording fed you wrong information and that you're ten minutes late. Still, you've already paid $1.50 to park and so what if you miss the start of the picture.

For some unfathomable reason you're hungry for some buttered popcorn, so you join the elbowing mob at the snack bar where two frenzied girls are trying to serve a dozen customers who are screaming for attention.

You get your popcorn all right but it's neither freshly popped nor freshly buttered. The assistant manager, before your very eyes, fills the popcorn machine with prepopped corn from a giant plastic bag; the butter warmer is filled from a can marked "butter flavored popcorn oil." Everything's artificial, you mumble to yourself, including the artificially high price: $1.25 for a bucket-sized scoop.

By the time you pay and look for a seat, the theater is mobbed and only the first four rows are empty. It's a sure bet you'll have eyestrain after just one feature. Meanwhile, some youngsters two seats away are jabbering and they refuse to clam up. Why don't the ushers toss them out?

The final straw: The film breaks two minutes before the ending, which is billed on the marquee as the "most sensational finale in motion picture history." Fifteen minutes go by and you're no longer spellbound, as the rave notices promised you would be.

And so it goes. Day after day filled with aggravating nuisances, rip-offs, infuriating encounters that seem to tear your sanity away piece by piece.

But there is simply no reason for you to go through life like a pussycat who's always having his tail stomped on. You've got the power to fight back, and you can do it without howling or clawing someone's eyes out. What's more, you don't have to transform yourself into a predator who will do-unto-others before they do it to you.

By the time you get out of basic training—and that's what I call Chapter 2—you'll be on your way to winning your black belt in consumerism. You'll be quiet, confident, self-assured, and proud. Sure, people will try to cross you and double-cross you. But they will only try it once.

FIGHT BACK!

Basic Training: Toughening Up Mentally and Physically

2

Welcome to basic training. I'm going to show you how to flex your mental muscles, stiffen your spine, and untie your tongue. You'll learn why it's important to sniff out the facts when you're spending money and how to defend yourself when you get screwed. I want you to become a tough-minded, cool-headed customer every time you buy.

Toughening Up

Let's start with your attitude. Right now, this very minute, I want you to make a personal pledge to yourself that you are no longer on anybody's suckers list. From this page forward, you're going to challenge every single person, merchant, company, or institution that tries to shortchange you, overcharge you, cheat you, or who refuses to deliver the value that you paid for.

This is a crucial commitment and you've got to make it. Before I can teach you specific fight-back strategies, you'd better be ready and willing to take the time and spend the energy required to rack up a victory. Sure you'll score some first-round knockouts. But in most of your battles, you'll need the psychological stamina to slash through the red tape, penetrate the bureaucratic briar patch, and cope with other people's ineptness and bumbling—all of which rob you of your dollars and your all-important self-esteem.

That's the key right there: self-esteem. When you allow yourself to be bagged—even for a dime—you lose another little bit of your self-esteem. Admit it. When you tolerate these abuses, you kick yourself, put yourself down, or you simply think you're not as good or as smart as that fast-talking friend of yours who always seems to come out on top in those sticky situations.

But that's a negative attitude. Dwell on defeat and you'll cripple your self-confidence. You've got to think positively, go all the way for the victory, no matter how much time or trouble it takes. Just remember: Everytime you win a showdown with a silver-tongued salesperson or a faceless corporation, you feel great. It's uplifting. Exhilarating. It's like finding money, even though you're only protecting your own cash or your credit rating. I personally cannot think of a better way of building your self-esteem than knowing that you alone stopped someone from bilking you on a purchase. You're elated and you should be.

To win in the marketplace, you must be indignant. I don't want you to get angry; I want you to become righteously indignant. That's civilized, rational anger. Indignation, according to Webster, is anger aroused by something unjust. And I ask you, what's more unjust than being manipulated against your will, cheated, huckstered, or otherwise ripped off?

Here's where you've got to make a conscious effort to help yourself. You've got to *learn* to become indignant, whereas anger is a normal emotion. It's only normal to get angry when you get taken for a financial ride. Instantly, you get hot and perhaps flushed and you can just feel your body temperature rising. I know I do. If you get really angry or enraged, you want to lash out at someone, but chances are you do nothing to vent that anger. You don't really want to risk a ruckus because someone might think you've lost control of yourself, so you punish yourself just by thinking how stupid you were for getting conned in the first place. And you try to strike back at whoever preyed on you by vowing never to do business with them again.

In other words, you throw in the towel. For instance, you drive clear across town to buy a $9.95 pocket calculator on sale and when you get it home, you discover the batteries didn't come with it. You go out and pick up a couple of penlight batteries and the damn calculator adds but it doesn't multiply. So instead of driving half an hour back to the store or mailing the purchase back and asking for a replacement, you take your anger out on yourself. You rationalize that it still adds and since it was on sale you should have known there was something wrong with it and you'll know better next time.

Why hurt yourself like that? Nothing is worse than getting angry and doing nothing about it. That's frustrating, and if you don't blow off the steam, those frustrations just ferment inside of you. So step two in changing your attitude, toughening yourself up, is to get rid of that anger in a positive way. I want you to focus it like a laser beam on whoever took advantage of you and make that vow to get satisfaction, get your money back or your money's worth.

I can't emphasize it enough. Instead of getting angry, get indignant. Rather than burying your wrath in the pit of your stomach and adding to your anxieties, I want you to ask yourself: "Who in the hell are they to try and pull a fast one on me? What right do they have to push me around?" That's righteous indignation. That's healthy anger and that's a powerful weapon on any consumer battlefield.

Sure, I know it's easy for me to tell you to get indignant, but I am also aware that true indignation isn't exactly easy to summon up. What's more, indignation is one emotion you can't fake. If your opponent thinks you're bluffing, he's gotcha. If that garage owner can't tell from the wrath in your eyes, the firmness in your voice that you mean business when you threaten to file a complaint with the attorney general's office over that bad brake job, he'll try to pacify you. Or he might stonewall all the way and tell you to kiss off even if he's wrong. He knows he has the upper hand since most motorists don't know a cotter pin from a carburetor jet.

To achieve righteous indignation, you have to be willing to make a scene, to speak up. But making a scene is also contrary to everything we've been taught all of our lives, and as a result we fear unpleasant situations.

From childhood we've been told over and over to behave, don't act up, don't speak out of turn, mind our manners and "be nice." In our teens and twenties we're continually warned by parents or influenced by social pressures to never complain, to control our emotions, bite our tongue rather than badmouth anyone.

And above all, we've had it drummed into us never to do anything to embarrass ourselves or anyone around us. It's gentlemanly and ladylike, we've been told, to overlook the aggravation and turn the other cheek.

But in today's world, which is becoming more impersonal, more automated, you can't go through life hoping not to offend anyone. You shouldn't submerge your feelings day in and day out, trying to win the approval of your friends, strangers, and anyone you come in contact with. You'll become too meek, too wishy-washy, and you'll find it almost impossible to speak out. You're setting yourself up.

For each day, in a dozen ways, we're beset by a raft of rip-off experts, corporate con artists, and plenty of honest people who simply make human errors *in their favor.* And when you sit still for it, you're only playing into their hands. I'm firmly convinced that all the childhood training we've had that taught us, in essence, to avoid embarrassing situations, shrug them off, or forget them is the reason so many of us go through life with our anxieties bottled up inside. Promise yourself now that you're going to stand up and speak out.

Becoming Aware

Hardening yourself psychologically is only one part of basic training. You need the personal armor, but it's just as important for you to become an informed and shrewd consumer. Whether you're buying a $10 electric hamburger broiler or a $10,000 automobile, you have to read labels, warranties, and every word in the fine print.

Shopping hard for automobile loans, for instance, can save you money. Most auto dealers have arrangements with a bank or consumer credit company that allow you to finance that car once you sign on the dotted line. But if you take the time and investigate credit unions or perhaps search out a bank that's hungry to make automobile loans, you might save 2 to 3 percent on the interest rate. And that can be a bundle of bucks considering the soaring prices of automobiles and the longer payoff periods most lenders are promoting.

On the other hand, if you don't shop around, compare prices, check out the companies, merchants, financial institutions, and professional people *before* they latch on to your money, you could be ripped off in a variety of ways—and it's your own fault.

Worse yet, if you fail to do your homework and then get suckered, it's pretty hard to muster up that righteous indignation that gives you the incentive to fight back. For instance, if you fall for the same mail-order scheme that has already burned thousands of people across the country you're just another hapless victim. Nobody is going to gallop to your defense.

Here's the bottom line. It takes a little brainpower and a lot of energy to be an intelligent, aware, informed consumer. Most people just don't want to invest the time and research before they buy. Although you would never think of letting your paycheck ride on the pass line at Las Vegas, how many times do you gamble with your cash and hope that "everything turns out all right"? You hope the new power lawn mower will last a lifetime although you never bothered to check it out in *Consumer Reports*. You hope the plumber installed your new bathroom sink correctly, yet you found him in the Yellow Pages and never asked for references. You hope that painful tooth of yours really needs to be pulled instead of just filled.

I have found that too often people just want to "buy it and get it over with." They rely on luck or a salesperson's spiel or a doctor's judgment instead of knowledge, common sense, and some healthy skepticism.

Is it any wonder that ill-informed consumers get ripped off the worst? They are helpless prey for swindlers who can spot a pigeon a mile off. And these same people are often the victims of an honest mistake made by a confused or untrained clerk. Many never even spot the error that was made.

Speedy spenders do themselves in. One woman wrote to me complaining that a savings bank had "stolen" her interest from a two-year certificate of deposit that she cashed in after 18 months —it turned out she had overlooked the fine print in the advertisement warning of a "substantial penalty for early withdrawal."

Getting smart is just as important as fighting back. If you don't arm yourself with information before you walk into the consumer arena, regardless of what you buy, you're really diving headfirst into a shallow tank of hungry sharks. So beware.

Actually, though, we've all been ripped off—by our educational system! Students are required to take biology, American history, U.S. government, and other basic liberal arts courses that are designed to prepare them for the world. But nowhere are students taught how to get a black mark erased from a credit rating when an oil company's computer mistakenly reports them as a slow pay. Most people today were never taught how to spot and shun the slick, subliminal sales tactics practiced by those wizards of mind manipulation, the Madison Avenue crowd.

That's right. American education has let us down when it comes to turning out smart consumers. There's nothing wrong with being able to quote the English poet John Milton. But you should also know the names of the local, state, and federal agencies you can turn to when your stereo breaks and neither the retailer nor the manufacturer will fix it to your satisfaction.

You're the Vital Link

That means it's up to you. As a consumer you've got to start taking charge and stop asking to be victimized. Just because we've been shortchanged in the schoolroom is no reason for us to march in lockstep through the marketplace like an army of ants, allowing ourselves to be trampled.

Fortunately, I was trained for marketplace combat at a young age by my mother Dora, whom I call Captain Consumer. She always has been the ultimate consumer. Still is. She's an inspiring person because she has the three crucial traits of a smart consumer: awareness, common sense, and the guts to speak out.

My family and I lived in a tiny, one-bedroom apartment in a melting pot New York City neighborhood where people had more street smarts than dollars. There was my mother, father, two sisters, and a brother. We had the supreme motive for trying to make every penny a dime and stretching that dime into a dollar. It's called survival.

It was a way of life for my mother to question everything, to look for the best price, the best quality. She did her homework and she never let herself get talked into anything she didn't want to buy. She spoke up and she never wasted words. She would have made a great bootcamp drill instructor.

My mother was the typical Jewish mother stereotype. She carried me around like I was her most prized possession, so I was exposed to the way she shopped—haggling in the markets, reading the labels. If there was anything on a label she didn't understand, she didn't buy it.

I can still remember one of my first lessons in consumerism. I was about 6 or 7, and I'm recounting it here only because I believe it crystallizes the essence of my philosophy: Be a smart consumer and don't be afraid to fight back when you get ripped off.

My mother had taken me to a produce stand to buy some fresh fruit. The produce man was offering a two-for-a-nickel special on oranges, which normally sold for 3¢ apiece.

"Why," my mother asked, "are the oranges two for five cents?" She had a knack for opening a conversation with the deceptively naive question.

"Because," the produce man explained, "you buy two oranges and you get a discount. You get one orange for 3¢ and one for 2¢." Like a bad chess player he had already lost the game with a weak opening move.

"What's the difference between the orange that costs 2¢ and the one that costs 3¢?" she wanted to know.

"There's no difference," he admitted. "They're the same."

"Then why should I pay 3¢ for one and 2¢ for another?" my mother asked.

"Because you're buying two and if you buy two oranges, you get a penny off."

"But that isn't a fair discount," she insisted.

"Then maybe I shouldn't sell them to you—two for a nickel," he said, more than a little disgusted by now. But my mother could smell victory.

"Why don't you sell them for 2¢ apiece, and then you're giving a real discount," she said.

"Lady, how many oranges do you want?" he finally asked.

"I'll take the one for 2¢," she said firmly. And he sold it to her.

The story doesn't end there. Despite the fact that my mother poked and squeezed and studied that orange she bought for 2¢, when she sliced it open at home, it was dried out; it had probably been sitting in a warehouse somewhere. In a flash, she scooped me up and marched right back to that produce stand, indignant that she had been tricked. While the owner quickly gave her another orange, she waved a pointed finger under his nose and threatened to turn him in to the Health Department for selling old fruit and promoting it as fresh. She never again got anything less than the freshest fruits and vegetables from that produce man. Believe me, he personally saw to it that my mother went away happy.

3The most important lesson of all didn't dawn on me until years later: Whenever she shopped, no matter what she was buying, my mother never, ever had a moment's doubt that she was an important consumer entitled to the best for the money, no matter how little money she had to spend.

I've never forgotten that and neither should you. This is a vital part of your basic training. You, the consumer, are the most important link in the economic chain. Without you the manufacturers, packagers, shippers, wholesalers, and retailers might as well close their doors. Without you spending your money, the entire economy would collapse. And if you don't think you're important, consider this: In 1978, just 100 of America's leading companies spent nearly $9 billion in advertising to convince you, the consumer, to buy everything from soap powder to sailboats, curling irons to Hawaiian vacations.

What Do I Do?

I know you're saying to yourself: "What difference do I make? I'm only a single voice, a lone consumer, and if I'm cheated, who cares besides me? American business doesn't need me when there are millions of other Americans out there who are ready, willing, and financially able to buy what they make."

But that's precisely the point. Today, more than ever before, you can make a difference, your voice can be heard. Just ask the coffee producers who felt the full force of an American boycott not long ago. They lowered their prices. Just ask the sugar growers who tried to stick it to the American public when a drought wiped out their crops one year.

A boycott is a powerful form of retaliation, but it takes a nation-wide ground swell of indignation to make it effective. As an individual, though, there are still plenty of ways for you to take action when you feel you've been legitimately wronged and no one is willing to remedy the problem for you.

One is to have tenacity. A woman in her late fifties bought a disability income policy from a reputable insurer and injured her leg a year later, which kept her from work. When she went to file her claim, she discovered her insurance agent was now selling cars. So she filed the claim direct. A month went by. No benefit check. She called the claims department and got the runaround —no one could find her file, the claims manager was on vacation.

But this woman fought back. She checked with her state insurance department, found out the name of the insurance company's president and called him person to person. If she didn't reach him it wouldn't cost her a dime. She pushed her way past the secretary by telling her it was a "personal matter" and told her story to Mr. Big himself. Of course, she mentioned that she had spoken with the state insurance department.

The president listened. He knew the value of customer goodwill, and he didn't want to see some lower echelon snafu or human error cause a problem for a policyholder. A half hour later a vice-president called, apologetically, and three days after that a check was in her hand. You may not always be able to get to the president of the company, but it's still worth the try. That's action and this normally placid senior citizen fought back and felt triumphant about it.

Hopefully, by now, you should be making some real progress. You've made a personal commitment that you're not going to allow yourself to be bullied and robbed any longer by consumer bandits. You are willing to stand up for your rights *when you are right*, despite what anyone says and no matter how much of a scene you have to make.

Never again will you be embarrassed to send back that veal dish because it didn't measure up to the delicious description you read on the menu. And you are not going to let that glaring waiter intimidate you and ruin a meal that you will have to pay for.

That's right, you are amassing some real power. But remember that responsible consumerism is a two-way street. You must be as fair as you would want the merchant to be. What you are defending are your rights. You're not looking for revenge. Too often, customers vent their anger and frustration by ripping off the businesses they patronize. They figure a successful corporation can afford it, so why not take advantage?

Let me tell you something: The capitalistic free enterprise system doesn't work that way. Businesspeople aren't patsies either, and I can assure you that every time they're ripped off by dishonest customers, they pass that loss along to you, their honest customers. You pay for it in increased prices, skimpier service. Whenever you think you've gotten something for nothing the truth is you haven't received the bill yet.

Okay, we're about to get down to the real nitty-gritty. Who precisely is screwing you and what specifically can you do about it? You've survived basic training and you're about to go out and do battle. But are you really up for the fight? Ask yourself, do you really think it's worth all the trouble and bother? Aren't we only talking about a few pennies here and there? If you feel that way, fine. Then you deserve what you get.

If you're not willing to concern yourself with the pennies, nickels, and dimes that add up to dollars, you're begging to be nailed to the wall. If that happens, don't scream to the consumer protection agencies because you are the one that allowed it to happen.

But if you don't think it's cheap and demeaning to lock horns over the smallest rip-off, and if you are a person of principle, then it's time to move on to Chapter 3.

The enemy is out there just lying in wait for you.

FIGHT BACK!

Rip-Off Artists: How to Spot Them and Stop Them

3

You wouldn't walk down a dark street in a bad part of town or through a deserted park at three in the morning. But you might go into a grimy garage and let a total stranger look at your new automobile that "isn't running right."

You wouldn't pick up an unshaven, grubby hitchhiker on a lonely road. But you'd let a door-to-door photographer come into your house to take a portrait of your six-month-old daughter because he promised you a free 5-×-7 print.

You wouldn't buy a $600 color television set from someone selling out of his automobile trunk. But you might let a fast-talking stereo salesperson load you up with $1800 in components when you just wanted to *look* for a new turntable.

Throughout life we've been trained to beware of dangerous situations where we can get physically ripped off—robbed, mugged, or worse. But how do you identify that person, store, manufacturer, or government institution that's ready and willing to assault you? It's plenty tough, but in this chapter you're going to learn how to spot the con artists before they spot you.

Skepticism Will Get You Everywhere

For openers, you have to be skeptical today of almost everyone and everything. Unfortunately, an excellent reputation fostered by years of dedicated service and millions of dollars in advertising doesn't mean that a company has your best interest in mind. In the business world, sales and profits are *uppermost* in a corporate chieftain's mind; the customer is second. Although most companies want to keep their customers happy and spending money, if they can, at the same time, cut a corner or two and save bucks, most will do it.

Even General Motors, world's largest automobile maker, was caught cutting corners rather blatantly in 1977. GM, which trumpets its "mark of excellence" in all its advertising, was installing Chevrolet engines in Oldsmobiles, Pontiacs, and some Buicks without telling the buyers about the little switcheroo.

Joe Siwek of Chicago took his automobile in for a checkup, discovered he had a "Chevymobile," with a 350-cubic-inch V-8 made by the Chevrolet Motor Car Division under his hood, and Joe fought back. He went to the Illinois Attorney General who, along with attorneys general of 46 other states, sued the automaker. The actual dispute was over misleading advertising; Oldsmobile's ads and commercials promised a "Rocket 8" powerplant. General Motors, which never denied the charges, argued that substituting compatible parts was a common cost-cutting tactic in the automobile business. This is true, but the company failed to publicly announce the mid-year substitution. It finally agreed to rebate $200 per automobile to more than 100,000 buyers nationwide.

Now this doesn't mean that General Motors is a corporate charlatan. On the contrary, it has built outstanding automobiles for eight decades and generally offers reliable, professional maintenance service nationwide. It's just that someone within that giant worldwide industrial concern probably said to themselves, "Hey, why build so many different engines when we can standardize some models and save a bundle."

The same thing happens every day on Main Street U.S.A. Erik Cutler of Marina del Rey, California, a busy young businessman in his mid-thirties, had this habit of dashing into the dry cleaner's, dropping off his dirty laundry, scooping up his clean clothes, and sprinting off to work. He never took the time to check his bill. He just paid it and ran. One day he took a minute, added up the bill, and discovered he was overcharged $1.25. A mistake, said the owner and blamed it on the countergirl. Next time Cutler double-checked again and found he was about to be stung for $1.70. Another mistake, insisted the owner, who mumbled how difficult it is to "get good help." Four days later, on a Saturday, Cutler was again almost overcharged, this time for $2.10.

The woman behind the counter—not the owner—freely confessed that the dry cleaner had two sets of prices, one for regular service, another for pickup-and-delivery service. Neither set of prices was posted. The clerk admitted that since most people never check over their laundry bill, the owner had instructed all counter clerks to charge the higher prices "once in a while." If the customer was sharp enough to catch it and complain, fine, they could always subtract the overcharge. If the customer never wised up, the owner pocketed the couple of extra bucks.

Do you see my point? We're a nation of sheep. We've become too trustful. We never question anyone we do business with. It's fine to be on friendly terms with your neighborhood butcher, dry cleaner, or shoe repairman, or to put your faith in nationally advertised brand-name merchandise. But you can't let people take advantage of your customer loyalty. Don't be lulled into thinking that just because you see your corner gas station dealer once a month at the Chamber of Commerce meeting he won't tell you your six-month-old shock absorbers have to be replaced. How do you know he isn't being pressured by his oil company to "move more TBAs" (tires, batteries, and accessories). Dealers get pressured like that all the time.

Now remember, I am not making a sweeping indictment of every merchant, manuf turer, or businessperson you spend money with. Today's ma tplace is not the crocodile swamp it once was. But neither is it free of scamsters and con people. It's up to you to defend yourself.

In ferreting out the potential rip-off, think of yourself as a pioneer, an American settler. Now this may sound a little melodramatic, but the pioneers were constantly on guard against attack from highwaymen, rustlers, and other bandits and hostile forces. They were rugged, self-reliant people who protected home and family when they were challenged. They studied a situation closely and carefully before they spent their money. They were traders and bargain hunters who stood their ground to survive.

Now I want you to keep that image in your mind everytime you spend your money.

A Little Knowledge Goes a Long Way

Okay, so how do you nail those hucksters of shoddy service and defective products before they nail you? For starters, I want you to open your eyes, your ears, and your mouth. If your television suddenly goes black right in the middle of your favorite show, you want to get it fixed fast; so you usually pick up the telephone and call a repairman. Research shows most people don't have a television repairperson like they have a dentist or a family doctor. And most television stores farm out the repair contracts. So, people end up taking a blind flyer in the Yellow Pages.

A lot of people think any company or service advertising in the Yellow Pages is guaranteed to be legitimate by the telephone company that publishes the phone book. Well folks, that's just not true. While all member companies of the Bell System and most independent phone companies have various standards and practices that a Yellow Pages advertiser must meet, they do not investigate the company placing the ad. It's just too big a job.

Once again it's buyer beware! And beware is just the right word. For example, in the past consumer groups in certain areas have found that some doctors who were listed in the "Physicians and Surgeons" segment of the Yellow Pages didn't even have licenses to practice medicine in that location. That's really scary for people who look up a doctor in the Yellow Pages rather than checking with their county medical association for a referral. And is the contractor who advertises that he can add a room to your house licensed by the state? You've got to check him out yourself because the phone company did not.

Now I'm not saying that phone companies have fallen down on the job. If they find an advertiser who misrepresents his company or service, or makes false claims in a Yellow Page advertisement, they will ban him from future directories. And if the telephone company receives a complaint, it'll act fast and conduct a thorough investigation.

But it's up to you to complain. Any company that fails to live up to claims it makes in the Yellow Pages should be reported to the telephone company of the area in which the directory is published. Any company that overtly rips you off after you responded to an ad in the Yellow Pages should also be reported.

Yellow Pages are a convenient and helpful American institution, but advertisers do not carry a seal of approval. We consumers cannot take them for granted.

Instead of crapshooting with your money, take ten minutes and call a few friends and neighbors. Ask them who repairs their television. Have they had good experience with that repairman? Is he prompt? Does he give an estimate first and does the bill match that estimate? Try and get a consensus *before* you call in the repairman. So you miss the movie of the week. The time you spend may save you money.

If none of your neighbors can recommend an honest repairman, call one, but ask for references first. If he hesitates to give you the name of satisfied customers, forget him. An honest, reliable repairman knows that good word-of-mouth wins a lifetime of customer referrals. Be persistent and keep calling. Don't forget, the time you spend is an investment because if you strike up a solid relationship with a reputable repairman today, you won't have to go looking for one the next time you blow a tube.

You are going out to buy a used car. You don't want to spend a fortune but you don't want a clunker that falls apart every week. There are two ways to buy: from a private party or from a used car dealer. Both are fraught with dangers, but if you're willing to ask tough questions, you can avoid the rip-off.

Here's the way I'd buy a used car. Find one that fits your budget and check out its "references." That's right. You wouldn't hire a stranger off the street to manage your company or guard your cash without finding out his background—calling former employers, credit references. So why go in and buy some expensive item blind?

If the car of your dreams is sitting on the lot, ask the salesperson for the name and phone number of the former owner. He doesn't have to give it to you, but you can make it clear you aren't about to be seduced by the gleaming wax job or the spotless interiors sprayed with that aerosol "new car smell." You want to check out the new car's "roots."

If he balks and the registration isn't in the glove compartment, copy down the license plate number and check with the local office of the department of motor vehicles. For a small fee most states will give you the name and address of the registered owner. Look up his or her phone number or drop them a note and arrange for a brief but serious consumer-to-consumer discussion about the "health history" of the automobile they're now rid of. Try to find out the name of the mechanic or service station dealer who worked on the car for them.

Finally, have a mechanic that *you* trust inspect the car and check it out or take it to one of the AAA approved diagnostic/repair centers. Its worth the small fee. If the car salesperson refuses to let you do it, walk off the lot. You can suspect that's a lemon rotting away right before your eyes. If that commission salesperson knows the car is in tip-top mechanical shape and you looked like a serious buyer, he shouldn't hesitate to cooperate. Overall, your investigation might take two hours but that sleuthing could save you months of grief and hundreds or even thousands of dollars.

Once you get in the habit of playing detective, instead of being played for a sucker, I guarantee you'll enjoy taking the time to shop, question, sniff out the phonies, flakes, and parasites that feed on consumer ignorance.

For example, your doctor has given you a prescription for some allergy pills. Normally, you just drop it off at the pharmacist, who fills it and charges you what always seems to be an exorbitant price. Well, that has to stop.

Today, a pharmacist will give you prices over the phone on the most frequently prescribed drugs. Call him before you climb into your car. More pharmacies are also posting prices. Or simply go in and ask the pharmacist if there isn't a generic drug which can be substituted. That means that the drug has the identical chemical structure, but costs less. Currently 41 states have laws that allow this type of substitution to be made by the pharmacist. You should also check to see how much you'll save if you buy in larger quantities.

Shopping shrewdly by phone for prescription drugs instead of automatically trudging off to have the prescription filled can save you hard cash. And don't be afraid to quiz your pharmacist; he's becoming more consumer-minded, but his prices still vary and widely at that. An undercover reporter for the *Los Angeles Herald Examiner* once shopped over 75 drug stores and pharmacies for a list of 12 prescription drugs that should have been selling for approximately the same price. Amazingly though, the most expensive pharmacy charged $55 more than the cheapest drugstore, and for the exact same items.

Anytime you beat a price scalper, you're doing more than saving money. You're retraining your shopping habits. You don't just smarten up and save on that single purchase. For the rest of your life you'll ask those probing questions and you won't feel intimidated. Figure out the money you'll save on prescriptions alone and you'll be surprised. Remember, you can't afford to be a pawn in someone else's get-rich-quick game plan.

When you go to a restaurant, you don't have to eat the meal to know whether you're going to have a great dining experience or be shoved through the meat grinder. Just look for the red flags. Are you ushered into the cocktail lounge for a couple of drinks before you're shown to your table? Are the waiters and waitresses mechanical robots or are they smiling and friendly-faced? Can you cut that steak, roast beef, or sliced chicken with a fork? If so, it's probably restructured meat, the cheapo vittles favored by fast food and chain restaurants which are obsessed with bottom line profits and portion control.

Just because you can cut the steak with your fork is no guarantee it's restructured. But if it "flakes," that's a dead giveaway. It's an inexpensive cut of meat so tough it can't be broiled. Instead, it's flaked and hydraulically pressed together into something resembling a steak.

Restructured roast beef combines beef chunks, fats, and vegetable protein in a mixture that is stuffed into a sausage casing and then transformed into a solid piece of meat. Veal, turkey, and chicken can be "manufactured" the same way. That's OK as long as the menu indicates it in some way. But if it doesn't and if you have any qualms about the meat you've been served, send it back to the kitchen and ask for the real thing. Get up and leave if they complain. Why pay for something you're not getting? Once again, you spotted the fraud before you spent your money.

And you know something—you can investigate every other financial transaction you make the same way.

There's an enticing mail-order advertisement in your local newspaper offering strawberry plants that bear fruit almost instantly, and you love strawberries. In fact, you'd love to have a garden full of strawberry plants. But it sounds too good to be true. Since none of your friends has ever ordered the plants or heard of the company, you check it out with the Mailorder Association of Nurserymen, Inc. in Medford, Oregon. This is a trade group that wants to weed out anybody who doesn't fulfill orders or deliver what the advertisements so rapturously promise.

If you can't dig up the trade association, you can contact the Direct Mail Marketing Association in New York City. The DMMA represents most reputable mail-order concerns and can give you a reading on the integrity of the company offering strawberry plants. If all else fails, contact your local postal inspector to see if there are complaint letters on file. By the way, some states, such as California, have laws forbidding the importation of certain plants and fruits. Check with your state Department of Agriculture before you order, although reputable nurseries will tell about such exclusions in their advertising.

Essentially what you're doing is taking yourself off the mail-order sucker list by investigating before you spend. You're buying "insurance" free. You're ensuring against the hazard of losing your money or getting stuck with a misrepresented product. And your fears are well founded. The Post Office Department is awash with complaints from people who have ordered "dormant" tree seedlings that show up dead in the mailbox.

So consider this every time you feel like responding to a mail-order offer, no matter how legitimate or tempting it sounds: Would you mail money to a total stranger, even five bucks, if you had no idea what you were getting for it or even whether you'd get anything at all? Of course, you wouldn't.

Not all mail-order offers are frauds. Shopping by mail is a respected reliable way to market products. And there are hundreds of nationwide, impeccably credentialed mail-order companies that stand behind their offers with money-back guarantees. But even the biggest catalog companies goof and inadvertently slip it to you—like sending the fireplace heat distributor, shown assembled in the catalog, in 30 pieces.

However, in recent years it seems that an army of swindlers have taken to the mails. The get-rich-quick chain letters are among the biggest rip-offs. They promise fabulous riches and a lifetime of good luck to anybody who sends cash, savings bonds, or money orders to the name at the top of the letter and who then mails the letter to a specified number of their friends. The catch, of course, is that the names at the top turn out to be the perpetrators of the scheme—they take the money and run. Chain letters are illegal under both federal and state laws and the only person who really makes money on the chain letters is the person who dreams it up and his partner; they usually work in pairs.

Crooks

The most frustrating mail-order problems are those where there is out and out fraud. Some crook puts an ad in the newspaper or magazine and advertises a wonderful bargain—not so cheap that you know it's too good to be true, but far below current market value. He opens a bank account under a false name, rakes in the money, deposits it, withdraws it and runs. The bunco squads are kept busy with these scams, but by the time they get enough complaints, the con artist is gone and has picked up a new name elsewhere. Even when they catch these people, they usually find

the money has been spent and there isn't any restitution for the
victims. Two such schemes were the sales of "Tiffany-style" lamps
for $29.95 (there was a picture in the ad, but the lamps never
existed), and the nationwide sale of Christmas LED watches in
1977. You're better off to stick with the well-known national mail-
order firms. They can go bankrupt too (such as Dunhill Collection
did a few years ago) but your odds are still better.

Mail-order health insurance can be a waste of money if you don't
know what you're buying. Although often the insurance underwriters are legit, licensed by state insurance departments, their
lawyers and clever advertising copywriters have teamed up to
create alluring headlines but incomprehensible body copy. I know
of hundreds of people who've clipped their coupons and sent in
their premiums only to discover when they're sick and in the
hospital that they're not covered. They didn't bother to read the
fine print. For example, all health insurance policies have an elimination period—you've got to be sick for a specified number of days
before they start paying. But it makes a big difference to your
pocketbook whether that period is 7 days or 30 days! Also if you've
been treated in the past for a certain condition, that's known as
a "pre-existing illness." Some policies will pay off for treatment of
these conditions after only 6 months, but some make you wait up
to two years before you can collect anything, and some policies
have a "coordination of benefits" clause and only pay off after the
policyholder's other health insurance benefits have been paid.
Thanks to some clever weasel wording and our natural aversion
to fine print, people wind up buying supplemental or extra health
insurance when what they really wanted was immediate protection for their hospital and doctor costs.

Sometimes you answer an ad and an agent comes to visit you—
or you get on a mailing list. An FTC commissioner testified recently before a congressional committee about the abuses of
agents selling supplementary coverage to senior citizens. They are
told that the policies will cover everything Medicare doesn't pay,
but this is often a vicious lie. The victims are persuaded to cancel
their old coverage and buy a new policy. Then, when they do get
sick, they find that they aren't covered because they haven't yet
met the exclusions and waiting periods which had already been

fulfilled under their old coverage. An 84-year-old woman was sold 23 health and accident policies over a two year period—to the tune of $15,000. The FTC says that there are so many of these policies offered that there is almost no way to make a comparison of benefits and premiums. Hopefully, there will be some protective legislation soon. Meanwhile, be super-cautious about cancelling what you have for something that you don't completely understand. Take a copy of the policy and study every word of it before you buy. And you might want to especially look for the policies that are written in "plain language." A number of insurance companies have stopped using legalese and it's a big step forward.

Before you send in a premium, take that direct-mail offer to a reputable insurance agent and have him explain the terms and limitations of the coverage. It's possible he's going to try and sell you *his* policy so be ready for his spiel. But if he can prove he can offer you better coverage for less money you may want to buy it. Or if you want another objective appraisal of the policy, take it to the credit manager or business office of your nearby hospital. Someone there will give you a straight explanation of the benefits and limitations. Also the FTC has a superb booklet on the subject of mail-order insurance available for 15¢ from the Government Printing Office in Washington, D.C.

The cruelest mail-order scams of all, though, are those that prey on our own sense of greed. Anytime you're offered "valuable government land dirt cheap"—beware. There's no bargain in government land or these promoters would be gobbling it up themselves. What they're selling you is remote acreage at market value prices. Before you bite, check out those peddlers with the Federal Bureau of Land Management, the Department of the Interior, and the real estate licensing boards in your state.

At least the government land schemes are selling something tangible. What about those self-proclaimed "millionaires" who want to give you their secrets on how you too can become a millionaire? The spiel is truly inspirational. They were once down-and-outers, teetering on bankruptcy. One day they made this "great discovery" that brought them fabulous wealth, a luxurious home, and beautiful cars, and they want to share it with you. Their "secret" is they made a fortune suckering in people who paid

$9.95 for what turned out to be a mimeographed pamphlet of common sense investment tips or complicated financial schemes. Meanwhile, when these con men are indicted for fraud, investigators often find them broke and in debt; they can't even manage the money they bilked out of their would-be disciples.

That $9.95 is nickel-and-dime stuff compared to what some promoters are going for. Recently the government has been cracking down on some "free" investment seminars where you supposedly learn how to make big money by investing in second mortgages. The rip-off comes at the end of the first free evening. If you want to continue with the full "course" you have to pay—often hundreds or thousands of dollars. What's more, government investigators claim the "inside information" they teach you can usually be found in real estate books available at any library.

Of all the rip-offs, though, these mail-order hypes are the easiest to spot. Anytime someone says they want to give you something for nothing, a loud fire alarm should go off in your head. In life in general, and in mail order in particular, nothing is free. Nothing. And whenever you think you just got something for nothing, remember this: You just haven't been billed for it yet.

Don't think those money-back guarantees are any protection on a risky offer. Time and time again I've found the guarantee in an advertisement is worthless when it comes to getting your loot back. Those kinds of promises are easily and often broken. But I'll take a closer look at that in Chapter 9.

Common Sense Can't Hurt

Let's face it, you can't check out every single purchase you make before you buy. You have to rely on your "secret weapon": common sense. Common sense tells you the automobile you're buying from that private party might be ready for the scrap heap because the current owner has a lawn full of weeds, a backyard full of trash, and grease stains all over his driveway. So you've fallen in love with his car—doesn't he look like the type who would probably drive his car into the ground and then pray that it holds together until he can pawn it off on some unsuspecting fish?

Common sense. You've got it. Use it. Does the auto mechanic keep his garage relatively clean and swept up? Is there pride on his face when he talks with you about his work or does he simply reel off the repairs required and the approximate cost? Your common sense will tell you if he sounds like he wants you as a customer or whether he sees you as a mechanically helpless soul and your money in his cash register.

The same holds true for doctors and dentists. If you know nothing about a specialist other than the fact that your family physician referred you to him, and you have no way of investigating, look for clues in his office. Is his nurse happy or harried? Is the waiting room jammed with grumbling patients who've been waiting a half-hour past their appointment? Are the other nurses scurrying or scrambling while the doctor barks instructions?

In short, if that doctor's office looks like a scene out of *M.A.S.H.,* get up and walk out. You know that his mind is on more than his patients' ailments. Too many doctors today are worrying about the outrageous cost of their medical malpractice insurance, the cattle breeding scheme their investment adviser got them into, or the "age" of their accounts receivable, or they have a dozen other anxieties that distract their minds while they're treating you. Maybe I'm old-fashioned, but I prefer the one nurse-one doctor office where you know he or she is not trying to build a financial dynasty at your expense and where the doctor takes the time to show a personal interest in your health problems.

I can't emphasize enough just how much you can do to save your own financial hide before you spend your money. Take, for instance, that package tour to Hawaii. The brochure is a rhapsody of adjectives describing the trip: "the breathtaking Hawaiian sunsets you will experience, the tropical lushness of Diamond Head and its spectacular view of Waikiki." But buried deep in the fine print, so small it's hardly readable, is a clause that says if a certain number of seats are not sold, the tour will be cancelled. Even if you get your money back, you may be forced to buy a full fare plane ticket since you've already made all your plans contingent on the dates of that tour.

There's nothing illegal about this; the charter operator spelled it out in black and white although it wasn't exactly in bold print.

The brochure also may promise a specific hotel "or equivalent." I can assure you that maybe three out of ten people spot all the fine print limitations but even they go ahead and send their money in, and if the trip doesn't get off the ground, they'll be the first to scream rip-off.

If you're going to Europe or South America, don't expect a "first class hotel" to be anything like a Hilton in this country. The travel agent's brochure will be perfectly legal and you won't be entitled to a refund if the foreign country has classified the hotel "first class," but you can end up staying in a dilapidated place in a poor location. The hotel may qualify because it has a dining room or restaurant, phones and bathrooms in the rooms and a concierge's desk—all of these things are counted in the government ratings. If you know this in advance, you won't howl after you've checked in. There are other "deluxe" and "luxury" categories of hotels which can usually be depended upon to be luxurious, but they are rarely included in package tours.

Anytime you sign anything or buy anything, read and reread the fine print until you understand it. That includes contracts, guarantees, warranties, labels, or any agreement. And if you don't *really* comprehend it, go to someone for a translation. Hopefully, the day will come when consumers will never have to walk barefoot through the briar patch of thorny legalese every time they spend their money.

Meanwhile, in the next chapter, I'll introduce you to some of the people and organizations who are ready and willing to join forces with you, to be your ally in every one of your consumer disputes. They'll stand beside you and punch it out. They're tough, powerful, and wired in at the highest possible levels. You're going to meet them and learn how to use them.

FIGHT BACK!

You're Not Alone: Whom Can You Trust? 4

If you get ripped off, remember this: You're not out there alone and defenseless. You've got important friends in powerful places. You have more muscle and brainpower at your fingertips than you can possibly use. There's a virtual army of tough, action-minded people, organizations, and governmental agencies just waiting for you to sound the alarm.

They're ready to come to your rescue. From hard-nosed organized housewives to smart government attorneys, top executives to dedicated civil servants, helpful consumer lawyers to sworn law enforcement officers. They'll advise, intercede, negotiate, pressure, and generally go to bat for you. What's more, it probably won't cost you a nickel in fees, retainers, or bills for "services rendered." They want to help. Often it's their job to help. And believe me, they get a lot of satisfaction knowing they've helped you put some clip joint or con artist out of business. And very often that's all they can do. Government agencies, no matter how tough they are on unscrupulous businesspeople, are not allowed to actually represent consumers like a private attorney. If it's at all possible, they will ask for restitution when they bring the case to trial and the judge can order the criminal to pay back what was stolen from the victims, but most of the time the defendant just goes to jail or is fined and perhaps stopped from cheating others. And usually when he's caught he doesn't have the money anymore.

But it's up to *you* to rally these troops, to map out a battle plan, to get yourself up for the fight. I've said it before and I want to say it again: When you get cheated you've got to take action. You have to take your cue from Howard Beale, the TV news anchorman in the movie *Network*. Remember how he urged people on nation-wide television to fling open their windows and shout to the world, "I'm mad as hell and I'm not going to take it anymore. I'm mad as hell and I'm not going to take it anymore."

Now, I'm not urging you to shout out your anger. In this chapter I'm going to show you how to channel that anger productively to get results. But you have to pledge the time and energy it takes to fight back. You've got to be willing to dig through details, follow policies for filing complaints, and persist, persist, persist.

Basic Strategy

Before we find out whom you can trust to help you and how you can find them, here's a basic fight-back strategy that could help you if you've been ripped off on a product or service. These guide-lines aren't cast in concrete, but with them you can lay the ground-work for a real showdown if it's required.

First, call or go back to the person or company that sold you the defective item or didn't deliver the service as promised. Most companies are in business to stay in business so you shouldn't run out and call some consumer agency before you confront the people you feel have shortchanged you. Any company which is really dedicated will go all out to remedy the problem without hassling its customer.

Most importantly, have all the facts at your fingertips. Go armed with a sales slip, a warranty, or a guarantee. And don't forget the product itself; the store will want to inspect it to make sure you are not trying to pull a fast one.

If you don't get your money back though, or fail to get a replacement, or if you think you're getting the cold shoulder or polite runaround, raise your voice but do not shout. Be firm, plant your feet, and stand your ground. Your body language alone might persuade the salesperson you mean business.

Here's where you get indignant and determined. Make it perfectly clear that it's not just a question of dollars and cents, it's a matter of principle. Then, if you can't resolve the dispute on the spot with the clerk, ask to speak with the department manager and, if you're still not satisfied, the store manager. Impress upon him or her the fact that you won't hesitate for a minute to contact the president of the company if you can't get your legitimate complaint resolved right now.

Then, if he or she does try to smooth you over without rectifying your grievance, ask for the names of the president and chief executive officer of the company (or the owner) and the vice-president of operations. And ask for the address of the company's headquarters. Don't let them refuse to give you those facts. But if they do tell them flat out you can get them elsewhere and in your letter you'll convey to the top man just how uncooperative his employees have been—and that you'll mention them by name.

By the way, you can get the president's name and address from plenty of sources. The easiest is from the store's switchboard or the local chamber of commerce and there are consumer books at the library with the addresses of all major company headquarters. After you get the information, fire off a letter spelling out your gripes. (In the appendix on page 246 we spell out how you can write a complaint letter that will get action.) Make sure you send carbons of your complaint to the legal department and the public relations department of the company.

Wait four weeks for your reply but no longer. Then send a registered or certified letter to the president restating your case. Include copies of your earlier correspondence, copies of all the documentation originally sent, and any other facts you can furnish to support your claim that you were ripped off. You should get a return receipt proving the letter was delivered to someone in authority at the company. Save that too.

Remember, the more detailed and complete your complaint, the more you'll convince the president that you mean business and you won't stop with him. Just for good measure, tell him if you don't hear from him in "seven working days" you'll be forced to take "appropriate action."

Now at this point, he doesn't know if you're threatening legal action, a complaint to local or state consumer protection units, or a call to a newspaper, radio, or television reporter who might want to make your case a cause célèbre. And that's fine. You don't want to tip your hand. For if you threaten to go to your brother-in-law at the Associated Press and the story never appears, he knows you're all talk and no clout.

But what happens if the company stonewalls all the way and you've exhausted your arsenal trying to settle your complaint at the retail and corporate level? Here's where you have to take action and go to the people or groups you know will help you.

Better Business Bureau—Better but Beware

Ten years ago I would never have referred anyone to the BBB. In my estimation, they were toothless, pencil-pushing groups funded by businesses and corporations, the very groups they were trying to patrol. Hence they were largely ineffective. But in 1970 the 149 locally operated bureaus reorganized into what's known as the Council of Better Business Bureaus, Inc. (CBBB), and today they can sometimes be a muscular ally.

A Better Business Bureau performs two basic functions: maintains files on companies and handles gripes. The files are built largely on public inquiries and complaints (some 8.2 million in 1977), but unless someone complains about a specific company's transgressions, no file is available. What's more, other companies cited for violations often have no BBB files.

Still, you should always lodge a complaint with your local BBB office—just to keep its files updated and accurate for your fellow consumer. For the bureau nearest you write Council of Better Business Bureaus, Inc., 1150 Seventeenth Street, NW, Washington, DC 20036; telephone (202) 862-1200. When a local bureau gets enough complaints on a company, it "profiles" the concern, including its record in handling consumer complaints, and it details any lawsuits the company's been slapped with. Those profiles and other file information are available to you free. Also available, some 65 pamphlets costing 15¢ to $1.50. Write or call your local BBB for an order blank.

If you've been ripped off, fill out a BBB Customer Experience Record form. Don't expect any legal help. Also, the BBB won't get involved in a fraud action or in any other cause where you allege some illegality. The bureau will send your CER form to the company and ask for an answer and that's all. The company can answer it and settle the dispute, offer its own version of the dispute, or ignore the request and the form entirely. The BBB has no enforcement powers; its strength comes simply from an implied threat of blackballing rip-off companies.

If you and a member company have genuine differences over who screwed who, the BBB will, in many states, conduct an arbitration. But both parties have to agree to arbitrate. You don't need an attorney. And the outcome—the arbitrator's decision—is generally legally binding in a court of law.

In the end, don't place all your faith in your local Better Business Bureau. Some are tougher than others. Some are pressured by their members. While the CBBB claims that 77.5 percent of all complaints filed were "settled," that doesn't mean the consumer was always satisfied. The BBB counts any "reasonable offer" by a company or rejection of an "unjustified claim" as a settlement. So beware.

Consumer Action Panels—The Industry's Referee

There was a time, not long ago, when rip-offs were so rampant in certain industries that Washington threatened to step in with a regulatory sledgehammer in order to defend the consumer. Industry took the hint. Since business hates legislation telling it what it can and cannot do, many industries voluntarily cleaned up their acts and formed their own Consumer Action Panels. Get to know them before you need them; some can save you a lot of money and anxiety. Others are a waste of time. Theoretically, they forward your complaint to the "right person" at the company that's ripped you off. Some CAPs, however, see themselves as a "court of last resort" after all other appeals for satisfaction have failed.

Major Appliance Consumer Action Panel (MACAP)

This was the first Consumer Action Panel organized. It was set up in 1970 to handle what was then an avalanche of consumer gripes over faulty appliances. Three brawny and influential trade groups sponsor it: the Home Appliance Manufacturers, Gas Appliance Manufacturers Association, and the National Retail Merchants Association. MACAP works on consumer complaints about refrigerators, washers, dryers, dishwashers, gas and electric ranges, room air-conditioners, garbage disposals, trash compactors, water heaters, humidifiers, dehumidifiers, and gas incinerators.

Before contacting MACAP, you must try to settle the dispute at the store where you made your purchase or with the manufacturer. If you get the runaround at the retail level and the manufacturer won't respond to your inquiries, call MACAP toll free at (800) 621-0477 or, if you live in Illinois, call collect to (312) 236-3223. Or you can write to MACAP, 20 North Wacker Drive, Chicago, IL 60606, and furnish your name, address, telephone number; the brand, model, serial number, and type of appliance you purchased and when you bought it; the name and address of the dealer *and* the service agent; plus a detailed factual description of your problem.

MACAP will go to a top executive at the retailer or manufacturer and ask for an explanation or a response. If there's no response, the panel, composed of people outside the appliance industry, makes its own recommendation at one of its monthly meetings. MACAP claims 90 percent of its complaints are eventually resolved and both parties are satisfied. But take heed: Don't try to flim-flam the panel; MACAP claims that more than half the complaints that go to the panel for a "recommendation" are deemed unjustified.

Automobile Consumer Action Panel (AUTOCAP)

Consumer experts claim the automobile is one of the biggest sources of consumer complaints today. Every year more people complain about faulty repairs, warranty disputes, and new cars that simply do not run right. And for most of us, it's the most frustrating dispute to settle. Many people feel that car dealers, no matter how honest they actually may be, have a little larceny in them. Some more than others. And since the salesperson is paid on commission, we know he isn't going to waste his precious selling time trying to help us.

What's more, we often feel we have to "take on Detroit"—or Japan or Germany or wherever the car is made—to get satisfaction, and that's intimidating.

Automobile dealers realize they're too often seen as the villains, so a few years ago two major groups, the Automotive Trade Association Managers (ATAM) and the National Automobile Dealers Association, set up a network of state and local complaint handling boards called AUTOCAP. All states don't have them, but there are approximately 40 statewide, regional, and city groups. Theoretically, they use "peer pressure" to get action, calling the head of the dealership or a senior executive and trying to settle it at the top. You can find the address of the nearest one by writing National Automobile Dealers Association, 1640 West Park Drive, McLean, VA 22101, (703) 821-7000.

The pitfall here is that not all AUTOCAPs have a panel to mediate disputes. About half do, and you should ask about this important point before you get deeply involved. What's more, each "panel" is supposed to have at least three dealers and two customer representatives to mediate disputes, but not all AUTOCAPs follow these guidelines. Often the panels are loaded with auto industry types. You've got to wonder if you're going to get a fair shake. Investigate before you complain.

Furniture Industry Consumer Advisory Panel (FICAP)

Organized in 1973 by the Southern Furniture Manufacturers Association, which produces about one-third to one-half of all furniture sold in the United States, FICAP doesn't pounce on consumer complaints with the same zeal that appliance manufacturers and automakers use when tackling disputes, but the organization is getting tougher. FICAP deals only with its own members. But if the seams are coming apart on a sofa manufactured by a non-member company, send a complaint anyway. Those furniture makers are a tight-knit fraternity, and FICAP might pass along a complaint on your behalf. Write FICAP, P.O. Box 951, High Point, NC 27261 and include the same factual information that MACAP requires, plus copies of any correspondence you've had with the dealer or the manufacturer.

Trade Groups

Virtually every industry and professional trade organization will handle consumer complaints. Some of the more enlightened, better funded groups have Consumer Affairs Departments at their national headquarters. Others pass beefs along to their state and regional staffers. Still others pick up the phone and call a member or write an "action" memorandum to someone with clout to clear up the problem. I can't think that any trade association official would throw your complaint letter in the trash. If he does, the members who pay his salary should sack him.

Some trade associations are doing outstanding jobs in serving their members and their customers. Others just haven't yet gotten the message that satisfied customers are their greatest asset, and dammit, they should do everything humanly possible to keep them happy.

But don't be misled. These industry and trade associations aren't punching it out in your behalf out of the goodness of their hearts. They know how devastating bad publicity can be. And they want to keep the heat—government, action-line reporters, and consumer activists—off their backs. But that's fine with me. Anything they do to resolve a legitimate complaint should be applauded. Still, it's up to you to try and settle the rip-off first, where it happened—with the dealer, manufacturer, or retailer.

Better Hearing Institute

Few people need help faster than a hearing-impaired person whose hearing aid doesn't work right. The Better Hearing Institute knows this and it investigates consumer complaints fast. It even mediates disputes, and claims to resolve 90 to 95 percent of the gripes it gets. Call the Institute's toll-free WATS line at (800) 424-8575, or in Washington, DC, call (202) 638-7577. Or write the Institute at 1430 K Street, NW, Washington, DC 20005.

There may soon be new laws requiring a prescription from a doctor or qualified audiometrist before one can purchase a hearing aid. It may cost the consumer something for the hearing exam, but it will save millions of people from paying as much as $2,000 for a hearing aid they don't need or which can't help their condition.

Blue Cross and Blue Shield

If you have a complaint over a Blue Cross or Blue Shield bill or payment, and you can't resolve the hassle at the state or local level, write their national Office of Consumer Affairs. Remember, the local plan has to give you a reason for denying your claim if that's the problem. Otherwise, after you've sought redress locally, the Washington office will appeal the complaint for you. If it's an emergency, call, and a consumer affairs staffer will call you back on the WATS line. While they cannot force a settlement from the local Blue Cross and Blue Shield plans, the national association has considerable clout. Write: Blue Cross/Blue Shield, Office of Consumer Affairs, 1700 Pennsylvania Avenue, NW, Washington, DC 20006. Telephone (202) 785-7932.

Carpet and Rug Institute

This trade association had a consumer action panel called CRICAP but disbanded it in 1974 because of the preceding year's financial crush. A spokesperson said CRICAP generated only several hundred complaints despite the panel's efforts to contact consumer action lines and consumer publications to drum up gripes it could settle. Now the Institute's Office of Consumer Affairs takes complaints and passes them along to the "appropriate person" at the manufacturer, regardless of whether they are a member of the institute. It just no longer mediates and follows up. Write: Director of Consumer Affairs, Carpet and Rug Institute, Box 2048, Dalton,

GA 30720. Telephone (404) 278-3176. The Institute is involved with domestically manufactured carpets only; it does not handle complaints on Oriental rugs.

Direct Mail Marketing Association

This 3300-member trade group represents most of the legitimate mail-order marketers, and it tries hard to get complaints settled. Its Mail Order Action Line will contact any mail-order company which bilked you and lobby to get your money back or get the product you ordered. The DMMA can pressure direct-mail companies, but it doesn't have police powers over its members or, obviously, any non-members. Nor does it have a mediation panel like some other trade groups do. But it does pour a lot of energy into complaint handling, and its staff seems dedicated to ridding the world of mail-order scamsters. Write and send all appropriate data including the direct mail or direct response offer to: Direct Mail Marketing Association, 6 East 43rd Street, New York, NY 10017. Telephone (212) 689-4977.

Direct Selling Association

Nothing is more exasperating than not getting what you've ordered and paid for or than trying to find a door-to-door salesperson you think sold you a bill of goods. Many states have a three-day "cooling off" period on door-to-door sales. You have three business days to cancel your order in writing and you're entitled to all your deposit money back. There is also a federal law which allows you three days to cancel any contract which can result in a lien being placed on your property at a later date. This would include any kind of repairs you might contract for, such as roofing, siding, installation of air-conditioning and such. The contract has to state the terms of the cancellation privilege, so read it carefully and comply exactly. It's a good idea to have a chance to think over whether you really need that set of encyclopedias or that new room added after the high-pressure salesperson has left. If you can't get satisfaction from a company that sold you something direct (that is, where no store or retailer is involved), contact the

Consumer Affairs Department of the Direct Selling Association. This group represents 200 of the largest direct-sales concerns— Avon, Encyclopaedia Britannica, Sarah Coventry, Amway, Time-Life Libraries, Mary Kay Cosmetics to name a few. DSA has a rigid code of ethics and has an "outside code administrator" who will pursue your complaints with members and will contact non-members. DSA contends that it resolves 95 percent of the disputes it gets. Write: Direct Selling Association, Director of Consumer Affairs, 1730 M Street, NW, Washington, DC 20006. Telephone: (202) 457-4900.

Electronic Industries Association

This association seems to take consumer complaint handling seriously. Its Consumer Electronics Group has a four-person staff to tackle your problems with televisions, radios, high-fidelity and stereo equipment, reel-to-reel and cassette tape recorders, CB radios, and other home entertainment electronic goods. EIA maintains a cross listing of 3000 manufacturers, brand names, and trade names, and will follow up claims on non-members as well. Before you contact EIA, try to resolve your differences with the selling dealer or the manufacturer. If that fails, send EIA the dealer's name and address; the brand, model, and serial number of what you bought; copies of any correspondence; work orders; and a statement of the resolution you're seeking. If it's a matter of safety, EIA will take a collect call. In 1977 the association handled 2673 complaints. It satisfied 71 percent and reached a compromise in 21 percent of the valid cases. Critics, however, claim that EIA is slow to respond. Write: Electronics Industries Association, 2001 Eye Street, NW, Washington, DC 20006. Telephone: (202) 457-4900.

International Fabricare Institute

The next time your neighborhood dry cleaner ruins a new dress or shirt and won't pay you for the damage, contact the BBB or your local department of consumer affairs. It, in turn, will contact this institute. It has a novel way of resolving who's to blame in a dispute. It costs $6 and IFI will chemically analyze the garment to determine who or what caused the damage. Sometimes the cost is paid by the cleaner, but other times by the consumer. Write the Institute at 12251 Tech Road, Silver Springs, MD 20904, or telephone it at (301) 622-1900.

Magazine Action Line

Here is one of the most effective complaint-handling services in operation today. Operated by Publisher's Clearing House, a reliable outfit that sells magazine subscriptions at a substantial discount, Magazine Action Line will go to work on your complaint immediately, even if it didn't originally sell you the subscription. MAL will either find you a suitable replacement for the magazine you didn't get, or, frequently, it will get your money refunded. Contact MAL at 382 Channel Drive, Port Washington, NY 11050 or telephone (516) 883-5432.

National Association of Furniture Manufacturers

This Washington, DC-based trade organization does more lobbying than consumer complaint handling. It will shoot off your letter or formal complaint to the manufacturer, but it will not stay on top of the case to make sure it gets resolved. That's up to you. Send all the information to NAFM, 8401 Connecticut Avenue, Washington, DC 20015 or telephone (202) 657-4442.

National Home Study Council

If you ever enrolled in a home study course and suddenly the lessons stopped coming in the mail or the outfit skipped with your tuition, check first with the school, then contact the National Home Study Council. NHSC accredits 96 home study schools such as La Salle Extension University, International Correspondence Schools, McGraw-Hill Continuing Education Center, and Art Instruction School. To get action for you, it will contact the school, whether or not it's NHSC accredited, and will usually follow the complaint through to a settlement. Their consumer spokesperson says that 80 percent of the problems are resolved. Write: National Home Study Council, 1601 18th Street, NW, Washington, DC 20009. Telephone:(202) 234-5100.

National Paint and Coatings Association (NP&CA)

The major complaints I get about house painting come from people who have had their houses done by companies which specialize in "texture-coating." This is a thick substance which is sprayed onto the house and supposedly eliminates the need to paint again for 15 years. The job ordinarily comes with a 15-year warranty against flaking, chipping or peeling. But the catch is if the surface isn't prepared properly the stuff will start dropping off soon after the job is completed. The manufacturer won't be responsible because his product wasn't defective and the contractor may not come out to re-do the job.

Those particular contractors go in and out of business every day and their guarantee isn't worth the paper it's written on. This is one of those times when you should get a list of satisfied customers and talk to them before you sign on the dotted line. Since these jobs can cost thousands of dollars, you'd better spend the time checking out the contractor. Your state contractor's licensing board can tell you if the company is licensed and how long it's been in business. You can find out from the customers whether the house was properly sandblasted or scraped and whether their outdoor plants and patio furniture ended up being texture-coated along with the stucco.

NP&CA is another trade organization that forwards complaints to its members but doesn't follow up. If your paint or wallcoverings peel or prematurely fade and you think the manufacturer wasn't paying attention to quality control, write NP&CA, 1500 Rhode Island Avenue, NW, Washington, DC 20005, (202) 462-6272.

National Tire Dealers and Retreaders Association

This national association is doing a commendable job of gearing up to respond to consumer complaints at the state and local levels. The association, made up of independent tire dealers (not affiliated with a major oil company), is trying to organize Consumer Action Panels among its 32 members at the state level. The national office of the NTDRA will pass along your complaint to a dealer whether or not it's a member of the association, and that's a real service, but it rarely follows up. Write NTDRA Field Operations Department at 1343 L. Street, NW, Washington, DC 20005. Telephone: (202) 638-6650. Associations in two states have set up their own CAPs—it's a start, but the CAPs are far from efficient. They are the Indiana Tire Dealers and Retreaders Association, P.O. Box 2104, Indianapolis, IN 46203, telephone: (317) 631-8124; and the Wisconsin Independent Tire Dealers & Retreaders Association, 1109 N. Mayfair Road, Wauwatosa, WI 53226, telephone: (414) 781-1244. The latter, however, has been deflated by a lack of interest.

Opticians Association of America

If you have a problem with eyeglasses or contact lenses, and an optician handled your prescription and fitting, this group will channel your complaint to its members. The problem is that it doesn't represent optometrists, who seem to sell the lion's share of corrective eyeware today. Still, this association claims to settle most of the complaints lodged against its members, so write: Opticians Association of America, 1250 Connecticut Avenue, NW, Washington, DC 20036. Telephone: (202) 659-3620.

Professional Insurance Agents

By far, the most consumer-minded organization in the insurance industry, the 35,000-member Professional Insurance Agents, Inc., set up a pilot Consumer Action Panel to mediate disputes, but it was scrapped in 1976 after 17 mediations when insurance companies and state insurance departments failed to support it enthusiastically. Today, the PIA will "pass along and follow up" on your complaints, and it will give you the name, address, and phone number of the president and chief executive and the consumer affairs officer of the insurance company you feel ripped you off. It will even point you toward your state insurance commissioner and give you specific tips on getting redress. Plus, it is a central source of insurance information that is yours for the asking. Some trade groups give lip service to consumer complaints; PIA really helps, particularly on automobile insurance. Write PIA, Office of Consumer Affairs, 400 N. Washington Street, Alexandria, VA 22314. Telephone: (703) 836-9340.

Photo Marketing Association

This trade organization is made up of 4100 retail camera stores and photo finishing companies. Its Consumer Affairs Department claims an 80 to 90 percent success rate in finding film lost by photo finishers and in getting retail beefs resolved. Often it will recover the cost of your lost film and finishing. It will write a letter on your behalf, or call the dealer if it's an emergency. And it will follow up. This organization is thoughtful enough to have a toll-free WATS line: (800) 248-1140, or, within Michigan, call (517) 783-2807. Or write to Photo Marketing Association, 603 Lansing Avenue, Jackson MI 49202.

Again, these are just the industry trade associations that have formal procedures for handling consumer complaints. Hundreds of other associations do not have official "consumer affairs" offices, but they do try and get disputes resolved, largely on a catch-as-catch-can basis. They can be effective if you present your gripe in a comprehensive package—all the facts, copies of supporting documents, and a detailed statement of what you would like to have resolved. Don't just write, call and yell for help.

Although there isn't enough space to list all the local, regional, state, and national trade groups, you can dig up their addresses and telephone numbers with a little investigation of your own. In all cases, direct your complaint to the executive director. And follow up.

You've Got Friends

The problem is finding who to go to with a complaint and knowing what they can do for you. In the appendix at the end of this book, you'll find a gold mine of information on whom you can trust. We've compiled a directory, starting on page 271, of the major, active consumer protection agencies that are known to the U.S. Office of Consumer Affairs.

We've also included in the appendix the latest list of non-governmental consumer affairs organizations. These are groups formed by bright, aware consumerists who realize that by banding together they gain political muscle and persuasive powers far greater than they ever imagined. For instance, one of the nation's most effective grass-roots consumer organizations, San Francisco Consumer Action (26 Seventh Street, San Francisco CA 94103, telephone 415/626-2510), publishes its own gutsy informative newsletter. What's more, the group is a no-nonsense defender of consumer rights in the San Francisco Bay area.

At the federal level, the U.S. Office of Consumer Affairs (Washington, DC 20201, 202/245-6164) is your watchdog in Washington. Unfortunately, massive lobbying by pro-business groups has kept it largely an advisory and coordinating agency that accepts *general* consumer complaints and refers them to the appropriate governmental regulatory agency for action. Sometimes, however, the consumer affairs office will write a letter on your behalf, pressuring a manufacturer to get on the stick and resolve your complaints.

Other governmental agencies such as the Federal Trade Commission work on specific complaints (FTC works on warranties, misrepresentation, and price-fixing—among other things), and you can save time and frustration by writing them directly. But remember, before you write that letter, be organized, have all the facts at your fingertips, know exactly what action you want taken, and be persistent. Don't give up and don't get clutched if you don't get an answer in four days. Bureaucratic wheels grind slowly, but your persistence will keep them greased. A complete list of federal agencies, their addresses, phone numbers, and jurisdictional areas begins on page 250.

If you're confused by the bureaucracy, check with the Federal Information Center in the city nearest you. This is a little-known free service that helps you find a government expert or agency that will answer your question or help you solve your consumer problem. Some cities have toll-free telephone numbers. A list of the phone numbers of federal information centers nationwide starts on page 255.

Tell The World

Rip-off artists hate publicity. A manufacturer, retailer, or any company who stubbornly refuses to satisfy your complaint suddenly becomes more cooperative when the press comes calling. After all, a good reputation is a fragile commodity and bad publicity can shatter it.

Newspaper action lines get results, but your complaint should be unusual or frustrating enough to stand out from the hundreds of gripes that pour into the paper's office each day. Find out who actually edits your action line locally and write that person a concise one-page letter accompanied by the facts to substantiate your claim.(In the appendix beginning on page 257, we list the newspaper and radio and television action lines.)

If your daily local newspaper doesn't have a consumer action line, write a letter to the city editor or business/financial editor, briefing them on your story. A responsible newspaper is always looking for solid news with a local, human interest angle. Big Business stepping on the Little Man is always newsworthy if there is a new twist. *Newsworthy* is the key word here. You can't expect an editor to get fired up if you have a squawk with the supermarket manager over a tough steak. But if you find that a dozen doctors in your community, including your own, simultaneously boosted their fees—that's news. Or if a local bank seems to be denying loans to creditworthy women—that's news.

Radio and television are excellent forums in which to air your consumer complaints. In fact, many radio broadcasters throughout the country support a non-profit referral and action service called, appropriately enough, Call for Action.

When you call in your problem (and they don't *have* to be consumer gripes), a volunteer confidentially records the information and refers you to a source for help. The CFA volunteer calls you back two weeks later to find out if the problem was cleared up. If it hasn't been, Call for Action staffers will zero in on it.

National headquarters of Call for Action is at 1785 Massachusetts Avenue, NW, Washington, DC 20036. The telephone num-

ber is: (202) 387-0500. The service is free and effective. CFA claims
it settles a good deal of the problems called in to it.

Radio and television generally are aggressive and competitive
news media in most American cities. And your complaint just
might spark a good story or a series of investigative reports. But
don't call the station and try and explain the circumstances of your
case; assignment editors are under immense deadline pressures all
day long. Instead, spell out all the details of your case in a memorandum to the assignment editor and point out how other lis-
teners/viewers might benefit from your story. The popular television program "60 Minutes" has been tipped off to some of its
better investigative reports by irate consumers.

One caution: Nothing makes an agency madder than spending
a lot of time trying to solve your problem, only to find out that it's
already been resolved by another agency. It's OK to write to
several agencies, but only one at a time. If they don't respond, or
you aren't satisfied, then try the next one on your list.

See Them in Court

Most people are scared witless of courtrooms. The mere mention of the word *courtroom* conjures up visions of high-priced
lawyers, stone-faced judges, and skeptical juries. But don't be
intimidated. In every city and county in all 50 states you have
access to what I call the "Consumers' Fight-Back Court"—
small claims court. Here, on neutral turf, you can challenge the
biggest corporation in a court of law and, if your case is valid,
beat them.

The beauty of small claims court is that you don't need a lawyer
to represent you. In fact, in almost all cases you're not allowed to
have one. It's do-it-yourself law and you're on equal legal footing
with your opponent. Filing fees are small, anywhere from $2 to
$15 depending on the state. And the court's decision is legally
binding although it can usually be appealed in a higher civil court,
and that's when the lawsuit gets sticky.

Small claims court is still the best way to fight the manufacturer
or retailer, or any other concern that refuses to take action when

you complain and they won't take your phone call, answer your correspondence, hear you out, or try to resolve a dispute. However, before you haul the outfit into court, be convinced that you are in the right and will prevail. Don't try to bluff—although a company will often resolve a dispute rather than tie up its lawyers to consult about what is dollarwise a trivial matter to the company but an important one to you. If you do bluff, be prepared to carry out your threat.

It won't take you that much time and effort.

What constitutes "small claims"? It depends on the state in which you live. It can range from $25 in a Louisiana city court to a maximum of $3000 in Indiana and South Carolina. Check with the small claims court in your community for details.

Collecting a Judgment

Even after you win your case in court, you may have difficulty collecting on your judgment. The courts will give you some assistance, but most of the work is up to you. You have to get copies of the judgment and then try to collect by attaching the person's bank account, placing a lien on his car or even posting a marshal in his place of business to collect the money as it comes in. All these things take time and cost money (which can also be recovered from the debtor if your efforts pay off). But smart con men know how to weasel out of all these legal methods of collection and sometimes your judgment represents a hollow victory.

Fight or Mediate?

Settling a dispute through mediation is probably the most civilized way to get a seemingly irreconcilable problem resolved. It's a serious and little understood alternative to the courtroom. But before you plunge into mediation you should realize one thing: The decision can't be appealed in a court of law. The mediator is the final word.

The Consumer Action Panels we discussed use mediation to solve consumer/manufacturer differences. But the American Arbitration Association's Community Dispute Service is probably the best example of how a third-party neutral can intervene between two battling parties and produce a final decision.

The San Francisco office of the AAA (690 Market Street, San Francisco, CA 94104. Telephone: 415/981-3901) gets cases from the district attorney and arranges the mediation. Both parties have to sign an agreement to arbitrate as they do in labor/management disputes. You can get a hearing in ten days and it doesn't cost either party a cent. What's more, the neutrals or arbitrators have a background in the issue being disputed. Basically they act as a catalyst to get you to bury the hatchet and come to some kind of agreement. However, if you can't work it out with your adversary, the neutral arbitrator can render a decision that's often binding under state law. For information on how or if you can settle *your* consumer complaints through arbitration, write the American Arbitration Association, 140 W. 51st Street, New York, NY 10020, telephone: (212) 997-2998.

As I said at the start of this chapter, if you get ripped off, don't think for a moment you should shrug off the loss and forget it. You've got some heavy artillery at your disposal, more firepower than you can use. But you've got to supply the ammunition.

FIGHT BACK!

Advertising: How to Sift Out Fakes, Flakes, and Flim Flams, Label Liars, Warranties

5

Here's a statistic that will stagger you. One hundred American companies spent $8.8 billion in 1977 to advertise their wares. That's just one hundred advertisers. All companies together—manufacturers, retailers, anybody marketing anything—spent an estimated $43 billion, says *Advertising Age,* the bible of Madison Avenue, which incidentally is published in Chicago.

That's right. Forty-three billion bucks are poured into television, radio, newspaper, magazine, direct mail, and billboard advertising. It includes sales spiels on benches and on the backs of buses and taxicabs. It doesn't include "reminder" advertising inside matchbooks or on the bottom of the calenders your insurance agent or hardware store sends you each Christmas.

Think about it. Forty-three billion dollars spent for a single reason—to sell you something. To convince you to buy. To persuade you to purchase.

With that kind of money flying around, it's no surprise that some of the advertising that bombards us, seduces us, or simply talks to us is misleading, overblown, or just plain crooked. Granted it's a small percentage of the advertising you see. And for good reason.

Top executives running big corporations usually won't tolerate advertising rip-offs. Morally, they're opposed to it. Financially, they know how devastating the consequences of getting caught on a false-advertising rap by the Federal Trade Commission or by some fangs-bared consumer group can be. It just isn't worth the hassle.

But that's not always true on Main Street U.S.A. Across the country, in air-conditioned malls, in suburban and downtown shopping centers, even at the corner grocery, you find some of the most blatant examples of phony advertising. These are sales pitches that suck you into the clutches of a merchant who won't deliver what you came to buy.

Think I'm exaggerating? A recent nationwide survey of 2513 households by the U.S. Office of Consumer Affairs in Washington, DC, found that the most common consumer gripe was stores not having a product that was advertised for sale. More people complained about these come-ons than about rip-off auto mechanics or shoddy workmanship or worthless warranties.

I'm not surprised. You show me anyone who hasn't been duped at least once by the Big Bargain that was "sold out" by the time you got down to the store. Or the "going out of business sale" that pumped you up with visions of bargain snatching, and then deflated your wallet with "markdown" prices, prices that were marked way, way up, and then marked down. But you never take a hard look at the prices because you are so swept up in all that promotional hoop-la and frenzied buying that you're psychologically convinced you are getting "a deal." But are you?

Last year, the New York City Department of Consumer Affairs went "shopping" in fourteen "going out of business stores" and handed out 42 summonses. The charges: misleading sale advertising, failure to post prices, failure to substantiate sale claims. The commissioner who personally headed this consumer SWAT team was shocked. He denounced some of the stores as "menaces," preying on bargain-hunting shoppers and tourists. The agency found that one out-of-towner was charged $5000 for two Polaroid movie cameras, projectors, and film—double the list price. Another woman, a New Yorker, paid $133.92 for two computer batteries that sold for $7 apiece.

Now some cynics may argue that anybody who is stupid enough

to pay $133 for two $7 batteries deserves to be ripped off. But that kind of thinking only encourages merchants to gouge. The truth of the matter is simply this: When a company advertises a clearance sale it should be a bona fide discount of at least 5 percent and the sale merchandise should be honestly marked. Unfortunately, though, you cannot and should not trust sale signs. Thanks to greedy and corrupt merchants, the word *sale* has lost its meaning.

Take the case of a hardware store in California that posted a huge sign proclaiming "Everything On Sale." Townspeople and passersby flocked in the doors scooping up everything in sight. Suddenly, one shopper noticed the prices were the same if not higher than another store in town. She complained to the county district attorney who came down, took a look around, and told her the merchant was telling the truth. Everything in the store was "for sale" and therefore, "on sale." Nowhere did the proprietor claim that he cut prices.

How do you know if you're being sold down the river at a "sale"? Do your homework. Check the prices at a reputable department store first on items that you are *likely* to buy at the sale store. Then you have a basis for comparison. Otherwise, you'll come home with sale merchandise you would never buy in a hundred years but that you snapped up because you *thought* it was a bargain. How many unused gizmos do you have stashed in closets or collecting dust in a garage that you bought because you thought you were saving money?

Watch out for giant discounts. The $1000 sofa slashed to $199.95 may still be a rip-off at that price. Don't laugh, but it could be stuffed with straw or upholstered in a fabric so flimsy it won't stand up for 30 days of normal sitting. And the frame could be made out of old packing crates. Don't let the merchant play on your sympathies by plastering his windows with "sale" signs proclaiming that he's selling everything at half price to raise cash to save his store.

While these hometown sob-sister salespeople are preying on your sympathies, some national advertisers are playing with your head. These companies should know better. They are spending big bucks on television advertising and have a nationwide reputation. They can't afford to waylay the consumer.

But they're doing it. The most overt misrepresentation of facts by a television advertiser has to be a margarine commercial that shows a taste test in which everybody preferred that brand of margarine over butter. I just couldn't swallow that claim, so on my "Consumer Buyline" show we took a television camera out to a nearby supermarket and conducted our own taste test.

We had ten people taste that margarine and we had the same ten people taste butter. Surprise! Ten out of ten picked butter. The misrepresentation took place when the margarine maker did not show or tell the viewers how many people they "tested" to get the five or six people who actually picked margarine over butter. For all we know the ad agency and production company shooting that commercial could have "taste-tested" 200 people before they found the margarine freaks. But we will never know because they'll never tell us.

Yet it was worth the wait for the margarine company. For their patience, they were rewarded with a half-dozen shoppers who look just like you and me and who raved over margarine when a camera was pointed their way. The subconscious conclusion they want you to draw is that margarine is so good that the "average person" not only can't distinguish between the two spreads, but he or she likes margarine better. The margarine people would have loved to have shown famous chefs who couldn't tell the difference between margarine and butter; that would have been a powerful testimonial for their product. But it would never happen. So they use the "slice of life," just-plain-folks spiel. Well, don't fall for it.

The Pepsi Challenge commercial isn't as misleading because we found in our test that more people did prefer Pepsi than Coca-Cola. But again, the Madison Avenue boys are meddling with your mind. They try to convince people watching this commercial that they are in the majority when they buy Pepsi. More people prefer Pepsi, the commercial claims. In doing so, it subconsciously asks, "So why should you drink Coke?"

Obviously, a lot of people do drink Coca-Cola. Again, we set up our impartial, independent taste test and poured a glass each of Pepsi, Coca-Cola, and several other colas for 11 people. Seven picked Pepsi, three picked Coke, and one chose Dr. Pepper because he didn't like either of the other two. But in their commercial you never see the confirmed Pepsi drinkers who picked Coke.

The most bizarre commercial that I've ever seen in ten years as a consumer reporter—and as a television watcher for that matter —was a TV spot for Krazy Glue. The commercial showed a man wearing a crash helmet that was Krazy Glued to a steel girder. That's right, he was hanging by his head.

I challenged the Krazy Glue commercial on television not only once but twice. I followed their directions explicitly. It didn't work either time. I was going to hang from an I-beam but it wasn't going to be nine feet above the ground. No way.

Our television test contradicted the affidavit Krazy Glue filed with Los Angeles television station KNBC claiming the product worked, and KNBC yanked the commercial off the air until further substantiation was received.

Outright lying in a television commercial is rare. Far more common are visual gimmicks and tricks designed to convey a subliminal sales message that the advertised product is something it really isn't. It's that deceptive subconscious sell that you've got to watch out for. And the biggest companies are sometimes the guiltiest.

For instance, one Hunt's commercial claimed its tomato sauce was so thick you could stand a spoon upright in the can. Now, unless you listen with your mind as well as your ears, chances are they zinged one right by you, making you think the sauce is thicker than it really is. If that claim didn't touch off any bells in your head, it isn't at all surprising. We hear so many commercials, read so many advertisements, and get pummeled with so many promotional plugs, we're practically immune to the meaning of the words.

Yet, while we're submerged all day in a sea of spiels, the craftiest and most creative seep into our subconscious and sit there just waiting to spring forth as part of a buying decision. That's fine if the commercial portrays the product honestly. But when it tries to dupe you or brainwash you, you've got to get agitated.

When I saw that Hunt's tomato sauce commercial, my personal fire alarm sounded a consumer alert. If it's that thick, I said to myself, let's prove it on television. I challenged the commercial but I couldn't make the spoon stand up in the sauce. I invited other people to come up on camera to see if they could make the spoon stand up—on either end. They couldn't do it. It was a gimmick. The advertisers later told us how to stand the spoon up using some centrifugal force trick but as far as I'm concerned, it was a misrepresentation.

What worries me most, and should worry you, is the way some advertising misleads children. A classic example is the commercial that claims a Tonka truck is so strong an elephant can't crush it. Now most youngsters and many adults seeing the elephant perched on the truck would believe it. You're looking at it with your own two eyes. And even if you think it's a bit farfetched, how many people have pet elephants so they can recreate the test?

You guessed it—we had to see for ourselves if Tonka was trying to pull a fast one, so we challenged the commercial. We took a film crew over to the Los Angeles Zoo and rolled a Tonka truck in the path of an elephant. The big beast stepped on it and flattened the toy. It didn't break the truck apart but it did crush it.

Now, I'm not knocking Hunt's tomato sauce or Tonka toys or Pepsi Cola. They're all fine products. What I object to is the sleight of hand and the shell game trickery used to sell these products on television. Advertising is a great informational tool to spread the word about a good product. But there's no need to hoodwink a consumer with a commercial that only a Merlin could create.

You can imagine how the advertisers I've challenged howl. They argue that their commercial demonstrations are filmed "under laboratory conditions." And you know what I tell them? I tell them the consumer's home is no laboratory and every product should perform for you the same way in your kitchen as it does in a commercial production company's "kitchen."

Then there are commercials and advertisements that make meaningless claims, concoct outrageous demonstrations, or use superstar salespeople to convince you to shell out your cash. Does the fact that one catsup comes out of the bottle the slowest necessarily mean it's the tastiest or the best? Who cares if actor Robert Conrad uses a certain kind of flashlight battery. Is that any guarantee they are long-lasting and powerful? And Joe Namath selling pantyhose—more mind manipulation. Namath, a heckuva football player, is almost as well known for his off-field activities as the swinging bachelor no woman has been able to tackle. The not-too-subtle psychological message to women is that if they buy the pantyhose Joe Namath is hawking, they might just wind up with a sexy, athletic, elusive man-of-their-dreams bachelor like Joe.

The same is true for the elephant-proof toy commercial. Regardless of whether the truck can support an elephant's weight (which we proved it could not do), you want a toy that a youngster can't destroy. Tonka toys, as far as I'm concerned, *are* that sturdy so why bring on the elephants?

You can save yourself some real money if you become a little more skeptical of advertising claims, especially those that crow over the superiority of the product. And you don't have to be a consumer reporter to verify those claims. In fact, you can test products yourself and challenge the commercials in your own home.

One of my favorite commercial challenges was the time I tried to verify the claims of the Duracell battery commercial for long life and dependability. The Duracell spot showed 14 battery-operated toy dogs barking. I made it very clear that our test was not a scientific one. And we used both regular carbide batteries as well as the more expensive alkaline batteries to make the dogs bark. Then a member of our staff stayed awake all night long to see which dog barked the longest.

Next morning, my staff member reported the results: the best buy in batteries in terms of running the longest in our non-scientific test was the Ray-O-Vac alkaline.

When I announced our test findings on the air, there was an immediate commotion. A representative for P.R. Mallory & Co., Inc., which manufactures Duracell batteries, its lawyer, and the agency vice-president in charge of the Duracell account, flew to Los Angeles to see me. They tried to persuade us not to repeat the test on the air because department stores and other retail outlets where batteries are sold were making a fuss.

My answer to that was, "Well, that's your problem. We didn't say anything negative about Duracell batteries either. We said they work great. But if you're going to buy a battery that's going to last a long time then according to our non-scientific test, the best buy is the Ray-O-Vac alkaline."

Beware too of television commercials that are as emotion-packed as the programs they are sponsoring. One such sentimental sales pitch was the heartrending commercial featuring the little lady touting Madria-Madria Sangria. Buy her family's wine, she pleads, and she won't have to make more commercials. She would be freed, presumably, to attend to her struggling family's needs. A bit of investigation unearthed the fact that the "struggling little family" goes by the name of Gallo—one of the world's biggest winemakers, known as "The Coca-Cola of grapes." And her husband is the nephew of the famous and wealthy Ernest and Julio Gallo.

By now you probably think only television commercials can be misleading. Not true. It's just that television is the most powerful and penetrating advertising medium. In truth, you have to remain vigilant to any advertising claim that looks or sounds too good to be true.

For example, the head of a San Francisco group calling itself the Starving Artists, who advertised sidewalk art sales, admitted the group isn't starving at all. In fact, they were getting fat selling cut-rate paintings. Yet strolling along the sidewalk "galleries" you subconsciously feel that unless you buy a painting from these artists, they won't eat tonight. Naturally, we all want to help the downtrodden, and that desire—you might call it guilt because we're not starving—intimidates you to buy. But here's the irony of it all: Many of those so-called starving artists don't even paint the pictures they're trying to peddle. They buy from wholesalers who obtain the art from Europe, Asia, and South America. In Texas, a similar group known as Southwest Starving Artists Group of Dallas changed its name when local lawmen slapped it with a deceptive advertising suit.

If you put your faith in advertising without checking out the claims, you can be royally ripped off today, especially on high-priced, technical products. Advertisements for home stereo equipment are a prime example.

Technics, made by Panasonic, once ran an ad for a stereo

AM/FM receiver in a national women's magazine, headlined, "Knowing what you want in a receiver is one thing. Being able to afford it is Technics." Clever, eh? But being able to understand the advertisement itself is something else.

For instance, that receiver, also called an amplifier or tuner, talked about "our 3-stage direct couple phono equalizer section. It gives you a phono S/N ratio of 90 dB at 10mV (IHFA). . . ." And if that isn't mind boggling enough, it goes on to purr about the "kind of sensitivity you get: 10.8 dBf (1.9 uv IHF'58). That's impressive. That's the result of Technics-developed fla-group delay filters and a Phase Locked Loop IC in the MPX section."

Now I defy anyone other than a hi-fi buff or a sound engineer to understand what that advertising copy says. The manufacturer may claim the ad is designed to inform the reader. I think it's designed to confuse and intimidate. But advertising, even for something as technical as stereo equipment, doesn't have to intimidate you to sell you. In fact, another stereo manufacturer, Pioneer Electronics, ran an advertisement in the same women's magazine that was designed to reassure the reader. Its headline was even more eye-grabbing: "How to Buy a Stereo Without Going Through an Interpreter."

Even more refreshing was the copy that started off admitting, "Shopping for a stereo can be a confusing experience. Those complex components and that audio jargon can make anyone feel a little intimidated. But take heart. Because you can buy a terrific (and affordable) sound system without learning a second language." Essentially, the Pioneer ad for its Centrex line says "trust your ears" and don't get rattled by all those Einstein-like equations that can only distort your mind.

Still, the manufacturer's ads that pound brand recognition into your brain, are just setting you up for the second part of that one-two sales punch—the stereo retailer's newspaper ads that are crammed with merchandise and "low-low" prices that they hope will lure you into the store. Here's where it pays to be wary. Those big "supermarkets of sound" are just like food stores. Giant stacked displays. Weekend specials. Visual excitement. Lots of buying activity. Plus they have one marketing ingredient food stores don't have, an army of salespeople hovering around who normally work on a commission basis.

This warning doesn't belong in the advertising chapter but since it was an ad that pulled you into the store, I want to stress this one point: You must be careful not to get razzle-dazzled into spending more on a stereo outfit than your budget allows. Retailers call this point-of-purchase pressure and it often works. As one former stereo store manager told me, "Don't buy stereo equipment with the most knobs, switches, and dials just to impress your friends with its appearance. Unfortunately, many people do just that. Settle on a dollar figure and tell the salesperson flat out that's all you are going to spend and you'll walk out before you spend a dime more."

Now there is nothing misleading or deceptive about either the stereo magazine advertisement that's chock full of audio gobbledygook or the newspaper ads screaming about discount prices (as long as they're actually discounted, and you can check that by getting the manufacturer's list price and comparing). But they can be confusing. Just like anything confusing, you must take the time and effort to understand what you are reading.

Verify claims. Don't fall for "puffery prose," no matter what you're buying. Words like "new," "excellent," "improved" are grabbers, and advertising copywriters use them loosely. But I'll guarantee you this: The same advertising copywriter will rarely challenge the client to prove the product's superiority. Chances are, he's not looking out for your interest. He gets paid to help sell that product. And if he works for an advertising agency, his first and foremost concern is to make sure his ad firm hangs on to the account. Certainly there are ethical ad agencies which care about the truth and don't write dishonest ads, but many of them flirt with the truth to keep the profits up.

Do Something

I could fill this entire chapter with advertising anecdotes. But what you want to know, and what I want to tell you, is how you can counterattack an advertiser that tries to sandbag you. How you can singlehandedly blow a misleading commercial right off the air, or at least help to do it. How you can let a company of con artists know that you aren't going to stand for advertising that promises bargains and value or something unusual and doesn't deliver.

First, understand this: False, misleading, and deceptive advertising is against the law. It breaks certain federal laws. It breaks certain state and municipal laws. It's not a question of ethics or bad taste. False advertising is against the law and anything you can do to bring these lawbreakers to justice will benefit you and your fellow consumer.

So get mad when you see a bad ad!

Now what are you going to do about it? In the case of television commercials that make outrageous claims, that insult your intelligence, write the television station asking for documented proof that substantiates the claim. The Television Code of the National Association of Broadcasters, which most television stations adhere to, categorically states:

"Broadcast advertisers are responsible for making available, at the request of the Code Authority, documentation adequate to support the validity and truthfulness of claims, demonstrations, and testimonials contained in their commercial messages."

When you write the television station, call and find out the name of the general manager and address the letter to him personally. Refer to the above section in the Television Code and make it clear you want proof, too. If you don't get an answer in ten days, write directly to the Code Authority of the National Association of Broadcasters, 1771 N. Street, NW, Washington, DC 20036, and explain that your first letter was ignored by the television station that aired the commercial. Point out that you consider that snub to be a "clear violation"—and use just those words—of the Television Code. Demand substantiation.

Step two in your fight back strategy is to write the sponsor. Address it to the president at corporate headquarters (and by now you should know how to find that name and address—call a stockbroker, check with Standard & Poors corporation directory, or call the TV station and ask). Make your letter short and to the point. Namely, that you think the commercial is misleading and if it's not changed you won't buy the product and you'll tell all your friends to do the same. Try to find the name and address of the advertising agency that created the commercial and send a copy of the letter to the account supervisor for the product advertised.

If enough people react that way with threatened boycotts it can do a lot to change the sponsor's thinking. But you have to *take the time to complain,* to write the letter, to look up the addresses, to follow up. One reason we see misleading and mindless commercials in the first place is because not enough people want to be bothered to do what I call "constructive bellyaching." They just sit back, look at the TV, and simply say, "What a bunch of crap." But they won't do anything about it.

There are other ways to torpedo deceptive and misrepresentative advertising. Contact the leaders of the advertising industry and let them know you're angry. Advertising executives are continually trying to police their own members because they know public outcries over misleading advertising makes all advertising suspect.

Where do you complain? Start with the National Advertising Division of the Council of Better Business Bureaus (NAD). This is an effective self-regulatory organization that also monitors advertising to keep it honest. Between June 1971, when it was formed, and April 30, 1978, NAD handled 1380 complaints. Some 530 were dismissed in favor of the advertiser; 474 were won by the person or group lodging the complaint, and the advertiser in question either modified or scrapped the ad or commercial. Incidentally, consumers aren't the only people complaining to the NAD. Other advertisers beef about their competitors; they hate to see another product's deceptive advertising steal away their share of the market.

If for some reason the NAD can't resolve the complaint, or if a decision is appealed, it will go to the National Advertising Review Board (NARB) (845 Third Avenue, New York, NY 10022), sort of the Supreme Court of the advertising industry. Actually, it's not a legal court of law; decisions rendered are followed voluntarily. But it's exceptionally effective. NARB panels hearing a case consist of three advertiser people, one ad agency person, and one member of the public. It's not exactly an unbiased forum but it gets things settled.

For instance, Zenith Radio Corporation claimed in a commercial that, "Every color TV Zenith makes is built right here in the United States by Americans like these." But the NAD, contending that 14.5 percent of total components/parts were foreign made, found the advertising misleading. When Zenith refused to change its advertising, the case went to NARB; Zenith quit stonewalling and withdrew the commercial. Spalding had claimed its Top Flite golf ball was the "longest ball." But when the manufacturer disclosed it used two golfing shots—a drive off the tee and a 5-iron second shot—to support its claim, the NARB turned thumbs down. Most people, the panel ruled, would assume the term "longest ball" referred to a single stroke off the tee.

Meanwhile, if you think a radio or television station in your community seems to be running a rash of shady commercials, or if a radio or TV station gives you the brush-off when you try and complain, let the Federal Communications Commission know about it. This is the federal regulatory agency that grants licenses to radio and TV stations, and a stack of gripe letters about a particular station could do some real good. Write: Consumer Assistance Office, Federal Communications Commission, Washington, DC 20554, or telephone (202) 632-7000.

You can sometimes get fast recourse on a rip-off newspaper or magazine advertisement just by writing the publication that ran it, especially if it's a reputable publishing house. Dow Jones, Inc., goes to great pains to weed out the fly-by-nighters who try and slip flaky investment scheme advertisements into the Wall Street Journal or Barron's. Dow Jones wants to hear from readers who feel they have been taken in by a scamster who is recruiting suckers by using their publications. Barron's and the Wall Street Journal were the first newspapers to reject ads from a commodities option firm called Goldstein-Samuelson when the advertising claims, subtly implying enormous wealth, couldn't be substantiated. Shortly afterwards, the high-flying Beverly Hills firm with 80 offices nationwide collapsed in scandal and the founder was packed off to jail.

Better yet, the National Enquirer, which writes hard-hitting exposés of consumer fraud and government waste, as well as Hollywood gossip stories, refunded money to every reader who could prove he or she was conned by an Enquirer ad for a new, low-cost coffee. That type of rebate is rare. But the Enquirer didn't want its readers to get burned just because a promotional sharpie got one past them.

Few publications are going to give you your money back, but you can ask. And by writing and complaining, hopefully you can get those advertisers blackballed from the publication's pages and save a few other lambs from the financial slaughter. The most effective way to fight back is to write the publisher (his name is usually in the front of the magazine or on the editorial page of the newspaper) and send a copy of the letter to the advertising director. If you've been burned out of some bucks, send photocopies of cancelled checks, a copy of the advertisement itself, and a lucid explanation of the facts.

Get a Little Help

Up to now, we've gone the gentlemanly route. We've advised the advertising industry how to clean up their act. But that doesn't put a dishonest ad promoter out of business or convince an errant corporation to quit bilking consumers. That is what the Federal Trade Commission is empowered to do and, believe me, today they are the commandos of consumerism.

If you feel you've been misled or hurt by false or deceptive interstate advertising (an ad heard or seen in one other state besides your own), or if you've been victimized by an advertiser located outside your state, contact the Federal Trade Commission's Bureau of Consumer Protection, Washington, DC 20580. Telephone: (202) 523-3727. The FTC will send you a complaint form to fill out.

But you've got to make the effort. If the FTC finds your complaint valid, it will go straight to the advertiser you're accusing and let it know that Uncle Sam's concerned. If it's serious and there are enough complaints, then the FTC will press for a consent order where the advertiser agrees to "cease and desist" or simply stop the dishonest tactics without formally admitting any guilt. Once the Commission approves the final consent order, it's legally binding and will be enforced.

Some of America's biggest companies have signed FTC consent

orders on false advertising charges. General Electric Co. agreed it would never again advertise that independent surveys showed its color television sets require less service than other U.S. brands; it just wasn't true. The National Commission on Egg Nutrition was ordered to stop advertising that there is no evidence that eating eggs increases the risk of heart attack or heart disease. C&H Sugar agreed to stop claiming it is different or better because it comes from sugar cane grown in Hawaii; the FTC said there are no differences in granulated sugar.

What's more, the FTC has ordered some companies to run "corrective advertising" announcing that a product does not do what the original advertising said it did do. The maker of Listerine, Warner-Lambert Co., was ordered to spend $10 million to advertise that their mouthwash "will not help prevent colds or sore throats or lessen their severity."

Interstate Bakeries had to take out ads telling consumers that Wonder Bread did not "build strong bodies 12 ways" as advertising had claimed. And in a landmark decision, the FTC persuaded actor-singer Pat Boone to hold himself financially and personally accountable for the claims he makes in hawking all of the products he endorses (hot dogs, skin care products, milk). Said the head of the FTC Consumer Protection Unit when he announced the agreement with Boone: "Our purpose is really not to stop celebrity endorsements but to make sure when a famous figure decides to lend his or her name and credibility to a product that they make sure they are telling people the truth. We do not want people to be duped."

The Federal Trade Commission is cracking down even harder on the advertising industry. The deputy director of the FTC's Bureau of Consumer Protection has said the agency must expand its efforts to assure truthful advertising. Instead of just monitoring an ad's written or spoken message, he wants to focus on what he terms sophisticated advertising techniques that seduce buyers with picture, music, or mood. In other words, he wants to check the truthfulness of the "non-verbal message," that is, the notion that if you buy the advertised product you will be young, beautiful, successful. The advertising industry, however, views this latest move by the FTC as "pure harassment." Either way, it's something for you as a consumer to be aware of.

But you don't have to go to Washington, figuratively speaking, to fight a crooked advertiser. You've got plenty of muscle right in your own hometown. In the appendix, you will find a list of some city consumer protection offices. Usually these offices are staffed with lawyers and committed consumerists. Their job: to search out, prosecute, and fine companies and people who rip you off. And nowadays, consumer protection offices are really zeroing in on anyone huckstering products with false and misleading advertising claims.

The San Francisco district attorney won what was believed to be the largest settlement of a false advertising case in California history when Bank of America, the nation's largest bank, agreed to pay $275,000 in penalties to settle a civil lawsuit. The Bank of America was advertising its interest rates on auto loans as "low" and "very competitive." But the San Francisco D.A. found they were among the highest in California, and Bank of America borrowers were being socked an average of 3 percent more interest than customers who were financing autos at competitive banks. Thanks to a complaint by San Francisco Consumer Action, 2000 borrowers each received an $85 rebate as part of the settlement.

You've got clout. Use it when you get ripped off. But don't go overboard, and make sure you've got a sound case before you start firing off complaint letters. An attorney for a northern California county consumer protection agency dropped a false advertising suit against General Mills when he was convinced that Olympic decathalon champion Bruce Jenner does eat Wheaties and had eaten the cereal for some time as he had claimed in a television commercial.

Spotting Rip-offs

It all boils down to a simple fact: Informed consumers can spot advertising rip-offs before they get stung. But some are not so easy to spot. I personally resent the psychological mind-meddling top designers are using to turn us into walking billboards for their name and product line. If you haven't noticed, quite a few designers and status-conscious companies will hire a public relations firm to come up with a distinctive logo and make their name "chic" or "trendy" or otherwise fashion a hot image for themselves. Then they plaster that name on everything salable from shirts to sunglasses to suitcases to sheets. Consumers are subliminally convinced that they can be high class, fashionable, and "with it" by buying, wearing, and using that designer item. What's more, the designer line is always more expensive than the same item without the name or the initials.

When are we going to wise up to those subtle promotional ploys and quit being walking sandwich boards for every fashion promoter with a smart press agent? But it's gone beyond fashion and apparel. Today people are ordering imported bottled drinking water that would cost $4 if you were to buy it by the gallon. Domestic bottled drinking water costs about 60¢ a gallon. And in case you're curious, that same 60¢ would buy you 1000 gallons of tap water in most cities.

The national love affair with premium-priced imported water is getting ludicrous. Think about it. You can't drink the tap water in France, Spain, and other European countries without getting the "trots." Yet these same countries are exporting their sanitary bottled water and we're paying up to $1.75 for a 6-ounce bottle in some posh restaurants.

But you want to hear something incredible? On my "Consumer Buyline" show, we did a taste test of imported and domestic bottled waters plus our own water, Sparkling Buyline. The winner was a domestic bottled drinking water. Sparkling Buyline placed third. And the costlier imported waters finished on the bottom of the list—from a taste preference standpoint.

By the way, in case you're wondering, Sparkling Buyline, which was judged third best, was nothing more than Burbank, California tap water that had been carbonated.

Warranties (Guarantees)—Read Them Before You Buy

The fastest way to get yourself bagged when you buy is to ignore the warranty. Ask yourself this question and answer it honestly: do you read and completely understand the warranty on every item you buy? Sure, it takes time but it can save you time and money plus anxiety later on. And don't depend on the TV commercials to spell out the facts in a fraction of a second in small, hard to read type.

Until 1974, warranties were often bear traps that snagged the unaware consumer who wanted to return, replace or repair a product that didn't perform. It seemed the alluring advertisements or persuasive packaging persuaded you to buy, but the ambiguous warranty got the manufacturer off the hook.

The Magnusson-Moss Warranty Federal Trade Commission Improvement Act of 1974 changed that. Warranties are no longer loopholes that protect primarily the manufacturer. The federal law requires the manufacturer or retailer to let you read the warranty on any consumer product costing $15 or more *before* you buy. That's why you now see warranties printed on the outside of packages as well as inside or in the owner's manual. And if you can't find the warranty, ask to see a copy before you lay out your dough or your charge card. The retailer has to have a copy available.

In fact before I buy anything where the price is significant, I take the warranty home and read it closely. Believe it or not many companies will let you do it. It's a great way to safeguard your cash. It may cool you off from making an impulse buy. Or it may reinforce the fact you're getting a good value plus iron-clad protection.

Full Warranties—Strong Protection But Read Them Anyway

There are two types of warranties under the new federal law. The first is the "Full Warranty" and it's strong but not impenetrable. A full warranty means that a manufacturer must fix or replace a product free for a specific period of time—90 days, one year and so on. That time or warranty period is spelled out right in the warranty so look for it. And the repairs or replacement must be made within a "reasonable time"—and that too is stated in the warranty. In addition:

• The full warranty usually covers anyone who owns the product during the warranty period. But this varies. Some fully warranteed products do not allow you to transfer the warranty.

• The manufacturer in some cases will pay all shipping and handling charges both ways. Plus you cannot be charged to remove or reinstall the product like a major appliance under a full warranty, if that's required to get it fixed.

• The manufacturer who fails to fix the product or who admits it cannot be fixed after the "reasonable time" that he's given to fix it must give you either a replacement or your money back when the product is covered by a full warranty. In my experience getting a cash refund rarely happens.

You are still vulnerable under a full warranty, however, if don't read it closely. For instance, the entire product may not be covered in full, only the components. The television set is the classic example where the main picture tube may be the only part that is fully covered under the full warranty; if something else in the set goes haywire, you may have to pay.

Limited Warranties—Proceed at Your Own Risk

The other type of federal protection is the "limited warranty." When you see these two words, it means "danger—proceed with caution." A limited warranty, for example, usually only covers the cost of the parts, not the labor when the product breaks down. Here are some other limited warranty points:

• The limited warranty is almost always non-transferable.

• It gives you only a pro-rated refund based on how long you've actually used the product instead of all your money back.

• It requires that you pay the shipping and often the handling charges to send the product back to the manufacturer for repairs.

All warranties—full or limited—must now be written in plain English and be printed in easy-to-read type. Before the Magnusson-Moss Act, you practically had to be a lawyer to decipher a warranty that another lawyer had written in legalese.

There are still plenty of pitfalls though. Even if you see words like "unconditional" or "lifetime" guarantee, they're virtually meaningless unless there is a full warranty supporting them. Don't let empty hype trick you into thinking the manufacturer is poised to respond to your every problem, until death do you part.

Personally, I'm very leery of warranties that force you to send a product cross country to get it fixed, especially if it was made outside the United States. Over and over again viewers complain they send products, like watches, back for repair only to be told the service center is out of parts and they're out of luck for a couple of months. Look for products that can be repaired locally or have regional service centers near your home. Many do. If you're not sure, ask the clerk the precise location of the service center that will repair the product you're planning to buy.

Don't just read warranties. Comparison shop them just as you'd comparison shop price. You can score some smart buys. Most major tire manufacturers no longer grant warranties to protect motorists against "road hazards"—glass, nails, or anything you run over that can blow out a new tire. The majors had touted road hazard warranties but got burned by too many replacements. Yet some private labeled tires and lesser known brands still give you a road hazard warranty to get you to buy. That's a major inducement as far as I'm concerned. Any warranty that protects you longer and better can easily justify a higher price, but in many cases the private labeled tires sold for less than the majors. The message here: shop warranties, read them and understand them. And if you don't, ask questions.

Implied Warranties—Look Out

The Magnusson-Moss Act doesn't require every manufacturer to issue a warranty. It just sets down tough guidelines for those that do. However, all states have what's known as "implied warranties" which are unwritten guarantees. A common one is the "warranty of merchantability." This simply means the seller—either the store or manufacturer or both—promises that the product will do what they say it's going to do. A broiler has to broil, a power mower must cut grass. If it doesn't keep this promise, and it can't be repaired or replaced to do so, you're entitled to get your money back. But you can get involved in a hassle about whether the seller or the manufacturer is responsible for the resolution of your complaint and once again, you have to read sales contracts and purchase agreements carefully. A seller can easily wangle out of an implied warranty by stating in writing that you are buying the product "as is." For that reason, you should almost always avoid anything whenever you see the disclaimer "as is." Unless you can personally repair any possible defect then those two words are telling you loud and clear there is trouble ahead for the sucker who buys.

Getting Action

Don't try to memorize the warranties of everything you buy. Just save them and file them away. (Personally, I don't send in the warranty registration card unless I feel there is a potential safety problem with the product and then I want them to know where to reach me in case there is a nationwide recall. I never fill in the blanks on the warranty registration that asks for my income, occupation and other sales-information unless they want to compensate me for taking my time to do their market research for them.)

If you do have to return the product for repairs, just know your rights under your warranty and specify them in your correspondence. If they're in any way violated, don't get into lengthy letter writing battles with a distant manufacturer. Write one more letter then go directly to the Federal Trade Commission or your state consumer protection office.

Let's wrap up this chapter with some fast facts—ammunition against advertising rip-offs—that apply in most states.

• Any merchant knowingly or intentionally using dishonest advertising to sell you something can be fined and/or sent to prison. If he commits outright fraud, the victimized consumer can sue. In California he can sue for three times the damages sustained. Check the law in your state.

• Bait and switch advertising is illegal. Retailers cannot advertise one item to draw you into the store and bring out a costlier item for you to buy. Watch out for ads touting "limited quantities available." But in many states if an advertised item is really sold out when you get there, you can get a "raincheck" and pick it up when a new supply comes in. That's also the law.

• Merchants advertising "easy credit" and then demanding higher down payment and stiffer finance charges than they would normally require of a good credit risk are breaking the law.

• A merchant cannot advertise something "free" and then force you to buy another product or pay any type of fee before you get the freebie. Nor can the merchant raise the price of sale merchandise in connection with the free offer. In short, there can be no strings or conditions attached to the "free offer" unless they are specifically spelled out in the ad.

• If you get a defective product at a going-out-of-business sale or a "fire sale" or any sale that proclaims "all sales final," you can take it back to the retailer and get your money back unless it's clearly labeled "as is." They cannot refuse to give you a refund. And if it is a true going-out-of-business sale, don't accept a credit. Get cash.

• The word *special* should be used only to signify merchandise temporarily offered at a price concession. Once the supply of sale merchandise is gone, the item goes back to its normal pre-"special" price.

• A "closeout" sale should include only merchandise that has been permanently discontinued by the manufacturer. The retailer buys the inventory at a reduced price and is passing the savings along to the consumer.

• When you see the advertising claim "up to 20 percent off" (or any other numbered discount), at least one-tenth of the items advertised should be reduced by the percentage figure.

• The phrase "comparable value" should be used when the product is similar but not identical to merchandise regularly selling in the same price range.

• The phrase "formerly sold at" should indicate that the merchandise was formerly sold in the same metropolitan area by principal retail outlets at the higher price.

• A "warehouse sale" can offer cut-price merchandise only in a warehouse. You can't hold a warehouse sale in a retail store. A "clearance center" should sell only goods previously offered in the retail outlets of the company that operates the "clearance center."

By now I hope you can see that it takes more than cash or credit to be a consumer. You must be alert at all times and wise enough to spot any attempt to hype you. Standing up to false and manipulative advertising is one form of consumer karate. Keep on reading and you will have your consumer karate black belt before you know it.

FIGHT BACK!

Automobiles: Who Is Giving Whom a Ride? 6

I'm convinced that 95 percent of Americans do not really buy automobiles. They fall head over heels in love with 3000 to 5000 pounds of steel, glass, rubber, and plastic and wind up staging their own shotgun wedding. Worse yet, even before the honeymoon begins, they're already making support payments.

If you've ever bought a new or used car and felt gypped, you know I'm not exaggerating. The moment you walk on the lot, there's old Marrying Sam, a smiling salesperson who welcomes you with open arms. He sees the lust in your eyes, and he wants to get this over with quickly so he can court his next customer.

So he begins the mating ritual by showing you row after row of sleek bodied high performers or quiet, dependable "econoboxes" hoping that one may catch your fancy.

If you're like most car shoppers, he doesn't have to wait long. You spot the car of your dreams and your eyes announce the engagement. While he reassures you that you'll both have a long and happy life together, he tugs you to the "altar"—his stark sales office—and after a short proposal, you financially consummate the marriage. That's right, before you and your motorized mate get a chance to know each other, you fire up her engine and drive off.

I realize this is overly dramatic but I hope I've made my point. While few smart men and women plunge headlong into marriage on the first date, these same people will let their emotions steer them into a major financial commitment: buying an automobile. And once they've bought that car, and the infatuation wears off, a majority of people will not give the car proper care and attention and then the problems really start. What was once your pride and joy becomes an albatross around your neck and a parasite gnawing away at your pocketbook.

Or worse yet, you may buy a "lemon," which the industry describes as "a fixable, production line goof up," even though you go in with your eyes wide open. You either ignore the danger signs or you do not know what to look for. And when that happens, you'll find yourself stuck with a lead sled that's squeezing you dry with repair bills.

Let me give it to you straight: Be a smart, skeptical shopper when you go out to buy a car or fix a car. And if you do get ripped off, I want you to fight back. Even if you think the odds are stacked against you, I'm betting that you'll come out on top.

To start off, you have to realize that a car is nothing more than transportation—a hopefully reliable means of getting you from here to there. Personal transportation that saves you from riding the bus, taking a cab, or straphanging on a subway. Despite the efforts and money spent on Madison Avenue to persuade you to buy "luxury," "freedom," "elegance," or "dependability," remember you're only really buying transportation, not a "heritage of automotive excellence."

And unless you are collecting classic cars, an auto is not an investment, so get that out of your head. Unlike a house, boat, piece of land, or even a mobile home or camper that either grows in value or holds its own, an automobile is costing you money every day you drive it. In fact, you lose a huge chunk of its value when you drive it off the dealer floor—depreciation you indirectly pay when a new car becomes a used car. With a new car, you're starting off in the red.

Do I sound grim? I'm just being realistic. The Bureau of Labor Statistics said it could account for only $46.35 in actual improvements in the quality of 1979 American cars, yet the average price was hiked $300 over 1978 models. And most of those improvements involved manufacturers' changes to meet tougher safety and environmental regulations. Is it any wonder a new car seems to self-destruct in three years?

No Money Down? No Big Deal!

The fender-pounding, motor-mouthed car dealer has almost become a celebrity in American life. All he has to do is buy enough television advertising, pull enough zany stunts, scream about "slashed prices" and consumers gallop to his lot. They rush in, ready to buy, dump money in his lap, or practically grovel at his feet to qualify for his "no money down—easy credit terms."

These high-powered pitchmen cut their teeth hawking used cars in the early days of TV. They've moved up to new cars and the folks are still flocking. Now, I'm not knocking auto dealers who advertise on television. I just want you to know that someone is paying for that promotion and that someone is you. What's more, those rock-bottom discounts might be nothing more than alluring come-ons to entice you in and set you up for the sales shaft you never feel until the contract's been signed.

Be wary of braggarts and big boasts. In Los Angeles recently, Lyons Buick-Opel-GMC, Inc., which proclaimed itself to be the "world's largest Buick dealer," was put out of business by the Los Angeles District Attorney and the California Department of Justice. The charges? Thirty-nine unlawful business practices ranging from misleading advertising, sticking the buyer with "dealer preparation charges" when the factory reimbursed Lyons for it, demanding "good faith" or "commitment money" and using high pressure sales tactics to get buyers to sign on the dotted line.

The Lyons case is almost a classic example of how you can get ripped off buying a new car. For instance, the dealer himself was well known in his area and was a popular member of the Jaycees.

First lesson: Don't let your guard down just because you think you're dealing with a pillar of the community. Law officers claimed the discounts were often on expensive models where

prices had been padded by tacking on options marked up sometimes as much as 300 percent.

Second lesson: Don't get sucked in by discount claims and stiffed
by markups on equipment you wouldn't normally comparison
shop, such as factory air-conditioning or power brakes.

This dealer also engaged in bait and switch advertising. Cars
offered at specific low prices couldn't be found when the consumer came to the lot. Or they were banged up. Or the dealer
would get the customer lathered up and ready to buy telling him
to "order yours today." Then he would announce a "six- to eight-
week factory wait" for that model in order to sell a car that was
already on his lot.

Third lesson: No matter how car hungry you are, if the dealer
can't deliver what he promised you, walk out.

Lyons Buick used a "turnover" sales-technique where customers had to deal with a series of people, each trying to trade him
up. It was pure razzle-dazzle, according to the district attorney's
office. A "greeter" salesperson would quote a price, then tell the
buyer he wasn't authorized to sell the car at that figure. Another
salesperson would step in, take over the negotiations and try to
boost the original "reduced price." By the time the buyer was
"turned over" to the "closer," a super salesperson or the sales
manager—he was often confused by what the D.A. termed a pure
"psychological ploy."

Fourth lesson: At the first hint of pressure—and you know what
it feels like to be squeezed—walk off that lot, even if the salesperson is writing up that contract. Walk out and forget the car and
the salesperson. You're not hurting his feelings. And don't let him
or anybody else give you the "guilties" with any sob story. Remember, you're going to be making those payments for a long
time so don't get rushed, hustled, or intimidated into buying a car
you're not 100 percent sold on.

Finally, Lyons's salespeople tried to wangle "good faith" or
"commitment money" out of customers *before* the final terms of
the sale were agreed upon. A deposit *after* the sale is made is a
lawful request. But before terms are finalized the dealer can't ask
you for a dime.

Fifth lesson: Don't just blithely give money to any merchant who asks for it before you've made up your mind to buy. The car dealer is trying to sell your subconscious mind so that it will influence your conscious mind and you'll agree to his terms. That "good faith" tactic is real mind manipulation so don't fall for it.

Now are you ready for the capper to this case? I checked with the Buick Motor Division of General Motors in Detroit to see if Lyons was in fact really the "world's largest Buick dealer" as he had bragged. While a Buick press agent explained that size can be measured a number of ways, he confessed that Lyons was perhaps "eighth or ninth biggest" in the United States. Asked if auto manufacturers monitor claims made by their dealers, the spokesperson said the dealer is "an independent businessman" who operates his own company.

What's the bottom line? It pays to fight back. The law, acting on consumer complaints, investigated and acted. It also fined the dealership $250,000 and Lyons president-general manager another $100,000. The judge further ordered the dealer to pay $3000 in restitution to one customer and $966 to another person who had been ripped off.

The Lyons case is a rare one but certainly not an isolated example of how you can be conned when buying an expensive item if you don't do your homework first. Or worse yet, if you don't know when or how to say no. If you have any doubts about the car, say no! If the deal sounds too good to be true, say no.

Watch out for the greedy dealer who hikes prices on popular models. This to me is one of the most sinister of all rip-offs. The Madison Avenue boys get you so revved with advertised and word-of-mouth hype that you make a beeline to the dealer and buy a $7000 automobile as if were a 39¢ bar of soap. But it's often the buyer's own fault. He hears everybody praising a particular automobile and he has to have one. Cars, sadly enough, have become fashion items and some people are obsessed with being fashionable.

But you pay a lot more for fashion. This happened recently when Mazda's RX-7 and the Honda Accord hit the showroom floors. Mazda's sports car looked so zippy and Honda's Accord delivered such great gas mileage and was loaded with such groovy electronic gizmos and standard accessories that the press headlines and promotional hoop-la brought in a stampede of buyers. The dealers were ecstatic. Since automobile dealers are independent businesspeople and free from factory control, they can set their own prices and it's not illegal. But wouldn't you know it—some chiselers jacked up the cost $1000 to $2000 over the sticker price and told buyers to take it or leave it. It's a prime example of how that basic fundamental of economics, the law of supply and demand, can work against us. Even with the inflated prices, people were willing to pay anything to get their hands on one of those cars just so they could be the first on their block to flash one.

Mazda, to its credit, tried to stamp out this rip-off, warning dealers in a letter dated May 23, 1978, that its "market position can be destroyed" if consumers are exploited. But no one can stop automobile price gouging more effectively than you, the customer. All it takes is some shopping around. And if you do find a dealer that's trying to cash in on the public's love affair with a certain automobile, march in and announce that not only are you going to boycott him, you're going to tell your friends, the factory, and the press he's out to bilk the public. That's right, tell the press. If you're the first to spot a potential rip-off, you've got a hell of an exclusive so don't sit on it.

But you have to complain. And by beefing you're doing your fellow consumers and yourself a big favor. You can get not only revenge—if you were financially victimized you might get your money back. For example, a high-volume Ford dealer in the West was zapped by city attorneys for failing to spell out the facts in sales contracts. They were important facts too, like the amount of down payment, total number and sum of payments, and the finance charges. The dealership also failed to state accurately the model years of the cars that it sold, whether they were new or used vehicles, and whether the down payments were refundable.

Now you might say an intelligent consumer shouldn't even sign a sales contract riddled with such obvious omissions. You're right but remember, even people who are otherwise informed are often putty in the hands of a skilled salesperson. Many sign just to get him off their back. These are people who have a difficult time saying no to anyone.

If you get rattled and you do sign on the famed dotted line and you sincerely feel you got ripped off, report it to your local governmental consumer watchdog. It may pay off. The Ford dealership that was snagged using incomplete sales contracts was ordered, as part of a stipulated judgment, to pay $1900 to three buyers who complained.

I could write a thick book on how to buy a new car. But some good ones have already been written. Instead, my mission in this chapter is to drive home two critical messages: Buy your new automobile from a dealer with a solid gold reputation for fairness, service, and satisfaction, and be an informed but skeptical buyer.

For example, how do *you* know if you're getting a fair price or a financial reaming from your friendly neighborhood dealer? Simple. A New York firm called Car/Puter International will send you a computer printout of the dealer's cost for a car together with the recommended retail price. You specify the model of the car and the options you want and for $11 the printout tells all. Write: Car/Puter, 1603 Bushwick Ave., Brooklyn, NY 11207. The company has a toll-free number, (800) 221-4001, so you can feed in the information and charge the printout to a credit card. *Consumer Reports* also tells you how to figure the dealer's cost on the car of your choice.

Armed with hard cost figures, you can figure out the dealer's markup and net profit. Remember, a dealer has to make at least $200 to $300 in profits when you buy one of his infernal combustion machines. On luxury foreign cars, he can make huge profits. To protect yourself, notes Car/Puter, you can order your Detroit-built automobile through its subsidiary, United Auto Brokers. United, it claims, will sell you a new car at $125 over dealer cost plus, in some cases, a $75 delivery fee.

Just because you think you are making a killing on the car's basic price, don't go hogwild ordering accessories and options. They add up fast, and that's where the dealer can make a lion's share of his profits. First, you don't have to buy the dealer's options. In fact, you're usually better off buying the radio elsewhere. Factory radios are generally overpriced and underpowered. The factory "upgrade" AM/FM stereo tape player is better merchandise, but the steeper price is no bargain. And would you really play tapes? Shop wisely and don't pay for options you'll never use.

You must always go in armed to the teeth with cost/price information. Know exactly the equipment you want. If you look and sound savvy, the salesperson might quote you a reasonably fair price right off. He works on a straight commission and doesn't want to waste his time playing the offer/counter-offer game if he sees you're aware and leery rather than ignorant and eager.

Keep your guard up. Watch out for his "lowball" ruse to psychologically sell you before you consciously buy. Here's how it works. The salesperson tosses out a real bargain price and you pounce on it. Then his boss, the sales manager, nixes the deal and browbeats him in front of you, claiming, "You know we can't sell the car that cheaply even though you're trying to give these folks your best deal."

The sales manager quotes a much higher price, the salesperson sheepishly shrugs, and you feel sorry for the chastised salesperson and go along with the more expensive deal because you now consider him your friend. Another tricky tactic takes place when the sales manager finds a "mistake" in his salesperson's arithmetic and bumps up the price—*after* you have psychologically bought the car. If any dealer tries to suck you in with these old but effective con games, walk out. And don't let yourself be lured back.

A few final tips before you buy: Don't fall for the "highest trade-in/lowest price in town" dealer siren song. You can't get it at both ends so try to sell your trade-in car to a private party; you'll come out better in the long run. How do you set the price? Call the loan officer at your bank or credit union and they will give you the wholesale and retail price. They will probably quote from a Kelley Blue Book and that can also give you some idea what the new car you are buying is worth after it's been driven around the block and depreciated. Also check the classified ads to see what your current car is selling for.

Another smart piece of advice is to never rush out and buy an automobile that wins a "car of the year" award. Automotive magazines that bestow these accolades often award these "honors" to the manufacturer that buys the most advertising pages. And a "buy recommendation" or a "rave review" from an automotive columnist shouldn't sway you either. Automakers throw gala free-loading junkets or supply free perfectly tuned test automobiles for auto writers. Unfortunately, most auto scribes won't bite the hand that feeds them. For objective appraisals on autos, stick with the impartial consumer magazines that carry no advertising and never allow their ratings to be used in any ads for the top-rated items.

Test It Before You Take It

After you've haggled and bought, but before you take delivery, spend some time—at least two hours—and check out everything mechanical on that car before you drive off. Take it on a stiff test drive, not just a spin around the block. And make sure your salesperson rides with you. If he balks, call for the sales manager and ask him to ride along. Everything on your new car must work. Too many people swoon at the sight of all that gleaming chrome and painted steel and they can't wait to show it off. While you're at it, check for dings, rust spots and paint defects—and do it in the daylight, *not* at night!

Also, audit your bill of sale to make sure all of the options you bought and paid for are on the car. Last minute equipment switcheroos are not uncommon. In fact some people never get the car they bought and, worse yet, never know the difference. If you inspect the car and anything is wrong or does not work, write it out on a piece of paper, get the salesperson to sign it agreeing that he knows you're bringing the car back to get those defects fixed. If he hesitates, call the sales manager. Should neither person want to sign your "agreement memo," trouble is brewing, so leave the car. And if you discover a major mechanical flaw, don't accept the car no matter how badly you want to roar off in it.

Okay, the car is yours and you find mechanical defects while you're under the warranty period. Don't be surprised; most new cars have at least a few bugs. But before you storm back to the dealer take some time and read your owner's manual. It's must reading and will tell you how your new car works and what you have to do to keep it purring. However, too many eager buyers simply toss it in the glove box and never read a word.

After you've read it cover to cover, if you still think you have a problem, go back to the dealer service manager. You should get to know him on a first-name basis; he's the doctor for your new car and you're paying part of his salary. Describe every defect and make sure he logs every point on the work order. If it still isn't fixed to your satisfaction, don't erupt in a rage. Just calmly write the dealer a personal note and make an appointment to visit him. Odds are you'll settle your grievance on the spot when you talk to the boss.

Still no satisfaction? Take your case to the next highest level, the zone or district office. You'll usually find the address inside the owner's manual. Once again, write, don't call. Spell out the problems, include copies of correspondence, work orders, and other relevant data and describe specifically what you expect to have done to the car.

The automakers tell me practically every gripe is settled at the zone level. But if you're not happy, write the manufacturer and direct your beef to the chief executive officer. (A list of the automakers' top brass is found at the end of this chapter.) And, as you'll recall from Chapter 4, your local AUTOCAP (Automobile Consumer Action Panel) might help you with your hassle, through their voluntary arbitration efforts. Again, no guarantees.

Now if you think your new automobile is unsafe at any speed and the manufacturer, for some strange unknown reason, is foot-dragging on your complaint or is giving you a royal runaround, fire off a telegram (make it a night letter and save yourself a couple of bucks) or a mailgram or a detailed explanatory letter to the following places:

Chief Counsel, National Highway Traffic Safety Administration, Washington, DC 20570. (They have a toll-free auto safety hotline, too: 800/424-9393); Consumer Product Safety Commission, Washington, DC 20270 (toll-free hotline: 800/638-2666) or write the privately run Center for Auto Safety, 1223 DuPont Circle Building, Washington, DC 20036 (telephone: 202/659-1126). The Center, launched in 1970 by a Consumers Union grant, does an excellent job and has some real teeth, so keep it posted on any prolonged battle you may be having with a carmaker.

And don't give up. It takes stamina to complain effectively, and too many people throw in the sponge when Big Business stonewalls. But this ought to pump you up: The federal Office of Consumer Affairs claims automotive problems are the consumers' Number One headache. So don't feel you're alone in fighting back over a problem-plagued auto. You'll make headway if you hang in. In fact, a spokesperson for one of Detroit's big three automakers confessed to me that some fat lemons roll off automobile production lines—cars that simply cannot be fixed. If you're stuck with one and you complain long and loud enough, you might get it replaced. But it may be a long struggle and you may need an attorney before you're through. You can get an excellent pamphlet, the "Lemon Guide," for $1.00 from the Maine Bureau of Consumer Protection, Augusta, Maine 04333, which tells you how to go about it.

Used but Not Taken

Buying a used car is about as safe as swimming with sharks. If the new car dealer turns out an occasional lemon, the used car dealer turns out a groveful. And when you buy from a private party, are you getting the schoolmarm's carefully driven coupe or the salesman's worn out sedan? It's almost impossible to know unless you're a seasoned mechanic or a body and fender man.

That doesn't mean you have to be a sucker. You've learned to drive defensively just to survive. Now you're going to become a defensive buyer.

First, know what kind of car you are buying, especially when you deal with a private party. The California Highway Patrol claims the low-priced car that sounds like a steal may be just that —stolen. Check ownership certificates and identification numbers on any car or parts you purchase privately with the Department of Motor Vehicles or your local police department. By trusting a friendly face or leaping at a low price, you could be unwittingly buying a "hot car." Worse yet, you could wind up on the losing end of a "receiving stolen property" rap.

With an established dealer, you wouldn't have that worry. Many used car dealers have cleaned up their acts and you're less likely to get burned with a "wax job"—that's what car dealers call a clunker that's cleaned up and parked on the "front line." Smart, reputable dealers today wholesale out their high-mileage autos and borderline junkers to "iron lots"—car dealers who then peddle them as transportation cars. Before you buy, you might want to check the latest April issue of *Consumer Reports*—that's the Annual Auto Issue. It will list the "frequency of repair" records for the past 5 years on all popular cars. The ratings are based on actual reports from owners. They will help you steer clear of brands and models that have more than the average number of repairs and will indicate which system needed the repairs (transmission, electrical, brakes, and so on). You'll know that you can expect that car to spend a lot of time in the shop and you'll know which cars are relatively trouble-free.

But even then, there is no foolproof way to buy a trouble-free used car. You can't depend on the dealer to protect you. You must remain skeptical and wary and ask questions no matter what kind of car you're buying.

Beware of bargains. The sale-priced car may not be stolen but you could be shelling out your cash or signing up to finance an ex-police car, a company fleet car, or a one-time taxicab. If you find a car that you want to buy, hire both a mechanic and an auto body repairperson to inspect it thoroughly from stem to stern. You'll find out if the car has been in a major accident, if it has a damaged frame, or has been rebuilt and reconditioned to hide the wear and tear. Remember, this is a dose of preventive medicine; not immunization against being ripped off.

You can spot some of the red flags yourself. Oversprayed paint on wheels, around headlights, on chrome strips and corners is a good tipoff the car was once crunched. So is fresh welding under the trunk or hood. Body panels with mismatched paint are another danger sign. Check for rust. It spreads and cannot be covered by paint. If you find any traces of rust or prior damage or if the car is "full of plastic" as dealers describe a car that has once been "totaled," don't touch it.

Don't trust the odometer to tell you the true mileage. The National Highway Traffic Safety Administration says odometer fraud is a billion dollar rip-off despite a 1972 federal law banning rollbacks. NHTSA figures an unscrupulous car dealer can pocket

$200 to $400 for every 10,000 miles peeled off. While federal law states the seller must inform the buyer if the odometer has been tampered with, guess how many 'fess up? You're right. Almost no one. Besides nobody seems to be enforcing the statute.

You have to protect yourself. Look for frayed wires, belts, or hoses under the hood of a low-mileage car. Check to see if the tires are factory originals; they should be if the car shows 25,000 to 30,000 miles on the odometer. If you see a different brand tire on each wheel, watch out. Check the door to see if an overlooked lube sticker might reveal the actual mileage. Finally, try to contact the former owner if you are buying the car from a dealer.

But there are other warnings that should sound a consumer alert in your mind such as fresh oil or fluid leaks. To check for leaks, fire up the engine and let it idle over clean pavement. Also watch for white or black exhaust; it should be clear. Inspect the tread on the accelerator or brake pedal; if it's worn down and the car isn't very old, it's a safe bet the previous owner was a hard-driving leadfoot. Lean on the fenders to check the shock absorbers; too much bounce means they are shot. Finally, do some simple arithmetic. A car is usually driven 12,000 to 15,000 miles a year. If you come across a three-year-old car that shows 17,000 miles on the odometer, odds are you'll be taken for a ride if you buy it.

Before you buy that car, find out exactly what the warranty covers. They range all over the lot (no pun intended) but generally they don't give you much protection. Even reputable dealers offer little more than the 30-day "50/50" protection warranties on the "power train." That means if something breaks in the engine, transmission, or differential, you and the dealer split the repair costs. Some dealers will try and sell you extra peace of mind—a two-year warranty that pays 100 percent of the costs on parts and labor. But it too can only cover the power train and can cost you up to $250. Considering repair costs today, though, it might be a wise investment. Some dealers have special tags on their best cars and offer full warranties for at least 30 days. You'll pay more but it may be worth it.

Next, take that used car out and test drive it. Or have your mechanic drive it. Veteran car salespeople tell me there is no way you can check out a used car without driving it hard for five to ten miles. Yet too many buyers, either in a hurry or intimidated, will take the car only on the proverbial "spin around the block." That tells you nothing. Do the brakes grab or pull? Does the steering wheel have a lot of play? Could be a rip-off about to happen.

In many states, however, the dealer is required by law to make sure the car is safe. The horn, brakes, and lights all must work. The old "as is" sales contract is no longer valid in some states and it's not a good idea to sign one anyway. (In fact, don't ink anything without reading it slowly three times and questioning anything you don't understand.)

After you've worked out the financing (we cover that and insurance in Chapter 11), the car is yours. Here's the acid test for your dealer's reputation. A mechanical foul-up in the power train in the first month may be covered under the warranty. But what happens if a voltage regulator goes haywire three weeks after you bought the car? The honest, professional dealer will replace it for free or at his cost, no questions asked. He wants to preserve or enhance his reputation and he knows good word-of-mouth advertising pays fat dividends in new customer referrals.

Not all used car dealers worry about their reputation and some will try to stick you with that sick car. It's the old "you bought it sucker, it's yours" philosophy. Fortunately, many states are wising up to these con artists and now give you a chance to "reject" a ripening lemon. If you sense real trouble and the dealer won't fix it fast, reject it immediately and in writing. By driving it around town for three weeks before you gripe, a shady dealer can claim you "accepted it" and you're stuck. And by then the financing will have cleared, making it tougher to cancel the deal. So if you smell a rip-off on a used car, complain to your state department of motor vehicles, the agency that issues dealer sales licenses and is empowered to suspend dealer crooks and cheats. Or complain to the zone office if you're buying a used car from a factory authorized dealer.

Meanwhile, you'll be happy to learn that your Uncle Sam is trying to put the brakes on fraud and deception in the used car business. The Federal Trade Commission recently proposed tough new regulations that would force used car dealers to tell prospective buyers everything that's mechanically wrong with the automobiles they're trying to peddle.

The FTC wants the dealer to inspect the car mechanically before it goes on the lot. If the FTC wins out, the dealer will have to paste on a window sticker disclosing any mechanical problems, the car's past use, actual mileage, warranty terms, and whether the car has ever been "totaled out" by an insurance company because of an accident or flood damage. Any mechanical system listed as "not OK" on the sticker will have to include the approximate cost to fix it.

As I'm writing this book, the National Automobile Dealers Association is fighting this proposal. But we need this protection. The FTC says 10 million used cars are sold annually, and at least 10 percent—a cool one million autos—are defective. If these proposals are enacted it could be a giant step forward for consumerism, and I salute the Federal Trade Commission for helping us fight back.

Auto Repair Rip-Offs: A Short Drive to the Poorhouse

Here's a statistic that will make you sick. Consumers spend a whopping $50 billion a year on car maintenance and repair. But the National Highway Traffic Safety Administration claims $20 billion of it is wasted on incompetent mechanics and needless fix-up jobs. In other words, a full 40 percent of the bucks we spend to keep our cars running right is cash thrown out the window.

Hell, for that kind of money, we could hire chauffeur-driven limousines most of the year.

But we still keep on flushing that money down the drain. Most of us who don't know a timing chain from a thermostat continue to offer up our sick cars—and our cash—to mechanics and repair people and pray to the Almighty that we don't get ripped off. We're convinced the mechanic is out to chisel us and we only hope we can get away with our cars and wallets intact.

That's the wrong attitude. You're admitting to yourself you're an ignorant turkey and you quickly assume every mechanic is a crook ready to carve you up.

From this moment on, you're going to take the upperhand in dealing with auto repair people. No, I'm not trying to turn you into a master mechanic and suggest you fix your own car. Actually, I'm trying to turn you into a master consumer who, I hope, can spot a greedy or bumbling mechanic at 20 paces.

I know this sounds like I'm singing my same old song but you have to be aware and informed. You wouldn't let just any doctor operate on you. But too many times motorists will freely let *any* mechanic, or for that matter anyone toting a wrench who claims to be a mechanic, stick his head under their hood to diagnose and cure precision machinery that has a thousand or more working parts.

Why invite a rip-off? That self-professed expert might look at your dead engine and press you to buy an alternator or a new battery when all you really need is to have your battery terminals cleaned. If you take that "expert's" advice, you can quickly spend a hundred bucks or more when any legitimate mechanic or service station would clean off your battery terminals and cables free.

How do you find a mechanic you can trust? Essentially, you have 6 choices: the new car dealer's service department, an independent mechanic who owns a garage, the corner service station mechanic, the shopping center auto repair center, the major department store's auto departments, and the moonlighting mechanic who offers to fix your car at night in his own garage at "his cost."

Forget the last guy unless he's a blood relative. It could cost you plenty. You have no guarantee he'll fix your car right and you have no recourse if he botches the job.

As for the service station, you may be better off to do business only with a national oil company station operated by an independent dealer who actually does the mechanical work himself. Make certain he's been there for several years and is not a johnny-come-lately. Some gas stations are operated by the oil company itself and these "company ops" are staffed by salaried employees who are putting in their time and don't have their own dough on the line; they can be transferred to another station tomorrow. The advantage here is that if you *are* ripped off, the major oil company will step in to help resolve the complaint. Most major oil company stations are operated by an independent businessperson who has sunk his own money into that station and his livelihood depends on repeat business and favorable word-of-mouth. That's to the good, but if there should be trouble and you complain to the oil company, you'll be told it can't interfere because it doesn't own the station—it just supplies the products.

In trading with a national oil company, you've got some built-in protection against rip-offs, especially if you've paid for the repairs by credit card. You can fight back by filing a formal complaint, subtract the disputed amount from your monthly statement, and, by law, the credit card company must step in and settle the dispute.

Just because you're dealing with a franchise dealer is no guarantee that the transaction will be a totally honest one. Recently, a Mobil Oil dealer was fined $1250 and placed on 12-months probation when undercover police investigators were sold a new carburetor and were not supplied with a detailed service invoice on a perfectly running car that simply had a spark plug wire disconnected. The Los Angeles City Attorney's Consumer Protection Section, acting on a consumer complaint, handled the investigation and won the judgment when the dealer pleaded "no contest" to two counts of attempted petty theft.

The shopping center or franchised repair shops are convenient, usually spotless, and over advertise specials. But unless you personally know the mechanic doing the work or know someone who has tested their guarantee, be cautious. Heavy advertisers usually have a volume quota to meet and bargain prices can often lure you into the shop where mechanics just happen to find you need other expensive repairs. If it isn't on the work order specifying original repairs you came in for, get indignant. Say you will check it with your "own mechanic." Even if they tore the engine down to start on that just-discovered ailment, make it clear you won't pay for it and will complain loudly if they try to charge you for putting the engine back.

But you do have some assurances at auto centers operated by Sears, J.C. Penney's, Montgomery Ward, Firestone, and other nationally known concerns that usually stand behind their work. These names have become globally known because they keep people happy with their guarantee policies. But ask yourself: Is this a mechanic who has a stake in the community or an employee who just looks at you and your car as "another job"?

The mechanic at your automobile dealer might be advisable if you want a true specialist who generally works on only one line of cars. He doesn't have to advertise because people who buy new cars there normally have them serviced and repaired where they buy. But generally his parts and repair prices are steep because the service department has to pay its share of the hefty dealer overhead. Besides, you never know if you're going to get the same mechanic twice unless you call ahead and reserve him.

Finally, there's the local, independent garage owner. He can't afford expensive newspaper or television so he relies solely on word-of-mouth advertising spread by satisfied customers. On the other hand, he doesn't have a giant corporation standing behind him. But then neither does your family doctor. However, if he has been a part of your community for at least five or ten years, keeps his garage reasonably clean (it shouldn't look like a grease-soaked auto graveyard) and you personally know a few of his customers, chances are he is trustworthy and competent.

How do you find a top-notch qualified mechanic? Check with the National Institute for Automotive Service Excellence, 1825 K Street, Washington, DC 20006 (202/833-9646). NIASE will furnish you with a directory of mechanics who have taken their voluntary certification program. This is a tough test of mechanic's skills and while it isn't a surefire guarantee that you'll go away happy, NIASE itself will respond to any complaints you may have with its graduates.

There are two other trade associations that are hard at work trying to scrub up the mechanic and garage owners image. One is the 3700-member Automotive Service Association, 8311 Shoal Creek Boulevard, Austin, TX 78766 (512/485-5353). This 28-year-old association has recently teamed up with the Better Business Bureau to establish arbitration panels in some states. The other group is the 5000-member Automotive Service Council of Independent Garage Owners, 188 Industrial Drive, Elmhurst, IL 60126 (312/530-2330). You can spot its members by their blue and white IGO sign. In addition, the American Automobile Association offers some measure of security with its 4000 "approved" repair shops across the country. AAA-approved mechanics give you a limited 90-day or 4000-mile guarantee on all AAA work, and they will referee hassles. Write AAA, 8111 Gatehouse Road, Falls Church, VA 22042 (703/222-6671).

Even if you are able to avoid auto repair clip joints, here are some solid tips on how not to get ripped off no matter who you do business with:

• Describe *all* your car's ailments to the mechanic but don't try to diagnose the cure. That's what you're paying him for. Hopefully you've chosen a mechanic who has electronic and mechanical diagnosing testing equipment and the know-how to use it. A well-equipped garage is a good sign you're dealing with a pro.

• Get a written estimate on all of the work he prescribes. Read the estimate closely and question him on anything you don't understand. Be concerned, not blasé; it's your car and your money. Give him the go-ahead but leave a number where he can call. Some state laws won't let him undertake additional repairs without your okay. If your state has such a law and the final price exceeds the estimate without your blessing, you don't have to pay him for it.

• Tell him out front you want all the parts he replaces. Even if you don't want them, take them with you. On the offhand chance something might go afoul, old parts are good evidence. And if you don't make the request in advance, the mechanic isn't required to save the old part.

• Make it clear you want factory replacement parts. There's a wave of cheaper priced, foreign-made parts flooding the United States. Some mechanic might be tempted to install them in your car and charge you the going price plus his markup for factory replacement parts. If you're getting the car fixed, don't skimp on parts.

• If you think you are in for major repairs—valve and ring job, transmission, front end or engine overhaul—get at least two and preferably three estimates unless you know your mechanic intimately and trust him. Many motorists who blow transmissions wind up at the nearest transmission shop because they don't want to spend the money to have it towed elsewhere. If your car breaks down and you limp into just any repair shop, you might be a duck about to be plucked.

You might want to check and find out whether your mechanic charges "flat rates" sometimes called "job rates." The new car shops usually do. They claim you'll save money because if they charge a flat fee for a certain job, you won't pay more for a slow mechanic or a pesky delay than you would if they charged by the hour. Some states are trying to outlaw this, but they haven't succeeded in most cases. That's one of the reasons it's a good idea to get estimates. The mechanic who charges by the hour knows just how long it will take him to do the job and you could save money.

Don't be duped by gas station gypsters. Despite warnings by lawmen and consumer organizations, highway travelers today are continually conned into buying unneeded tires and parts. These bandits are only a cut above child molesters; they squirt grease on shocks and wheels and prey on your fears by telling you the master brake cylinder is shot or your shocks will throw the car out of kilter and you'll never reach the next town. If that happens thank them for their concern and check out the alleged problem with the two other gas stations up the road.

• Ask the mechanic exactly what his guarantee covers. Don't be embarrassed to discuss it before you turn your car over to him. It can save you a lot of grief later on.

A word of caution: If your car is under warranty, you must have the repair done by a factory authorized repair shop. If you're out on a Sunday and the car breaks down and you drive into a gas station, you won't be reimbursed for the repair. Furthermore, if something else goes wrong with the same system, your dealership may blame the mechanic who worked on it for doing the job wrong. Even though it may be inconvenient, try and wait until Monday and take the car to the dealer.

If you're on a trip and you have to be towed into a small town, you have to call and get approval for repairs if there isn't an authorized dealer. An independent garage can be authorized to do the work. The emergency numbers to call are usually listed in your new car handbook. Be sure you have it handy in the glove compartment and that you read it!

As you might suspect, there are hundreds of ways you can be cheated by a crooked auto repair person and I don't have the room to cover them all. But if you do legitimately feel you've paid for a bad repair job, what can you do about it?

First, go back to the mechanic who did the work. Don't jump down his throat. Simply tell him your car is not running right. Mechanics are only human and today's cars are extremely complex, so he could have made an honest mistake. Give him the benefit of the doubt and ask him to fix it without charging you. I want to underscore this point: The vast majority of the merchants you'll meet are not rip-off artists but trustworthy businesspeople who value you as a customer and hope you'll refer your friends.

However, if he refuses to make good your repairs, don't throw a fit. Walk out and complain to your local police department or the Bureau of Automotive Repair if your state is enlightened enough to have one.

Secondly, if you paid by cash or check, go to a legitimate garage which stands behind its work and get your car fixed. Then get a written statement of the work done and what was wrong. With that, you can file suit in your local small claims court and the mechanic will have to reimburse you for the money you spent to get your car running again. Make sure it isn't more than the court maximum. It's worth the effort to fight that incompetent or dishonest mechanic in court.

You are in the best position of all, however, if you paid the first mechanic by credit card. Write the oil company or credit card concern that you were ripped off and you want the amount of the worthless repairs subtracted from your statement. As I've mentioned earlier, under the Fair Credit Billing Act, the credit card company must fight this battle for you. What's more, they can't slap you with late charges or interest payments on that charge while the dispute is being hammered out.

When you win the battle with this rip-off repair person (and you will if you fight back hard enough), you can't just take your money and gloat. You have a responsibility to your fellow consumers. Set aside some time and outline your experience in a letter. Then send it to your local Better Business Bureau, any trade association the repair person may belong to, local governmental consumer fraud agencies, and private consumer organizations, even newspaper and television consumer action lines. Spread the word! Sound a consumer alert.

As consumers we must realize we have to join forces, share intelligence, keep each other informed about out-and-out con artists in the community. If you can save someone from getting suckered by the same person who almost bagged you, you're performing a valuable public service. Hopefully, someone will return the favor and keep you from getting burned!

FIGHT BACK!

Appendix

If you can't get that new car of yours to work right or you had out-of-warranty work done at a dealership which you think the factory should pay for and you can't get any satisfaction from your dealer or the regional office, rev yourself up and go to the top. Write the president of the company and give him a blow-by-blow account of the situation complete with documentation to substantiate your story. Or call the president on the company's dime. Check with toll-free directory assistance (800-555-1212) to see if they have a free WATS line serving your state.

ALFA ROMEO
Aldo Bozzi, Chief Executive
   Officer
250 Sylvan Avenue
Englewood, NJ 07632

AMERICAN HONDA
MOTOR COMPANY
K. Yoshizawa, President
100 Alondra Boulevard
Los Angeles, CA 90247

AMERICAN MOTORS
CORPORATION
Gerald Meyers, President
27777 Franklin Road
Southfield, MI 48034

BMW OF NORTH
AMERICA
John Cook, President
Montvale, NJ 07645

BRITISH LEYLAND
MOTOR CORPORATION
Graham Whitehead,
   President
600 Willow Tree Road
Leonia, NJ 07605

CHRYSLER MOTOR
CORPORATION
Lee Iacocca, President
P.O. Box 1919
Detroit, MI 48231

FORD MOTOR
CORPORATION
Phillip Caldwell, President
Rotunda & Southfield
Dearborn, MI 48121

FIAT MOTORS OF NORTH
AMERICA
Claudio Ferrari, President
155 Chestnut Ridge Road
Montvale, NJ 07645

MAZDA MOTORS OF
AMERICA

(Western and Central States)
Toru Ogawa, President
3040 East Ana Street
Compton, CA 90221

(Eastern States)
Hideo Suetsugu, President
8313 Bay Center Road
Jacksonville, FL 32216

MERCEDES BENZ OF
NORTH AMERICA
Karlfried Nordmann,
    President
One Mercedes Drive
Montvale, NJ 07645

NISSAN MOTOR
CORPORATION (DATSUN)
H. Matjima, President
18501 Figueroa Street
Carson, CA 90248

PEUGEOT MOTORS OF
AMERICA
Pierre Lemaire, President
P.O. Box 607
Lyndhurst, NJ 07071

RENAULT, USA
Pierre Herrmann, President
100 Sylvan Avenue
Englewood Cliffs, NJ 07632

SAAB-SCANIA OF
AMERICA
Jonas Kjellberg, President
Saab Drive
Orange, CT 06477

SUBARU OF AMERICA
Harvey Lamm, President
7040 Central Highway
Pennsauken, NJ 08109

TOYOTA MOTOR SALES,
USA
Isao Makino, President
2055 West 190th Street
Torrance, CA 90504

VOLKSWAGEN OF
AMERICA
James McLernon, President
818 Sylvan Avenue
Englewood Cliffs, NJ 07632

VOLVO OF AMERICA
Bjorn Ahlstrom, President
Rockleigh, NJ 07647

SOURCE: *Automotive Age*, December 1978.

Supermarket Survival: Choice or Chance

7

Here's something to chew on next time you go food shopping. At this very moment, an all-out war is being waged between supermarkets and restaurants. They're fighting for your food dollar. And both sides—especially the supermarkets—are using psychological warfare to start you spending and keep you spending.

Billions of dollars are at stake. Americans today spend one out of every three of their food dollars on food cooked by someone else. And as we become more leisure-oriented (some call it lazier) we'll soon be spending two out of every three food dollars to dine out, experts say. Even though we know it costs more to have somebody cook for us, serve us, and clean up after us, we're willing to pay because it's easier.

This scares the hell out of supermarkets. Until recently, they have been the main source of food for most people. And because we spend more money at a food store than any other type of store, they've been able to push us around, harass us, embarrass us and make us wait in long lines like helpless pawns. But now, with fast food restaurants springing up everywhere, you can eat out almost more cheaply than you can eat at home. By the time you buy the food, pay for the energy to cook the food, buy the condiments to spice up the food and the water and power to wash the dishes, dining out looks like a pretty good bargain to busy people.

The supermarket industry knows this. But they aren't sitting still for his invasion and twiddling their turnstiles. They're battling back. The big food chains are calling in the reinforcements; they're hiring psychologists, motivational experts, advertising hot-shots and other merchandising wizards. They're bringing in these big guns to make sure we don't gratify more of our appetite for impulse eating at fast fooderies, restaurants, and food-to-go stands.

Fact is, the cracker barrel grocery store that became the stream-lined supermarket is slowly, quietly, subliminally becoming a big bucks battleground. Today, it's a marketing minefield, booby-trapped with would-be bargains and subconscious sales strategies that push buttons in your psyche when you walk down the aisles.

Supermarkets have turned predatory, not just because restaurants are stealing food shopping dollars. They're trying to survive. Unless supermarkets start selling more than just food where net profit on sales is a puny 1 to 1½ percent, one food store executive told me, they face financial extinction. Sure, grocery stores have always sold so-called non-foods and some clothing. But today, you're finding mini-clothing, hardware, appliance, toy, and drug stores under your supermarket roof. Record sections, garden shops, and small appliance departments are turning up there too. And all that merchandise has hefty markups. Some of the more imaginative marketeers like Ralphs Grocery Company in Tor-rance, California, have even opened restaurants staffed with wai-tresses and chefs right there in the store. Not a snack bar but a sit-down restaurant with a full menu. Supermarkets are becoming department stores that happen to sell food.

Meanwhile, as the war for your dollar escalates, the only real casualties are the consumers. Consider this: The American green-back lost half its buying power during the decade between 1968 and 1978. Yet grocery prices doubled, sometimes tripled during that same period. Groceries are almost becoming big-ticket items. Weekly grocery shoppers who could load up a cart and get out of the store for $25 or $30 a week a dozen years ago, now drop $70 if they are careful and $85 and up if they're careless or fall prey to the "impulse buying" that is subtly encouraged in every aisle and at the checkstand.

It seems that even the "ten items and less" checkout stand has become millionaire's row. And many markets are even accepting credit cards from bewildered buyers who are putting their food on the cuff and paying interest on it.

So what's the bottom line? Simply that supermarkets are doing everything in their power to take the biggest possible bite out of your wallet or purse every time you walk through their automated doors. And you know something. They're biting a lot of us to the bone and we hardly even scream. Either we're oblivious to the pain and meekly accept high food costs as a fact of life. Or we're numb from pushing a cart up and down supermarket aisles, like a rat in a maze, and being bombarded with pseudo-bargains or promotionally pummeled with enticements to buy.

But you can fight back! You can cut your grocery costs sharply. All you have to do is wise up to their game.

Advertising: Real Deals or Empty Hype

Supermarket advertising is a classic example of old-fashioned circus barking designed to lure you under their big top. You're dazzled with a jumble of prices and products, grabbed by games and giveaways, and almost always suckered into spending more than you had planned.

But supermarket ads can point you to a few bargains if you know how to read them. First, realize that only five to ten items at the most offer any real price reductions; most offer only a few pennies savings. The rest are simply placed in the ad so the store can collect "co-op" advertising dollars from the manufacturers, which it may or may not pass on to you.

Is it worth your time, then, to run around town scooping up these "loss leaders"? Not at the price gasoline fetches today unless you can stockpile those bargains in your pantry. And some supermarkets put limits on their weekend specials.

The same is true for some of the radio and television advertising gimmicks supermarkets are using today, apparently because the newspaper advertisements aren't pulling. One giant food chain claims it has the lowest prices in town and will pay triple the difference in cash to anyone who can dispute its claim.

At first blush, that sounds like a fantastic offer. Until you stop to think that since most supermarkets are competitive, chances are that another store would only be a few cents cheaper per item. Even if you found three items at 2¢ to 3¢ lower, would you waste your time running between stores for 9¢ in cash? Of course not.

It's bad enough the chain tries to get you in the store with that siren song, but there is still another catch. Once in there you have to spend at least $25 there on at least 25 different food items. Then, if you find another store selling these same items for less, you have to buy the 25 items and spend another $25. *Then* you get triple the difference in cash. The offer's legitimate alright, but how many customers have the time to roam the aisles of every store in their community to uncover 2¢ and 3¢ per item savings? Don't let yourself be hornswoggled by such hype.

Supermarket sweepstakes games have a mesmerizing effect on shoppers. Your chances of winning the Grand Prize are so remote it's ludicrous to think people choose a market in the hopes of winning a lifetime of groceries or a "round the world" jaunt. On the other hand, if the store where you regularly shop is promoting the game, play along because the cost is already factored into your food prices. You might get lucky but don't count on it.

What happens if your store is out of the advertised special by the time you get to the store? Don't fret. Ask for a raincheck. Don't accept a substitute item of lesser value. Few people ask and they're ripping themselves off. And if you're not sure if the advertising "special" really is a "special," ask the manager to show you the price book. And if two prices are stamped on the package, demand and get the lower of the two. In at least one state, Connecticut, there's a law forbidding increasing prices on items already on the shelf.

The Not-So-Hidden Persuaders

The minute you walk into the store, they're playing with your mind. It starts with the shopping cart. Today's cart is roughly 30 percent larger than it was ten years ago. It's deeper and holds more—and that is no accident. Research shows that many—certainly not all—but many people who food shop once a week will buy until they fill up their cart. Not until they buy what they need, but until their shopping cart is piled so high with groceries they can't squeeze in another can of peas or another frozen pie. And only when they can't push the cart around anymore do they finally head for the checkout stand.

How do you guard against that kind of spree buying? For openers, go in armed with a shopping list and stick to it. Next time you see someone struggling with an overflowing shopping cart, look to see if they have a shopping list. I spend a lot of time in supermarkets but I see very few lists. Ask anybody who's been through tough times how a shopping list has held a budget intact.

Without one nowadays, you can easily be a prime patsy for those hundreds, perhaps thousands, of in-store tricks designed to trigger impulse buying. Instead, spend ten minutes before you go to the store and inventory your needs. It takes discipline but I would bet you'll slice 5 percent at the very least and possibly 15 to 20 percent off your grocery bill weekly.

Look at it this way. Your supermarket manager never buys merchandise for his store without an order book and he wouldn't buy on impulse. His head would be on the block if he bought, say, 200 cases of canned armadillo meat because some salesperson offered him a nickel a can discount and then he discovered he couldn't sell the stuff.

No sir. Supermarkets order only enough of each item to keep the shelf filled until the next truckload arrives. And now, many food chains use a computer to monitor every item they sell so they don't overbuy and waste *their* money.

Write down specifically what you want to buy when you go to the store and add how much you expect to pay for it. This is great self-discipline. The more precise you can be, the more likely you are to stick to your list and save yourself money. By carefully "ordering" your groceries each week you'll buy less because you will think about each purchase.

Next, make sure your shopping list coincides with the layout of the store. If the canned fruit aisle is nearest the entrance, put fruit items at the top of your list. The worst thing a shopper can do is crisscross the store searching for items. That takes time and time costs money in a supermarket. Experts say you spend an average of 70¢ for every minute you are in a food store.

Worse yet, in randomly roaming the store, you discover dozens of items you had not planned to buy. Suddenly, for some unexplainable reason, you pick up that $9.95 picnic cooler that's stacked alongside the soft drinks. Never mind that you haven't gone on a picnic for three years and you hate ants. The "special purchase" sign convinces you it's a bargain and after all, you rationalize, you can always give it to someone as a gift. Now is it any wonder your "food" bill is so high?

Beware of Subtle "Stop Signs"

Do you hear gentle music at your supermarket. It's not piped in purely for your listening pleasure. The background music relaxes you, slows you down, makes you more receptive to merchandising ploys. The same is true of that free cup of coffee that some stores offer their shoppers. You're not going to push a cart and balance a cup of coffee at the same time. So you stop and sip and sweep the store with your eyes searching for more things to buy. Or you feel that your supermarket is being downright neighborly offering you a free cup of coffee and you are more predisposed to purchase without questioning.

But the next time you run across these subtle "stop signs," ask your store manager if he'll simply take a quarter off the pound of ground coffee you are planning to buy that day. That's the same pound of coffee that sold for 55¢ in the mid-1960s and was selling for $2.79 a pound in the mid-1970s and was still selling for that same terribly inflated price as this chapter was written.

A free cup of coffee and tranquilizing music do nothing but set you up for shrewd merchandising designed to stop you dead in your tracks every 10 to 20 feet. Everytime you stop, markets claim there's an 80 percent chance you'll buy something you hadn't planned to purchase. That's why you see towering end displays of 500 precariously perched cans where you gasp and grab. Or find dump displays in the middle of the aisle and are convinced it's a true close-out or special purchase, so you buy. And that's why you find lunch pails and vacuum jugs on a "tie-in" with soup and you buy all three.

Call them "stop signs," call them "impulse displays," they are built for one reason: to strike a responsive chord in your subconscious and dupe you into thinking you've hit upon a full-blown bargain bonanza, so why not buy.

But why be a pigeon about to be plucked? Everytime you're stopped, ask yourself, "Do I really need it?" Does your dog need a $3.98 rawhide chew bone that is displayed in the middle of the pet food table? Plenty of pooches got along for generations with an old house slipper or flat tennis ball. Now manufacturers sell dog toys shaped like a slipper or a newspaper. Or pet shampoo that's more expensive than human shampoo or pet vitamins that cost more than human vitamins—canny merchandising to make you feel guilty for "neglecting" your pet.

Supermarkets know that youngsters have clout. That's why you see high profit toys, comic and coloring books, and inflatables in the middle of the cereal aisles. Anything to get them grabbing. Newest profit ploy: the threefold, four-pocket vinyl notebook festooned with pictures of rock stars, movie stars or Star Wars characters that fetch astronomical prices. You buy because you think it will save you a trip to the stationery store and besides junior is about to throw a fit on the store floor. Well, let him throw one. The price of that notebook would give me fits.

Convenience Can Cost You Plenty

After that little episode and this headline, you probably think I'm going to launch into a tirade about the curse of convenience foods.

Well, you're wrong. You've heard the "Fables of the Freezer Section" before, so why should I harangue you with a rehash. Besides, I don't have the space in this book. Instead, I'm more concerned about the alleged convenience of non-foods. For one thing, they cost far more than the foods you eat, but it seems that if you buy them at a supermarket you're getting far less.

Personally, I resent the fact that many food chains are turning grocery stores into general department stores just to pump up profits. If supermarkets really cared about their customers, they would do their damndest to make sure the quality of dry goods matched the quality of their foods. But generally, the quality and value of the non-foods are second rate.

And it's easy to see why. Department stores have separate buying staffs for the linen department, men's wear, women's wear, housewares, gift items, and so on. Supermarket chains have non-food buyers, often have non-food warehouses, and cannot get first-rate non-food merchandise from top manufacturers who worry about tarnishing their quality image and angering the other stores that regularly carry their goods. Just check out the dishes, tableware, towels, pots, and pans in supermarkets. Dollar for dollar, you're usually getting gypped on value so why bother to buy?

On nationally branded household appliances and personal care items you could be getting a real value, but comparison shop at a department store before you buy. Buying everything under one roof may be just a convenient way to rip yourself off. Still, the worst of all possible buys at a supermarket is also a non-food item. I'm referring to those sales schemes where the supermarket encourages you to build a set of china, flatware, or encyclopedias over a 20-week period. To get you started they give you the first volume or the first place setting free or at a real bargain price, but you pay full retail for the rest of the set. While these are surefire ways to lure in new shoppers and keep old customers coming regularly, those who bite on the offer usually get themselves ripped off. Only one out of every three shoppers who starts the set finishes it. And then what do they really have to show for all their efforts? Usually an inferior set of encyclopedias or a cheap set of dishes or tableware.

In short, why fritter away your food dollars on things other than food? Even today most consumers seem to be buying everything but real food at the supermarket. I once surveyed all supermarkets in Los Angeles for a special television series I was producing and I was astounded to find the product purchased most often during a one-week period was a 5-pound bag of C&H sugar. Second most popular: a 32-ounce jar of Best Foods mayonnaise, then Tide detergent and Pampers diapers. The fifth most popular item was Coca-Cola in 12-ounce cans. Not until we got down to the fourteenth top-selling item do we even find real food: a 6-ounce can of Chicken of the Sea tuna. Now that ought to tell you something.

"Cents Off" Can Be a Rip-off

"Cents off" can be a genuine savings and I usually scour the shelves to find these discounted packages or products I use. It means the manufacturer wants to hype sales and he's giving you a break for buying. Or he's trying to stimulate consumer demand during a new product introduction. Sounds innocent enough, but take a closer look.

First, make sure that the "cents off" has been correctly subtracted from the regular price; don't assume it has. More importantly, make sure you really want the item in the first place and will use it. Would you, for instance, really buy that $2.65 frozen pizza if you weren't saving 20¢? Or are you being suckered by this supermarket scam and the pizza will sit in the freezer for six months?

Manufacturers often dangle "cents off" discounts to get you to try their newest discovery.

If they want to give you a free sample, fine, but do you want to risk a buck or more of your own capital on some soapmaker's newest fabric softening miracle just because he's kicking back a dime or two off the regular price?

However, if one of the leading soapmakers offers you a quarter off on a box of detergent, buy it and save. The Quebec Consumer Protection Office recently tested 21 different detergents including the 11 U.S. brands and concluded that for "all practical purposes, they all clean about the same." There is no need to pay top price for detergents.

So whenever you see a product with a "cents off" label, ask yourself, "Is there a real bargain in it for me or am I just being hustled to buy?" Sometimes "cents off" makes no sense and can rip you off to boot if the discount forces you to buy things you don't want or can't use.

Clipping Coupons: Are You Cutting Costs or Spending More?

We're getting showered today with money saving "cents off" coupons and the downpour is getting heavier each month. Manufacturers hit us with these cash credits through the mails, in magazines, newspapers—giving us a deal to get us to buy. Supermarkets entice us with coupons to pull us into their stores.

I collect coupons and cash them in, but only on products that I actually want and use. My wife and I just had a baby so you better believe I clip those baby food coupons. What fool wouldn't? But I would never buy a big jar of a new coffee "beverage" instead of my usual brand of coffee just because I found a 50¢ coupon in my mailbox.

Some food manufacturers try and force you to buy their product *twice* before they dole out that mini-rebate. What looks like a "cents-off" label discount is actually a come-on. The coupon is inside the package and it's only "good for your next purchase" of that same product. Unless I use that particular product, it's no bargain to me and I ignore that enticement.

But apparently many people are ignoring coupons altogether. In 1978, 70 billion coupons and refund forms were distributed by manufacturers but only a scant 3 percent were redeemed. Consumers who do not want to bother with these tiny pieces of valuable paper may be literally throwing money away; coupons are promotional advertising and the cost of them is factored into the price of the product. Since you've already "paid" for the coupon, why not use it—wisely?

Read the Label

As I said earlier in this chapter, supermarkets are designed to have a hypnotic effect on you. Walk in the door and you are instantly confronted with a forest of signs that shriek of bargains at every turn. Navigate the aisles and skillfully designed packages bristling with psychological stimulants visually leap off the shelf at you to block your path. A trip to the store can dull the senses and you can easily wind up a passive robot programmed to buy.

That's why it's important to read the label and personally question every purchase. These two suggestions alone are probably the wisest things you can do to stretch your food dollars today. For instance, there are at least three nationally known products masquerading as frozen concentrated orange juice in the freezer section of your supermarket. Read the label and you find "Frozen Concentrate for Imitation Orange Juice" and it contains no orange juice.

Label readers will make some fascinating discoveries. That some margarines contain as much fat as butter and are almost as expensive. That the supermarket's private label bleach has ingredients identical to those in the nationally advertised bleach yet costs considerably less. And know that labeling laws require foodmakers to list the calories, so you get an idea of what you're eating. But did you know they list the calories per serving? To calculate all the calories in the can or package, multiply by the total servings, then think twice about it before you buy.

Don't be misled by creative label writing. Some manufacturers will disguise the sugar ingredients with words like "natural sweeteners," "corn syrup and molasses," and "sucrose." But they all mean the same thing: there's sugar in it. Check the codes on a product for freshness. Today, you don't have to be James Bond to crack an "open code." Anyone can read it but few pay attention. Known in the grocery trade as the "pull date," it assures you that the item is fresh until that date. If you come across a code that you can't decipher, ask the manager for an explanation. They're not top secret anymore. If he can't or won't figure it out for you, forget it.

Are you buying expensive water or natural juices? The gross weight of the can is no yardstick to what's inside and canners now realize this. Fortunately, canners are now listing the "drained weight" on the label so you can find out what you're really getting. Brace yourself for a shock; sometimes 30 to 40 percent of what you think you're buying is water that gets poured down the drain.

Label sleuths can make other startling discoveries. Household bug sprays vary widely in cost. And while some of the prices will kill your budget, the ingredients are virtually identical. Buy the least expensive and save. And watch out for the metric system, which is now marching through American supermarkets. The wine industry has already found a way to hoodwink you; it replaced half gallons with liters. In most cases, the price is the same but you get nearly 12 ounces less.

Beware of words like *natural* and *organic* and other tranquil sounding terms that imply you're buying sugar-free health foods. The catch is there are no state or federal standards for certifying health foods. Any manufacturer can freely throw around the word *natural,* and many do. Ironically, lots of high-priced natural foods are loaded with sugar, but apparently that doesn't turn off buyers. If they read the labels, either the words don't register in their minds or they simply don't care. But that may be changing. As this is being written, federal regulations are being formulated that would give some real meaning to the words *natural* and *100 percent pure.*

Organic foods are also expensive, yet you can't trace their roots to certify the purity. The word *organic* suggests the food has been grown with natural fertilizers and without pesticides, additives, or preservatives. But again, there is no law to protect you against unscrupulous growers. Pesticide traces have been found on products grown in fields where pesticides were previously sprayed. Your best defense here is not "read the label" but "know thy merchant." Some health food store operators are pseudo-gurus, but the majority are honest and will tell you where their organic groceries are grown so you can check them out.

I can reel off a hundred other rip-offs that you can avoid by studying labels. Like the "old-fashioned chocolate chips" that are actually artificially flavored chocolate. You can still buy real chocolate chips but naturally they cost more. Is it worth it to you? We're also getting rolled by toilet-paper makers who are now selling one-ply instead of two-ply tissue at the same old price or higher. Has the roll shrunk? No, because it is often inflated with air.

But then some labels tell you absolutely nothing. One coffee claims to be "mountain grown," but the company doesn't tell you it considers a 2000-foot peak a mountain and then only 70 percent of its coffee beans are grown at that height. The other 30 percent come from other sources. Who cares where the beans are grown anyway? It's the taste that counts.

And did you know that at least 300 "standardized" foods like tomato catsup, tomato puree, and white bread are exempt from labeling disclosure laws? And how does that help a diabetic who has to avoid sugar in his or her diet? If you're concerned and if you eat these foods regularly, write the manufacturer and find out what goes in them. If you're offended by this favored treatment for a chosen few, write your congressman.

Finally, watch out for the bottled water companies who tout "pure fresh" water as if it were mountain spring water. In reality, it's city water that's been processed and treated. If the bottled water says spring water on the label, it has to come from a natural spring.

Just don't let them snow you.

Unit Pricing: Shortcut to Savings

Do you really compare value or compare prices? Until now it was almost impossible to know if you were getting a bargain unless you were comparison shopping for an advertised special. But thanks to a voluntary effort by some supermarkets, you can make an intelligent buying decision and stretch your food dollars.

It's called unit pricing and it's a handy shortcut to savings. Unit price, sometimes called price per measure, is the actual cost per pound, per quart, or per count. The unit price is usually posted next to the shelf price. In a glance, you spot the best value between two comparable products.

For example, if one French dressing costs 61¢ for an 8-ounce bottle and a different brand is 79¢ for a 10-ounce bottle, what's the best deal? The unit price tag points out the smaller bottle at a cost of 7.62¢ an ounce is a better value than the larger bottle that costs 7.9¢ an ounce.

Big deal you say? You bet it is! Watching pennies at the supermarket makes a lot of sense and cents. What's more, unit pricing explodes some old myths. Traditionally, we're told to buy the larger size and save. Sure, that's true many times, but not always. Unit pricing takes the guesswork out of comparison shopping.

Unfortunately, there's no law requiring unit pricing—yet. The markets doing it did it for public relations, and it's paid off. Others don't even want to be bothered with it because it takes time. And they are convinced that shoppers won't use it.

That's why you are so important. Not only should you use unit pricing to save yourself money, you should support the unit pricing concept to aid your fellow consumer. If your supermarket doesn't offer unit pricing ask the manager when he plans to institute it. He may claim he has no control over corporate decisions, and that's true. So write the president of the company politely requesting unit pricing as a customer service. Encourage your friends to write and pour on the pressure until you get some satisfaction. Remember, you're not asking for a gimmick or a game; you're asking for help.

Meantime, you can figure the unit price yourself with your small pocket or purse-sized hand calculator, which is as valuable as your shopping cart at supermarkets. To get the unit price on any item, divide the price into the weight and then simply compare the price per pound or per ounce or per weight to make the smartest buy.

No Frills Food—Costs Less but You Get Less

I don't care who you are or where you have been raised, you've been "brandwashed" all your life. That's the American Way and there is nothing sinister about it. Food manufacturers put their national reputation on the line everytime they stamp their name on a label or package. Their goal, apart from generating profit: a continuous standard of quality that you, the customer, can count on.

But you don't have to be a Harvard Fellow to know that quality costs money. And anytime a manufacturer invests in quality, someone—usually the customer—pays for it. No hocus-pocus here. But the big question you must continually ask yourself is this: Am I paying for those quality costs or am I paying for packaging and marketing costs that may create a reputation for quality which the product itself does not deserve?

Only you can answer that question. Examine the items you buy blindly (and those you don't buy blindly), that is, items you buy because the label is familiar and therefore reassuring or the commercial had a catchy jingle. The way food prices are soaring today, you can't afford the luxury of laziness. Know what you buy.

The popularity of private label grocery products proves that a lot of Americans don't care whether they're buying a nationally known and promoted can of peaches, roll of aluminum foil, package of flour, or bottle of salad oil. If they save money, they'll opt for groceries wearing the name of the supermarket that sells them. My advice? Check out the value with your own eyes; you can save anywhere from 5 to 20 percent over nationally known brands.

You'll also discover the quality difference is not that drastic between famous label and private label. Sometimes you can't taste the difference. Personally, I can see and taste the difference in catsup and canned soups; national brands are thicker and richer. But most private-label canned milk or frozen french-cut green beans look and taste the same as the costlier national brands to me.

But who cares how they taste to me. My message here is simply this: Don't automatically dismiss groceries that don't sport a recognizable name. Often, the national manufacturer actually makes the private label item that its own brands compete against. Look for value. And don't let yourself be intimidated by friends or family who only buy familiar brands.

If you're not hung up on national brands, you can save even more. Plain labels or so-called "generic" groceries can sharply slash food costs. Many supermarkets, fearing that high food prices are scaring shoppers away to discounters are now stocking these no-frills, stripped-down groceries and selling them for less—a lot less. According to the September, 1978, issue of *National Food Review*, generics can save you up to 25 percent off national brands and 15 percent off supermarket private brands.

But it's no secret that with generics while you're paying less, you're getting less. Some of the savings is in the packaging. No colorful labels, dramatic shapes and different sizes, or fancy lids or pop-tops. Labels carry just the basic information plus a straightforward description of what's inside, such as whole kernel corn.

But most of the savings are inside the can or package. The fruit and vegetables are standard-grade rather than the costlier extra standard or fancy grade packed by private labelers or national brand outfits. That means they might not be as ripe or tasty or as colorful, because no food coloring is added. Canned fruits and vegetables might contain broken slices or segments of uneven sizes. Toilet tissue is one-ply, not two, and it isn't perfumed or overprinted with floral colors. In short, the packaging and the products themselves are plain. But they all meet or exceed U.S. Department of Agriculture requirements for standard and extra-standard.

Frankly, I buy certain generic groceries and I'll keep on buying them because they save me money. In fact, once they're cooked, only a certified snob or a Cordon Bleu chef would know or really care if they're eating fancy-shmancy or standard grade. The decision is yours but you owe it to yourself and your food budget to give generics a try. If you can find them.

Not all supermarkets sell "no-frills" food. Some are resisting and questioning the quality. But executives of these holdout chains have told me privately they will change their tunes and sell the cheaper generics if the public demands it and if other chains are selling them too. Now there's your engraved invitation to speak up and save and I urge you to do it. Plain label seems to be the only tangible alternative we have to high food prices, the only way to dramatically cut our food costs. And by demanding generics, you will be performing a valuable service for your fellow consumers. Generic groceries give senior citizens who live on fixed incomes and other people who can't afford to buy the more expensive national brands the chance to eat just as well as anybody else.

If You Hate to Wait, Speak Up

Nothing is more maddening than weaving your way through a busy supermarket for an hour, then being forced to stand in long lines for 15 minutes when seven out of the ten checkstands are closed. If all the checkstands are going and you have to wait in line, well that is the price of shopping at a popular store. Be patient.

But if a half dozen checkers or stockclerks are stocking shelves or yakking on their coffee break, you're being ripped off. Your time is worth money and the supermarket is stealing it. When that happens to me, I'll politely ask the checker to have someone open another checkstand. If my request falls on deaf ears, I'll summon the manager and ask him or her to have someone open up. Usually that's all it takes and you're on your way.

Suppose, however, the manager in charge gives you the brush-off, claiming that all his clerks are busy filling shelves or out to lunch. Don't cave in, clam up, and burn up while you're waiting in that long line. The fact that he has to get his store stocked is not your problem. Let the manager know if he doesn't take care of customers first, his clerks won't have to worry about stocking shelves because nobody will be buying anything there once you're through spreading the word. Make it clear that you and your friends and acquaintances will find a supermarket where they are appreciated. If you're really angry, leave your shopping cart there and walk out. You'll feel better even though it costs you some time.

And I wouldn't stop there. When someone who is paid to serve sasses me, I write the supermarket headquarters and give the president a factual "instant replay" of what happened at one of his stores. You are doing a favor for your fellow consumers who shop there and are forced to wait in the same long snaking lines.

On the other hand, if the supermarket manager is always cheery, cooperative, and personable, throw him a bouquet the same way you threw that dour dude a brick. Take five minutes and write the president commending the manager or anyone else who bends over backwards to help you when you go in to shop.

Waiting in line at the supermarket can cost you more than your time. While you're standing there, the store has an extra five or ten minutes to seduce you into buying more. You see a towering end display of hair spray and think the price is a nickel cheaper than it was a month ago so you toss a can in your cart. It's the old "if-it's-a-special-display-it-must-be-a-special-price" roust and you fell for it.

Or, you see those ceramic cookie jars sitting there at the base of a mountain of "old-fashioned" cellophane-packaged cookies. Suddenly, you remember how your mother always kept a jarful of cookies for you and your friends. This rush of nostalgia overwhelms you so you scoop up not only the jar but the cookies too.

But when you're stuffing that expensive bag of packaged cookies into your shopping cart, here's another nostalgic thought: Your mother never used artificial chocolate chips or fake flavorings and preservatives you can't even pronounce. And they never sat in a warehouse for lord-knows-how-long.

You've inched your way up to the checkstand where the supermarket tries to make its last stab at your wallet. This is treacherous turf. You're hit with a barrage of candies, mints, gums, cigarettes, magazines, vitamins, film and other high markup or sugar-coated impulse items all silently whispering to you "Buy me, buy me— I can make you happy."

In researching television programs, I have planted myself there at the checkstand thumbing through a magazine or newspaper, and have seen people almost unconsciously pick up one, two, even three dollars worth of those instant gratification items. The supermarket ordeal has worn their resistance to a frazzle and they succumb to the final point-of-sales spiel.

Watch Those Flying Fingers

Most checkers are accurate but keep an eye on the register as they ring you out. Why tempt a larcenous clerk by burying your nose in a magazine. Besides, checkers do make mistakes; they are only human and if you stood there eight hours a day pounding a cash register, calling prices, and chatting with strangers grumbling over high prices, you might make an occasional mistake too.

But some checkers—a small percentage I hope—are out to rip you off. And unless you keep track of what you spend, you can be easily cheated. Here's how one scam works. Essentially, the checker checks out the person ahead of you who is buying perhaps $4 to $6 worth of groceries. He or she subtotals the cash register and collects for that order, say $6.35, then immediately starts checking out your full shopping cart. You wind up paying the grand total of both orders. Later, the checker pockets the $6.35. The register isn't short but you've been ripped off for more than six dollars. Worse yet, you never realize it.

Among the most difficult prices to check are produce prices. Many markets now "code" the produce with a number which the checker has to remember. Instead of pricing the item on the scale, the checker hits the code number on the computer type cash register, puts it on the scale, and gets a total. Suppose the code number is wrong. Then you could end up paying 59¢ a pound for something that should sell for 29¢. When you get the slip out of that register it looks like something Einstein was working on. This is where you really have to know the price and watch the scale.

It's good advice to check out the checker. Ask the person to slow down if you can't keep up. And if you have a question about any item you're buying, don't hesitate to call him or her on it. The supermarket isn't giving you those groceries, you're paying for them, so get your money's worth.

Just don't go overboard. If the total cost on your hand calculator doesn't match the total, don't demand a recount. But if there's a discrepancy of three bucks or more, speak up.

To Fight Back, Bring It Back

Of all the places where you spend money, supermarkets and food stores are probably the most skillful at handling consumer complaints. First, they get plenty of practice. Second, there's cutthroat competition among foodstores and no supermarket wants to lose a customer who spends $50 a week or $3000 a year over some silly $2 squabble. Third, most markets have liberal refund policies on groceries. From a profit standpoint, the stores have to eat some of the "spoils" or "bring-backs." But in most cases, they get full cash credit from their suppliers on returned merchandise so it doesn't cost them a nickel.

Besides, the savvy supermarketeer knows he can make a lifetime friend if he handles the complaint smoothly and courteously. As a reporter, I've witnessed some of the greatest acts of diplomacy not on Embassy Row in Washington or at the Palace of Versailles near Paris, but in the deli aisle of the Safeway or in the meat department of the A & P.

But just because you don't have to hack your way through a jungle of red tape and bureaucratic bungling at the supermarket, you shouldn't become a complacent customer. A victory in the aisles, fending off spur-of-the-moment spending urges, could turn into costly defeat in your kitchen if some item is bad or broken and you toss it away instead of taking it back.

We're back at the beginning. You have to convince yourself of the wisdom in that whiskered cliché: Pennies add up to dollars. If a 45¢ quart of milk is sour when you get it home, don't just shrug it off or fume. You're throwing a half a buck away if you pour the milk out instead of taking it back to the store. And why should you settle for tomato puree because the bagperson squashed your fresh tomatoes. But ask yourself, is it worth your time and gasoline to drive back and complain or do you wait until your next trip to the store. I've done both, but if I do go back to rectify their mistake, I'll really let them know about it. Some stores even give you a merchandise credit for your trouble.

Okay, you have taken the solemn Horowitzian pledge not to get ripped off by the supermarket. That you will return any item that doesn't give you your money's worth. Unlike fighting a faceless corporation you don't have to arm yourself with letters and warranties, but you should be prepared.

It's always wise to have your cash register tape as proof of purchase. But realistically, you can get a refund without it. A paper ribbon of numbers is not irrefutable evidence you bought the product there, so even if you didn't save the tape, take the item back. Many stores can recognize their price marking. And again, if you have an honest complaint, they're not looking to hassle you.

But they will if you bring back an empty jar of pickles and tell them the gherkins tasted sour instead of sweet. They will probably —and they should—put up a fuss if you walk in with an empty box of $2 wild rice and claim it was bug-infested. I know if I were a supermarket honcho, I'd be suspicious as hell if a shopper walked in with a hambone and told me the ham was tough.

My message here is obvious: Don't eat it all or use it all and then try to get your money back. You're ripping off the market, and while the manager may come across with the cash, you're hurting your fellow consumer who may follow you in with a legitimate complaint and get an icy reception. If it's rancid, tough, spoiled, moldy, mildewed, or just plain bad, bring in the proof and thrust it under their nose. And that means most of the roast, practically the full pound of bacon, 7 ounces of an 8-ounce bottle of salad dressing.

Here again, I'm sure you're thinking, David, you're lecturing me on something any 12-year-old should know. You're right, any 12-year-old should know that, but I've seen too many adults walk in with empty wrappers and packages and demand their money back. That's not fighting back responsibly; that's unarmed robbery.

You can also protect yourself from the financial ravages of impulse spending by returning the item to the supermarket, unopened. The professional salesperson calls it "buyer's remorse" but I call it smartening up after the sale. If you come home with that $1.49 2-pound bag of popped popcorn and realize you blew a buck-and-a-half on a whim, take it back. Take back that new $5.95 cannister set that you "discovered" on a floor stack in front of the baking mix shelf, then found your old cannister set looked better. And do you really want to spend $3.95 on some gourmet South African snails?

How do you get your money back if there is nothing wrong with the product? Just be honest with the manager. I wouldn't slink in like some Milquetoast and confess I didn't think before I bought (you'll only hurt your self-esteem). Or swoop in like a crazed Attila the Hun. I would simply take the unwanted, untouched merchandise and cash register receipt and ask for a refund. Be straightforward about it. Tell him you got carried away, went over your budget, and you don't want these products after all. Nine out of

ten times, you'll get your money back. If he refuses, go to the top
(which may be a regional manager if you're shopping at a large
chain) and repeat your request—unemotionally.

Or Send It Back

Unfortunately, supermarkets have become scapegoats for manufacturers. It's easier to trot back to the store with the frozen coffee
cake that was moldy when it thawed out than to write a letter to
the manufacturer. But that's a cop-out. If some food or household
product shortchanges you, or doesn't perform, tell it to the manufacturer. But send the product back with your letter. I've discussed this with dozens and dozens of manufacturers who retail
through supermarkets and I can assure you, your letters are read
and corrective action is taken. First, manufacturers are eager to
find out if their production quality control measures have a flaw.
Your complaint may be the clue. And because the supermarket
shopper is a repeat customer instead of a one-shot buyer, they
really want to keep you happy. If the product is defective, you get
either a refund, a replacement, or sometimes both. I know of one
soft drink manufacturer who delivers a whole case of merchandise
if a consumer buys a bum can.

But don't get the wrong idea. These big corporations aren't
pushovers for consumer con artists. Your request for a refund is
studied closely before a payoff is made. And you can't blame them
for being careful. I've heard story after story of how greedy shoppers try to rip off these corporations, not for just the price of a
single item. Just to give you an example of how crooked some
consumers can be, a spokesperson for a nationwide manufacturer
of frozen bakery goods based in Chicago told me that a California
doctor wrote in saying he bought 16 cakes for a party he was
throwing and his guests got sick. He didn't send in a receipt or the
name of the store where he bought the cakes. He just wanted
money. This company investigated and dug up the fact he was
trying to shake down a supermarket with the same ruse. A quick
check of the computer proved that no store in his area would ever
stock that many cakes in the freezer at one time. When the good
doctor refused to supply any more details, the cake manufacturer

politely told him to take a flying leap. And I salute the company for standing up to such blatant attempts at petty thievery.

And Don't Forget Your Uncle Sam

Not all companies, of course, will hear the consumer out. If you feel your complaint is valid and you get ignored by the manufacturer, write the Food and Drug Administration at 5600 Fishers Lane, Rockville, MD 20852, (301) 433-3380. Or check in the appendix for the phone number of the Federal Information Center nearest you. They can tell you if the FDA has a field office in your city for direct contact.

The FDA is the federal agency that assures us that foods are pure, wholesome, and safe; that drugs are safe and effective; and that cosmetics are safe. The FDA is the chief watchdog for misleading labeling. Consumer complaints have prompted the FDA to pull mislabeled, unsanitary, or otherwise harmful foods, drugs, and cosmetics off the shelves of supermarkets, drug stores, wherever the items are retailed.

An excellent source of information on grading standards and procedures plus a monthly update on which foods are in plentiful, adequate, or light supply is the Agricultural Marketing Service (AMS), an agency of the U.S. Department of Agriculture. The AMS does not fight consumer battles though. Still, for usable solid facts write Information Division, Agricultural Marketing Service, Department of Agriculture, Washington, DC 20250. Or call (202) 447-6766.

Summing up, you'll spend more time and more money in the supermarkets than you will in most other stores. Unless, of course, you're an oil sheik on a never-ending spending spree. But if you add up how much money you spend at the supermarket in a year and then include how much you spend to dine out, you'll find that you pocket some hefty cash just by carving 5 to 10 percent a year off your total food costs.

And that's not the impossible dream. You can do it if you stay aware, stay alert, and stay away from any overt or subtle scheme to separate you from your food dollar.

FIGHT BACK!

Restaurants: You Might Be on the Menu

8

Dining out should be a glorious adventure where charming people pamper you with attentive service and magnificent cuisine. But even in some of America's finest restaurants you're nothing more than a sitting duck in a shooting gallery and everybody seems to be taking potshots at you. What's discouraging is that you often don't even know when you've been hit.

Restaurant rip-offs are not nearly as obvious as the supermarket swindle where the government-mandated label tells you the 100 percent natural bread has sugars and processed flours. Restaurant rip-offs are not as blatant as the auto mechanic whose $125 final bill is fifty bucks higher than his $75 estimate.

You just never expect to be ripped off in a restaurant; you go in for a great dining experience not a fight; you're there for a squab not a squabble. So when an arrogant waiter gives you disappointing service or a profit-hungry host serves you frustratingly bad food, you usually swallow both without a whimper.

Well that's going to change. We have truth-in-lending, truth-in-labeling, truth-in-advertising, and now, truth-in-menu is beginning to take hold nationwide. And where investigators are cracking down, they are finding a shocking number of restaurateurs and fast food operators are not living up to the promises their menus make. But more on that later.

Moving Targets

More than 136 million people dine out at least once a day. But for most of us, dining out with family or friends is a special occasion. And at today's prices, we expect special treatment. Most restaurateurs recognize this. They know that gracious service and fine food can justify a stiff tab at the end of an enjoyable evening. But, unfortunately, other restaurants find they can squeeze out maximum profits if they run their restaurants like an assembly line. In fact, if you listen closely in some restaurants you can almost hear the bells and whistles.

I call these "buffalo restaurants." Despite the fact that you arrive five minutes before your reservation, they round you up at the door and try to herd you into the bar. They may want to avoid a traffic jam at the front door that might discourage "drop-ins" from waiting for a table. But more often the restaurant's main motivation is to get you into the bar to order a drink. It's no secret *that's* where they make their greatest profit.

Suppose you don't drink, yet they still shove you toward the cocktail lounge because there is no other place to sit (a trick more than a few restaurants try). Don't feel intimidated. Simply explain to the waitress that you don't drink but don't give up your table in the bar to someone who does. You don't have to order anything, but if you want to you can order a cup of coffee or even a glass of free ice water. That's right, even though some cocktail lounges will try to charge you steep prices for anything they put in a glass (such as a dollar for a plain cola or lemon lime), don't let them bloat up your bill just because you abstain.

Munchies are another cocktail lounge hazard. Sit there too long and you'll feed your face with peanuts, pretzels, and flavorless dip that fills your stomach and kills your appetite.

If you do order a drink, and you're not actually sitting at the bar, order carefully. Ask right up front what brands they pour from the "well." Better restaurants and cocktail lounges, as any spirits connoisseur knows, will pour a quality, nationally advertised brand. And they'll "free pour" it rather than use a shot glass, which usually works in the customer's favor. But, if they pour some private label hooch, you might want to spend a dime or two more to get a "call" of your favorite brand.

Now I'm not dispensing any great wisdom here, but I am sounding a consumer alert: If you don't like the drink you are served, send it back. If it's too weak, too strong, packed with too much ice, or if you ordered Jack Daniels and think you got a cheapo brand, return it. I've interviewed dozens of veteran bartenders and they all claim that a "short pour" or substituting some rotgut for an expensive call brand are old tricks for buoying up bar profits and they're still being used today. But these same bartenders all agree most people never even notice this little fraud or they're too embarrassed to speak up. Nonsense. You can't afford to be timid —not at today's prices!

Don't Let Them Stall You

If I have a reservation, I don't mind waiting 15 minutes past the time that I've been promised a table. But that's the limit. It's unfair to you and your guests to be treated that shabbily; too many people will sit meekly in the cocktail lounge drinking or grumbling rather than put the restaurant on notice that they just can't be stalled. Personally, I'll fight back. I wait 15 minutes, inform the maitre d', and leave on principle if I feel the restaurant overbooked that night. It's a hassle to do this, it's unpleasant, it can spoil your evening, but you've got to do it because that's the only way you'll make your point. You might end up the evening at a pizza house or fast food spot, but at least you'll feel good about yourself. On the other hand, I may be the whipping boy because other consumers have ripped off the restaurateur by making firm reservations and never showing up. Play fair. If you can't keep a reservation, cancel it.

What should you do if you're waiting for a table and the maitre d' seats a regular customer ahead of you, even though he just walked in the door. Personally, I would ask if that person had a reservation and require the hostess to point out his name and seating time on the waiting list. That may sound a little obnoxious but why should you get shoved aside just because somebody crossed the maitre d's palm with a five spot? That may be standard operating procedure in Las Vegas showrooms, but I resent it at a restaurant. Speak up! It's good for your blood pressure.

Does the Menu Speak the Truth?

I should take a breather here and repeat again that I am not pointing an accusatory finger at every restaurateur in America. The vast majority of individual restaurant owners know that a sterling reputation takes years to build, yet it can be tarnished in a flash if enough people get fleeced and start complaining. Even nationwide chains and franchised restaurants (and I'm not talking about fast fooderies) have a certain reputation to uphold; they get an operating manual from headquarters and they're supposed to follow it to the letter.

But restaurants have some profit quotas to meet to keep their doors open and even the most elegant dining establishment may try to meet them at your expense. That's right, for years even famous restaurants have shamelessly swindled their customers by promising certain foods on their menus, then serving cheaper substitutes.

Until 1975 this was a rather well-kept secret. Then the Consumer Protection Staff of the Los Angeles County Health Department started vigorously enforcing menu laws that had been on the books since the 1930s. Today, Los Angeles, New York City, and Washington, D.C.—three big restaurant towns—are all spearheading strong moves to protect you from menu fraud.

Fresh or Frozen? Taste Can't Tell

Here's what they're looking for and what you should watch out for too: rip-offs like frozen shrimp passed off as "fresh." A two-month survey of 141 Washington restaurants by the District of Columbia's Environmental Health Administration found that 100 percent of the shrimp advertised as fresh had been frozen. Why pay the higher price for fresh shrimp if you're not getting it? Fight back! If it's listed on the menu as fresh, ask the waiter if it really is. If he hedges or fidgets, and your mouth is watering for fresh shrimp, ask to see a copy of the supplier's invoice. The waiter may be taken aback but an honest restaurant won't mind substantiating a menu claim.

You can be ripped off in other ways when you order fish. Investigators found that turbot is often substituted when costlier halibut is ordered; rock fish for red snapper and ordinary shark for white fish or scallops.

Some of the more flagrant menu misrepresentations include pork soaked in milk or cream served up as veal; ground veal patty substituted for veal cutlet; smaller ocean shrimp for big Gulf prawns; and pork shoulder served as baked ham.

If you see the phrase "Idaho baked potato" on a menu, ask the waiter if it really is a big, tasty Idaho-grown spud. Los Angeles County investigators did and found that some restaurants were peddling California potatoes and charging higher Idaho potato prices.

Are you getting cheaper turkey salad when they advertise chicken? Imitation syrup that's described as real maple? Blue cheese dressing when you're paying for (and should be served) roquefort cheese?

Time and again menu fraud investigators found that non-kosher meat was sold as kosher or kosher-style; ground beef with 40 percent fat was served when the menu specified costlier, leaner ground chuck, ground round, or ground sirloin.

Truth-in-menu holds that if a restaurant claims foods are brought in from different parts of the country, customers paying for that quality (not to mention the transportation costs) better get "The Real Thing." If you have any doubts, question the waiter when you see Louisiana frog legs, Florida pompano, Wisconsin milk-fed veal, Chesapeake Bay oysters, eastern bay scallops, Gulf of Mexico red snapper, Nova Scotia smoked salmon, Monterey abalone steak, Lake Superior white fish, Maryland clams and scallops, and Idaho trout.

Yet terms like Denver omelette, New York steak, New England clam chowder, Italian spaghetti, and country fried steak describe a style of food, and truth-in-menu investigators rule that these terms are not misleading. The same holds true for danish pastry, french dip, and english muffin.

On the other hand, when you read rapturous menu merchandizing phrases like "finest lobster from Maine," "selected from choice Eastern-fed pork loins," "top of the choice," or "the fish you eat here today slept last night in Chesapeake Bay," summon the waiter or owner and ask him to prove it. After all, you're paying extra for that quality. How do you know whether you're getting it or the shaft?

Beware of Other Subtle Skullduggeries

Are you paying for butter and spreading on margarine? If they serve you "whipped butter," you might be getting half of each; it's an age-old profit-making trick that many restaurants use. Are you ordering fresh juice and getting frozen made from concentrate? If it's frozen, it isn't fresh.

Don't let restaurants cut other corners right off the food you order. The Los Angeles truth-in-menu squad found that some famous hamburger houses were charging customers for half-pounders but grilling up third-pounders. And then there is the "Great Soup Swindle" that I blew the lid off of on "The Johnny Carson Show" proving that sometimes the cup of soup and the bowl of soup hold the same amount of broth, with the bowl costing up to $1 more. Two Houston women got so stirred up over that when it happened to them that they called the waitress over to the table and recreated my entire demonstration in front of a packed restaurant. They fought back and got a 95¢ refund. A small financial triumph but a big psychological victory.

When it comes to menu rip-offs, you can put up a battle. If the restaurateur tries to sucker you and your friends and you've got reasonable proof (not just a chip on your shoulder because an expensive steak was overcooked), write the local or state restaurant association and file a complaint. These trade groups are super-responsive today. They do not want formal truth-in-menu laws jammed down their throats and they're trying to keep their members on the straight and narrow. Restaurant associations in Ohio and Michigan have already warned their membership to clean up their menus or face a full-fledged regulatory crackdown and possible consumer revolt. Some associations even have their own menu-writing guidelines.

However, if you find menu misrepresentation to be very widespread in your community, contact your local city attorney or county health department and ask for an investigation. Press your city council for truth-in-menu laws with some teeth in them. Tip off community consumer protection organizations to your discoveries.

Remember, you're not nitpicking or kicking up a needless ruckus. If some restaurant is slipping you a pressed turkey roll when its menu says sliced turkey, you can bet that every other turkey eater is getting ripped off in the same way. What seems like petty theft adds up to grand larceny; they're picking your pockets and putting it in their cash registers.

Worse yet, some of the substitutions are downright unappetizing. I don't think you would order those fresh breaded shrimps if you knew they were shrimp scraps, chemically glued and hydraulically pressed together, filled with preservatives, breaded, and deep fried. Yeecch! But thanks to "extrusion technology," manufacturers have found ways to mechanically flake and "restructure" beef, chicken, turkey, fish, even eggs. And buyers for volume-minded chain restaurants are gobbling them up because they are low in cost, offer uniform composition, reduce kitchen labor, allow restaurateurs to maintain strict portion control, and have a long shelf life. So what if the food tastes like soggy cardboard? As long as you keep putting it in your mouth, they'll keep pushing it down your throat.

Until restaurant-goers make it clear they will not tolerate such bogus foods, nor pay for them, they will flourish. It's only when enough people send food back that restaurateurs will stop ordering such junk.

If It Tastes Funny, Ask

Finally, there are other kitchen frauds that are almost impossible to detect. My rule of thumb: If it tastes funny, ask. Some restaurants, for example, claim to serve prime rib when the quality of the beef is not USDA Prime but USDA Choice, good, or a lower, cheaper cut. If it's not prime beef, that cut should be listed on the menu as USDA *Choice* prime rib. If it isn't listed that way and tastes tough, question the waiter and demand another slice.

Other restaurants will prebraise or precook food hours before it ever reaches your table. The reason is, they do such a land-office business night after night that orders would be backed up and patrons would be screaming if they didn't. I know of one popular San Francisco restaurant that prebraises its lobsters in the early afternoon and stacks them up on the kitchen floor. The diner thinks he is getting a live lobster. Ask to see it unless the clawed critter is fished out of a tank in front of you. Even then, at some restaurants your lobster simply goes back into a kitchen cooler and the prebraised item is popped into the microwave for final cooking. Technically, a customer is getting a lobster that was alive earlier that day, but he's not getting the one he picked and that's fraud. Incidentally, if you pay for lobster by the pound—a popular merchandising gimmick at seafood restaurants today—make sure the lobster you get isn't punier than the one listed on the menu. Inspect it closely. But again, in fairness to restaurant owners, consumers have forced them to take shortcuts. It takes time to prepare food properly, so be patient. We've become a heat-and-eat and hate-to-wait society, and we're only ripping ourselves off.

Who's Waiting on Whom?

One of life's great mysteries is what the waiter or waitress should do to earn the tip. I've got a simple solution to that one: provide spectacular service. But today it seems that we've been bamboozled into believing we should be thankful just to get the food.

Dump that hangup of yours right now. You're paying 15 percent or more of what can often be a substantial bill and there's no reason you should get anything less than red carpet service. Whether you're at a pancake palace or a bistro de haute cuisine, your money is the same color and has the same weight in the cash register as any VIP's.

For openers, when you sit down at the table, see if a waiter or waitress comes over (or winks or nods) within five minutes. Are you greeted warmly or do they simply toss a menu in front of you? Next, how long do you have to wait before they take your drink or food order? I think ten minutes is reasonable; you're neither hustled nor ignored.

Ask the waiter or waitress for the chef's specialty of the day but also ask the price. At the same time ask him or her what to avoid. If he or she sounds impatient and tells you everything's great, look out! A professional waiter or waitress is more than a two-legged conveyor belt; they take pride in knowing what's happening in the kitchen. Personally, I weigh a waiter's recommendation but I don't just let them order for me carte blanche. That's just a personal thing with me. If it's something I don't like but is prepared superbly, I've gambled and lost. When it comes to a crapshoot, I roll my own dice. But if you *do* let the waiter order, have him tell you the price of every item you're getting. Why? Because everything's extra in fancier restaurants and you don't want a surprise at the end—that'll ruin your evening.

One of the classier restaurant rip-offs is what I call the "living menu." It's the height of intimidation and psychological mind-bending. The living menu is usually foisted upon you in the so-called "IN" restaurants, those places that try to squeeze maximum bucks out of the diner by making the person feel important. You can spot it in a minute. The living menu is a well-dressed, courteous, sophisticated showman. You sit there spellbound while he or she poetically caresses your taste buds with what's going that day. Usually, the living menu is someone with a distinctive accent, too; you are so mesmerized by what's being said that you're afraid to ask what it costs. I have been in restaurants and watched a roomful of people be suckered in by this ploy without one of them asking the price. They all felt classy—until the checks came.

Other intimidations: The restaurants that hand women a menu with no prices. They're 20 years behind the times. Today, everyone has the right to know what it costs. If someone slips you a "priceless" menu, tell them to shove that chauvinistic menu— back into the drawer.

When you give the waiter your order, be prepared to wait. As I said earlier, good food isn't popped in and out of a microwave oven. As least I hope it isn't. To save you aggravation, ask how long it's going to take because you may not have an hour to kill. Also, check the menu; some restaurants will list the approximate cooking time for special entrees and desserts.

The meal arrives. If there is anything that isn't to your liking— *anything*—don't be afraid to send it back. Most good restaurants are delighted to be informed of that fact. And they'll replace it with a smile.

Suppose your waiter or waitress gets upset. Don't back off. *You* are the guest. If you get the lame excuse that the head chef is ill, or there is a problem in the kitchen, don't just accept the food. Their problem isn't your problem. In fact, I've told more than one restaurant if the chef's sick or the food's "off" that night, put a sign in the window warning diners: "Enter at your own risk."

But be reasonable. If you ordered a steak well done and you got beef jerky, you screwed up. You should have told the waiter you wanted it well but not incinerated. And don't eat the entire meal and then bum rap the chef. You're nothing but a freeloader and you'll ruin it for the rest of us.

You've finished the dinner and you want to sit back and relax. Are you getting the bum's rush? The fastest part of the service in many restaurants is the bill; right behind it is the waiter waiting to collect. But don't be rushed into paying. Here's where you become an accountant and audit your tab. Don't be ashamed to use your pocket calculator.

So what if the waiter is drumming his fingers while you calculate the check. And if there's anything you don't understand, or if you need his help to decipher a scrawl or a foreign language, speak up. I have found that about a third of the checks I get have at least one error—bad arithmetic, overcharging for an à la carte item that was included in the dinner, sometimes an extra glass of wine that I never ordered, or somebody else's food that shows up on my check. And watch out for the sales tax mistakes.

Some Tips on Tipping

If the service is really lousy, tip zip! That's right, not a dime. But let the waiter know why; that's consumer self-defense. It's a hard thing to look that person in the eye and tell him or her that the service was terrible. But be constructive and tell them where they went wrong. Don't just stiff them and slink out. Too many people do that. They say to themselves, "I'll never have to see that guy again because I'll never come back to this place." What's even worse, they tip 15 percent when the service was miserable, just because the waiter riveted them to the chair with his laserlike glare. But paying off when you get ripped off is the ultimate cop-out.

Almost as bad are those membership groups who take off without tipping but leave a card complaining about the service. That's just weaseling out.

If the service was superb, tip more than 15 percent. If someone made your evening a memorable one, remember him or her. Tip until it feels good.

Suppose the service was excellent and the food fell flat. Don't blame the waiter or waitress, especially if they tried to fight for you in the kitchen. Summon the owner or manager and let him know how you feel. Describe what went wrong but give him a chance to whip his kitchen into shape. Let him know you'll give his restaurant another try before badmouthing him.

And what about the maitre d' or the hostess? If you want to flip them something, go ahead, but I think it's a waste of money unless they really did something special for you. Like refereeing a dispute with the waiter or making sure you got everything you paid for. Then, how much you give them is up to you.

You Can't Always Trust the Critics

There is no foolproof way to pick a good restaurant. The chef could be feeling wretched and the waiters or waitresses could be preoccupied with personal problems. We all have bad days. For that reason, I never write off a restaurant after one visit unless the food and service were insufferable and the manager's attitude was worse.

Personally, I rely on recommendations of friends and business acquaintances or my own gut instincts in trying out a new restaurant. I'm very leery of restaurant "reviews" unless I'm convinced the critic is truly objective. And few are.

As a reporter, I've found that too many restaurant critics are nothing more than freeloaders who sing for their supper. They get a free meal and write "rave" reviews. Or the newspaper or magazine they write in sells restaurant advertising and if the restaurant bites for an ad, they get space for their press release or a glowing story in return. It's a payoff so don't be swayed by that kind of puff. Actually, it's the local newspaper that's perpetuating this practice; they should separate editorial and advertising so neither would be influencing the other.

Legitimate restaurant critics—and there are plenty of them—usually slip in unannounced, never call attention to themselves, scrutinize every aspect of the service and the food, pay their own tab, and, editorially, call it as they saw it and ate it. They normally try a restaurant two or three times before sitting down at the typewriter. You can usually spot these reviewers by their writing. They compliment *and* they criticize; if they rave, it's deserved.

You're probably thinking to yourself, "Horowitz, why did you devote an entire chapter to restaurants? If I do get ripped off, I won't get stung for a fortune." You're half right. You won't lose a lot of money. But experts say you'll soon be spending two out of three food dollars to dine out. And restaurants are the one place where we're least likely to fight back. We've been told all of our lives never to make a scene and we don't want to disrupt a room full of people who are having a good time.

But by speaking up, you're not making a disruptive scene. You're standing up for your rights. What's more, the restaurant is a laboratory for consumer action. If you can stand up and speak up there, you can assert your rights anywhere.

Otherwise, you'll continue to pay good money for second-rate food and second-rate service. And you'll always be a second-class consumer who never wins in the marketplace. It's enough to make you stay home and curl up with a fresh frozen TV dinner.

FIGHT BACK!

Mail Order: Merchandising a Dream or Nightmare | 9

Shopping by mail has ballooned into a $75-billion-a-year business and it's easy to see why. What could be more convenient than sitting in your own comfy home, thumbing through a colorful catalogue, then ordering on a form that practically flings itself back in the mailbox?

Thanks to the miracle of mail order you can buy almost anything without having to drag yourself onto crowded city streets or lonely country roads. You can avoid traffic jams, packed parking lots, and long, long lines. Shop at home and you are free of a hundred little hassles that strain your patience and drain your energy.

But don't get too smug. Don't think you, as a consumer, are totally protected, sitting there in the security of your own home. This ought to rattle your cage: Mail-order buyers get ripped off more than any other consumers. Mail-order companies generated more complaints than any other type of business in 1977 and were maintaining their lead in 1978 as this book was written, according to the Council of Better Business Bureaus. What's more, a recent survey of newspaper and television "Action-Line" reporters by Corning Glass Works found that mail-order selling produced more gripes than any other category.

And these aren't nickel-and-dime beefs. This isn't the classic example of buying a set of cookware through the mail, waiting patiently for four weeks, then discovering the corner store is peddling the same pots for less and you wouldn't have had to pay postage or handling.

No, I'm warning you to watch out for the dream merchants who promise you a fatter bank account, a thinner waistline, a richer social life, success and fame, and ask nothing of you except money. These are the real parasites of life—they feed on our fears and prey on our needs to be sexy and sought after no matter what our age.

Now, I'm not putting down the entire direct-mail industry; $75 billion a year includes a lot of sales and satisfaction. I am only blasting the bandits and bunko artists—the kind of crooks you find in any business. It's important for you to realize that direct-mail marketing exists for only one reason: to sell you something and collect your cash. If you go ahead and order and get real value for your money, fine. But if you get cheated, here's how to avenge yourself. Better yet, here's how to avoid it in the first place.

Beware of the 'Get Rich Quick' Boys

It seems the only person who gets rich quick from a "get rich quick" book is the person who wrote it and sold it. Yet each week thousands of people fall for those sincere sounding pitches from overnight millionaires willing to share their "secret" for achieving "financial freedom." That "willingness" should be your red flag. I've yet to find an instant, easy, lazy way to make a fortune. And if I did, would I throw away some of that money on expensive advertisements to tell the world. Hell, no. I'd be talking to an investment counselor or a banker, trying to build my nest egg.

But, to convince you they're really rich, these con artists prefer to brag about their block-long Mercedes Benz and their big expensive homes and yachts. Then they humbly claim "it wasn't always this way." They too were once "wage slaves" or "working stiffs who could never get out of debt" until they discovered the secret.

They all want you to say to yourself, "Well, if he can make it I can make it. So why not invest $9.95 and learn his secret?" There's your mistake. Plunk down your money and you usually get nothing more than a cheap booklet of common sense financial advice that any bank would have given you for free.

Many of these offers have a legitimate money-back guarantee. In fact, a guarantee is part of the come-on. The advertisers claim they will not cash your check for a month. But top direct-mail copywriters, the people who write these ads, claim that only a fraction of the people who send in money ever ask for it back. They would rather lose $10 than admit to themselves they can't make a fortune when other people are apparently getting rich.

Nonsense. If you order the booklet and get ripped off, get your money back. And if they refuse, contact the postal inspectors. The post office tells me they are itching to nail these flim-flam folks, but they're selling dreams and the public is buying. One scheme even goes so far as to tell us to repeat a prayer ten times and we'll get rich. It seems that, as a society, we're willing to believe anything or grasp at anything to make instant money. But in doing that, we're only feeding the con men and hurting ourselves.

Most Mail-Order Diet Plans Will
Only Lighten Your Wallet

Nutritionists and doctors tell us the only real way to lose weight is to cut down on our caloric intake and do exercise. But newspapers and magazines are riddled with a never-ending stream of diet plans that claim you can lose weight without making any effort whatsoever and without altering your diet.

Folks, that's just pure hokum. But notice how they try and sell you. They try to convince you this is the one diet that will work ("If you have tried diet after diet without success") and you'll be fat free forever ("You'll never be overweight again"). All you need is the secret contained in the doctor's incredible new book ("And incredible it is because it requires no starvation, no deprivation, and no exercise. Yet your surplus weight will disappear like magic and never return").

The only thing that magically disappears is your money. What's more, some of these diet plans boast of additional benefits: Once the weight tumbles off your complexion will clear up, your skin will be moist and firm and there will be no more sagging, menstrual cramps and constipation will be eliminated, and you will be saved from stretch marks. Now I ask you if that doesn't sound like the old snake oil salesman who used to work the medicine show circuit a century ago. When you read those outrageous diet claims (one "amazing discovery" swears you can "lose inches in minutes in your own bathtub"), why not write in and ask for the name and address of someone in your community who lost weight and kept it off using that "secret diet." Better yet, if you've got a weight problem, your doctor will have a diet for you.

Mail-Order Astrology: Harmless Rip-Off?

If it costs you money, you're harmed—in my book at least. Yet people will eagerly risk three dollars to see if their horoscope matches Jackie Kennedy Onassis' or if it matches that of some other person who suddenly found fame and fortune. Most of these ads are exactly the same: There is plenty of copy to read because copywriters have found that once a reader is hooked by the headline, he will sell himself over and over again; the longer the message, the more convinced he becomes.

The astrology pitches don't offer books. Their ploy is to give you a copy of a "special research report" on astrology for just a $3 "copying charge" plus handling. By the time you read this, you're convinced you're not buying anything, you're just participating in a "research program." But this is only the beginning. Once you bite, they know they have a sucker on the line. You receive a letter informing you that you've been "nominated" to join an astrological society. Although regular memberships are $50 a year, by acting now you can be "admitted" for just $25.

Now they have you in their psychological clutches. What started out as a $3 "copying charge" for a research report, winds up as a full-scale hustle. You get periodic letters from the society's "staff astrologer" who tells you that, as part of his ongoing research, he found that "some important event will happen in the near future" and he wanted to get in touch with you immediately. Then you are told he will prepare "special horoscopes" just for you to keep you apprised of that "important event."

Since no one can actually prove that astrology is bunk, the postal service can't stop these charlatans. The consumer can only protect himself or herself through awareness. In the case of astrology, who cares what Jackie O's horoscope said. Is that going to bring you fame and fortune?

Watch Out for the Mail-Order Medicine Men

Mail-order health schemes are among the cruelest of all rip-offs. They're aimed squarely at a sick person who is grabbing at any cure. Worse yet, these are often the very people who can't afford to lose the money these quacks are often demanding.

Once again they're selling miracles to the desperate. One ad promises to sell you a book containing the secret of "your body's natural healing powers" so you "can manage almost all but the most grievous illnesses entirely by yourself." Others offer a book by a doctor for curing arthritis in your own home. Still other books purport to tell you how "your nerves can cure themselves."

So how do these mail-order medicine men get away with it? First, they are all careful never to offer any drug or device. That would bring the Food & Drug Administration down on their backs in a moment. All they are selling you for $7.95 or $9.95 are their "secrets"—often nothing more than opinions, sugarcoated with some old-fashioned healing doubletalk.

Think about this for a moment: If these mail-order medicine men had in fact made a major medical breakthrough—a cure for arthritis, aging, prostate problems—you can rest assured that the entire medical profession would know about it and would be using it to treat sufferers. Right there you've got a tip-off to a rip-off.

Bust developers and wrinkle creams are other products that illustrate the fact that people are still looking for that miracle after medical science has come up empty-handed. There are only two ways to enlarge your bust: get pregnant or get them augmented surgically through implants by a reputable plastic surgeon. Hormones, too, have worked on some patients, doctors report. But those are prescription drugs, not available by mail. As for wrinkle creams, they're worthless. Again, a competent plastic surgeon is the best wrinkle remover.

Still, these mail-order gyp artists are convinced the public will buy anything. They have us totally psyched up because they know we want to lose weight, get rich, be healthy, stop aging, quit smoking, develop a winning personality. That's why the mail offers never stop. The only way to turn them off is to ignore them entirely.

Getting Your Money Back

As I said earlier, if it's too late and you've already sent them your money, remember this: You can fight back. On any mail-order purchase—whether it's from a tiny company or a nationally known giant retail chain—sit down and write a letter. Enclose that proof-of-purchase (copy, never the original), the offer itself, and the item if you want a refund. Write a businesslike letter and don't get emotional or make wild threats even if you were cheated. You want your money back first.

I would wait two weeks for a reply. If nothing happens and you have a phone number, make a collect call to the president. Chances are you won't get the top man, but perhaps a secretary will take down the information and process your refund. If the phone call gets no action, write a second letter, this time to the president (hopefully you got his name through the telephone call, but if you didn't, it's not important). Tell him firmly that if you don't get a refund in seven working days, you're going to contact the deputy chief postal inspector in his region. That should bring him around. But if it doesn't, you've got plenty of ammunition left.

The Mail-Order Folks Have an Action Line Too

Don't throw in the sponge just because you get the brush-off. Under the Federal Trade Commission's Delayed Delivery Rule, a mail-order company has only 30 days to send you your merchandise unless the advertisement specifies a longer wait for delivery. After four weeks, though, if nothing arrives and they still have your money (or if your refund request goes unanswered), contact the Direct Mail Marketing Association, 6 East 43rd Street, New York, NY 10017, (212) 689-4977. DMMA, the nation's biggest and oldest mail-order trade association, operates a Mail Order Action Line, and it will lean on errant mail-order outfits to find out what gives.

DMMA writes a letter or makes a phone call. Sometimes the association finds that the company in question is so swamped with orders that it can't fill them in 30 days. Here you have a legal out; the FTC says a mail-order company must notify you it needs more time to process your order, and offer you the opportunity to cancel it on the spot and demand a refund or accept the additional delay.

However, the DMMA can't force the company to cough up your order. Nor will it go for the jugular to protect you or your money. DMMA's clout is strong with its 3300 members, but it claims that 85 percent of its 1000 monthly Action Line complaints are against non-members. And as a trade group, it has no regulatory powers. So if you still haven't gotten satisfaction, call in the Feds.

"The Complaint Is the Key: Use It"

The U.S. Postal Service is far more than a nationwide army of dedicated people who handle and deliver mail and sell stamps. Behind the scenes, under the direction of the Chief Postal Inspector, is a crack team of 1700 law enforcement officers who are every bit as tough and effective as the Federal Bureau of Investigation. Located around the country, they investigate post office burglaries, hold-ups, mail-order pornography. But their real meat is mail fraud. They passionately pursue and prosecute any person or organization that tries to rip you off via the U.S. mails. Your Uncle Sam is not about to be a co-conspirator with some penny-ante or million-dollar swindler.

It all starts with the complaint. As a ranking official of the Postal Service in Washington, DC, bluntly puts it: "The complaint is the key [to busting a fraud]. Use it." And lest you think the government uses kid gloves on these presumably nonviolent and often white-collar con artists, here's how a postal inspector views his job: "We aren't interested in a wrist slap. We go for a federal indictment, a conviction, and a prison term."

According to a spokesperson for the Postal Service, consumers are certainly complaining. Some 161,741 complaints were received in fiscal 1978 and every one of them was read and acted on in some way. Postal inspectors were suspicious enough to conduct 5724 separate full-scale investigations. They arrested 2232 people on suspicion of mail fraud and convicted 2012 of them. That's a pretty healthy conviction ratio. In addition, some $9.1 million in monies were recovered.

But it's up to you. If you've got a complaint and the company ignores your first two letters and your phone call, don't wait any longer. File your complaint fast. Mail-order con artists often move around, dreaming up phony names and opening and closing post office boxes with amazing speed. Even though you may be embarrassed to admit you've been ripped off by some scheme, don't sulk about it. You've got to get righteously indignant and move quickly before they have a chance to scram.

Where do you begin? Postal officials in Washington, DC, suggest you submit a two-part, numbered Consumer Service Card (available at any post office) to your local postmaster; one half of the card is automatically mailed to the Office of Consumer Affairs, U.S. Postal Service, Washington, DC 20260. I'm told your local postmaster forwards the Consumer Service Card to the appropriate postal inspector, who will read it and take action. However, insiders tell me you should actually send it to the same zip code as the one in the address of the company you feel is ripping you off. Or you might check with your local post office for the divisional office of the postal inspector closest to that zip code.

I would also attach a letter to the Consumer Service Card, outlining your beef. If they took your money and didn't send you what you ordered, include a photocopy of the front and back of your cancelled check (never, never send anybody cash), plus a copy of the advertisement or offer and some evidence the mails were used. To clarify—on an ordinary "failure to deliver" case, try the DMMA first, but in a business scheme or possible fraud, go directly to the postal authorities.

That Tells Them Trouble Is Brewing

What happens next? First, a postal inspector will write or call the company on your behalf to find out why they haven't "fulfilled" the order—that is, sent you what you paid for. The Feds are not looking for fraud with that first letter or call. Mail-order companies are often swamped with correspondence and may just be slow in answering your query letter. Give them the benefit of the doubt. It could be the infamous "breakdown in communications."

Usually the postal inspector's letter gets results. "If you're in the mail-order business and get a letter from a postal inspector, you know trouble is brewing," Tom Ziebarth, a senior lawyer in the U.S. Postal Service's Consumer Protection Office, told me.

Once that first letter is sent, the mail-order outfit has 30 days to reply. If other consumer complaints are collected about the same company, that's a tip-off to a rip-off. Meantime, if there's no answer from the mail-order company within a month, and the post office gets more complaints, either a "final letter" is sent or the case is "jacketed" and a full-scale criminal fraud investigation is launched. But there has to be a batch of complaints before that happens. And that is precisely why it is so important that you speak up and don't give up if you're cheated through the mails. "Strength in numbers" is more than a tired, overworked phrase. It adds up to consumer clout and it works. Your letter might be just the one that triggers an all-out investigation; that may save a lot of folks a lot of money even if you don't get your own money back. For a 15¢ stamp and a little effort, you can put some mail-order scamster out of business or behind bars. Once the postal people find out the company is dishonest, it puts a "hold" on all deliveries to that address, so no more money or orders can be collected by the crooks.

Scratch Yourself Off the List

Some people feel loved when they come home to a mailbox packed full of direct-mail advertisements. They can pore over the latest pitches for something that strikes their fancy and order right there in the privacy of their own home. But most folks who find their box jammed with junk mail always ask me how they can get off the sucker list.

The Postal Service can't help unless you're getting ads hawking "sexually explicit matter." If that is happening, fill out form PS-2201 at your nearest post office and the porn kings will steer clear of your mailbox.

But the Direct Mail Marketing Association can try and turn off the flow of "advertising mail" (they despise the term *junk mail*) or at least cut it to a trickle. Write DMMA's Mail Preference Service at 6 East 43rd Street, New York, NY 10017 and ask for a "name removal" form. Your name and address is added to a computer list DMMA sells to big mail-order houses and mailing list brokers who then scrub your name off their list. It takes about 90 days before you'll notice the difference but DMMA insists this form should get you off 80 percent of the mailing lists—for a while, at least.

Naturally, not every mail-order merchant will shell out money for DMMA's tapes, so if the pitches persist, write the president of any company bugging you. On the other hand, if you want to be added to mailing lists—and DMMA swears more people want on than off—write and ask for a "name add-on" form; you'll get a choice of 24 categories of mail advertising.

Either way, take five minutes and take a stand. Strange as it may sound, mail-order companies are only too willing to purge you from their lists; postage and mailing costs are too high to waste even a single solicitation on someone who won't even read it. But if you're categorized as a known mail-order buyer, you might have a helluva time getting off lists. Your name is worth more because you've bought in the past; if you're hooked on mail order, they may not want to let you go.

Speak Up and Send Them to the Slammer

Some of the most insidious mail-order rip-offs prey on our patriotic pride. But don't be sucked in by a phony flag waver. Postal inspectors convicted Gary C. Halbert of California on 16 counts of mail fraud for his role in devising a scheme which duped 17,000 people into paying a grand total of $200,000 for bogus American Bicentennial memorabilia. Halbert created three fake companies with names that would have impressed any historical scholar: the Impressions of America Historical Society, the National Collectors Guild of Santa Monica, and the U.S. Historical Society. Using mass mailing, these three companies peddled the public $9.95 books and $15 decorative plaques to commemorate the American Bicentennial. This Bicentennial fraud scheme was busted by the Postal Inspection Service, and Halbert was sentenced to 18 months in prison.

The elderly are prime targets for fast-buck land hustles, but they too can fight back. In August 1978, George Apostol, convicted of 18 counts of mail fraud and three counts of perjury for operating a real estate investment scheme soliciting from senior citizens, was sent to prison for 12 years. For almost four years Apostol had used the mails to drum up investments in Pan American Land Research Inc. of Des Plaines, Illinois. According to postal inspectors, Apostol promised investors a guaranteed retirement income. The suit claims 41 elderly people lost half a million dollars when Apostol dissolved Pan American, pocketed the money, and paid no dividends.

A home improvement rip-off sent Ernest L. Bowers of Charlotte, North Carolina, to jail for five years on 11 counts of mail fraud. Postal inspectors say his construction company rented luxurious office space, advertised expensively in the television supplement to the Sunday newspaper. The ads offered a special discount on home remodeling when a homeowner added a room or modernized a kitchen. The hoax worked like this: Homeowners answering the ads paid one-third down upon signing a remodeling contract, another one-third when the materials were delivered, and the final third when the job was done. But sure enough, right after the contract was signed, the salesman banged on the front door to collect the next payment.

No work was performed, but the materials were delivered and the homeowner was then hit with a lien against his property filed by the materials supplier, even though the cost of the materials supposedly had been paid. That little charade cost Bowers five years in prison.

Then, too, a get-rich-quick scheme that supposedly used psychic powers to discover oil wells blew up and sent the promoter to jail, but not before 300 people had sunk a total of $3 million into dead holes. John R. Shaw, known to Dallas wrestling fans as "Ivan the Terrible," pleaded guilty to a single count of mail fraud. "Ivan," capitalizing on his nationally known identity, teamed up with a pro boxer and circus strongman who claimed to have inherited ESP powers from his mother, who originally received them from a Sioux Indian medicine man. The boxer psychic would allegedly advise his clients to invest in oil; never with Texaco or Exxon, but with smaller, more aggressive companies. Shaw's company was touted as small and aggressive.

As part of the ruse, Shaw, the psychic's "best friend and millionaire oil man from Texas" would coincidentally be visiting during the reading. The psychic would try to persuade Shaw to let his client invest in one of Shaw's oil wells; but Ivan Shaw would refuse. After some "haggling" Shaw would relent and the grateful client would whip out his checkbook. To seal the deal, the psychic and Shaw would really go into their act: Shaw would credit his "100 percent success" in striking oil to the psychic's uncanny knack for spotting winners through ESP. For his part, the psychic would claim that when he visited the drilling sites, his hands would bleed the moment he came on a sure winner. What's more, he would swear that such celebrities as Eddie Albert, Doris Day, and comic Judy Canova had made big money by investing with John "Ivan the Terrible" Shaw. Postal inspectors found this to be a lie. To top it off, the 30 holes supposedly drilled in West Texas had actually been drilled and abandoned by major oil companies who found they weren't worth further exploration.

Give Them a Hard Look

Some mail-order schemesters never give up—not as long as people keep taking the bait and sending in money. Here is a list of potential rip-offs and some good clues to help you know whether you're being conned or not.

Mail-Order Charities

If a charity puts the arm on you through the mail, be careful. Many send you small gifts or stamps to intimidate you into giving or to create guilt for not giving. Under federal law you can keep the trinkets and you're not obligated to send them a dime. Although many charities are respectable fundraisers, others are pure hustles. The American Association of Fundraising says a full 1 percent of the $14 billion given to charities in 1977 was wasted on phony or poorly managed groups. How do you know if it's legit? Check out the charity with the Council of Better Business Bureaus, Inc.'s Philanthropic Advisory Department, 1150 Seventeenth Street, Washington, DC 20036. For a buck and a self-addressed stamped envelope, BBB will give you a rundown on 400 charities. Or send a postcard to the National Information Bureau, 419 Park Avenue South, New York, NY 10016, and you'll get the appraisal free. Other tips for givers: Never "pay" what looks like a bill or urgent invoice (by law the fine print must tell you it's a solicitation); make sure it's tax deductible; send a check to the organization, never to an individual; and never send cash.

Unordered Merchandise

Some mail-order companies try to buffalo you into buying by mailing you merchandise you never ordered and neither need nor want. Then you're billed. Forget it. Under federal law you can keep the merchandise and not owe them a nickel. Only exceptions: book clubs and record clubs that use the "negative option" selling technique. If you don't decline their mail-order offer by a certain date, they can send out the product and legally charge you for it unless you send it back. However, if any other firms try to browbeat you into paying for merchandise you didn't order, turn them in to the U.S. Postal Inspection Service. Mail-order hucksters have no right to harass you.

Phony Invoices

Odd as it may sound, consumers and businesses pay bills and invoices almost automatically these days, fearing they might otherwise tarnish their credit. Some unethical mail-order firms take advantage of this fact and send solicitations disguised as invoices to small businesses, supposedly for advertising or for listing the company name in a directory. Read these invoices carefully because somewhere you'll find the wording, "This is not a bill." Don't let yourself or your company be psychologically pressured into paying. Tear it up and forget about it.

Work-at-Home Career Opportunities

Sounds great to be your own boss but "can you really earn big money in your spare time?" Almost never! Consumers have lost millions of dollars answering magazine ads that offer extra cash for stuffing envelopes or clipping coupons at home. Although some honest companies may be around, I've yet to see one legitimate offer to make money by stuffing envelopes at home. Beware of any offer asking you to buy expensive materials to get started, promising high profits with no experience, or asking for an up-front investment. Some companies sell you the equipment to make items which they'll supposedly buy back from you. But after you invest the money and manufacture the product, they'll claim it's "not perfect" and won't buy it back. With any such offers, always check with your local postal inspecter, state attorney general or the attorney general where the company is headquartered. Or check with the Better Business Bureau, or any governmental consumer affairs office.

Chain Letters

This isn't a potential rip-off—it's a full-fledged scam and you should never, ever invest even the price of a stamp to keep the chain unbroken. Chain letters used to be a harmless way of perpetuating "good luck." But when they promise a fortune and ask for money, it's a tip-off to a rip-off. Don't be impressed by famous names who've supposedly "kept the chain going" or be faked out by unbelievable stories of sudden wealth. Chain-letter promoters prey on the elderly and the lonely and bathe you in guilt for even thinking of snapping the chain. Well, break it and call in the postal inspectors. By busting the scheme you could protect plenty of people from getting hurt.

Giant Fruit, Towering Trees

Among the most blatant of all mail-order swindles are advertisements for a shade tree that will "soar two stories" in a single year, tomato plants "guaranteed" to produce 1000 tomatoes a season, "miracle pot-o-gold rainbow plants" that "turn your home into a riot of color" and "grow over 100 color combinations in a year." How about climbing strawberry plants promising berries "the size of a peach—twice as big, twice as tasty as regular garden strawberries." I've investigated these mail-order offers and others, and I can tell you most of these ads are deceptive; the guarantees are worthless. The tip-off: All the ads show you only a drawing of the fruit or tree and never an actual photograph. But there are plenty of honest mail-order nurseries around the country. To check out any offer that sounds "too good to be true," write the company and ask them for the names of people in your area who have successfully grown the plant. Tell them you want to look at those plants or trees with your own eyes and listen to their "amazing growth story" with your own ears. Meantime, the Mailorder Association of Nurserymen, Inc. can tell you which of the mail-order nursery offers are rooted in reality. Write to them care of Jackson & Perkins Co., Medford, OR 97501.

The "Free" Vacation

Of all the mail-order complaints I receive the largest number involving a single company has been against Columbia Research Corporation. I first started investigating the company in 1973 and 1974 when it was operating under the name of Market Development Corporation of Cincinnati, Ohio. It was conducting a nationwide mail-order campaign telling people they'd won a vacation at any of several resorts in Nevada and Florida. All the winner had to do to get the trip was send in $15. The company not only failed to deliver in many cases, but it misrepresented many of the items contained in its offering.

Finally, after many suits were filed against it, it went out of business. But within a few months, the mails were again flooded with similar offers by Columbia Research and upon investigation it turned out the power behind the Las Vegas vacation scam was back in business with a new name and Chicago address. This time, they tried to stay within the law. For example, it's illegal to tell anyone they've won something and then charge them anything to collect it. So they changed the wording and tell people that "this is their lucky day—they've been chosen by a computer to get one of these special holidays." You're offered three days lodging, meals, chips for gambling, free drinks, slot machine cash—it all looks fabulous until you send in your $15.95. Then you find out about the $25 you have to send in which you'll get back in casino scrip later, and that you have to make reservations 30 days in advance, you must be over 21 and have two people in the room, it costs you to get to the resort, you can't go on holidays or weekends, and on and on.

The point is that the offer isn't what it so boldly proclaims. And the "money back guarantee" doesn't apply unless you take the trip and are dissatisfied—by that time you've put out a lot of money and been frustrated by all the rules and regulations. If you'd bothered to check, you'd find out you could have gone to Las Vegas on any one of the special offers advertised in the papers daily—and it would have cost you the same amount with no hassle, or a travel agent could probably get you a better deal.

Commemorative Coins

Mail-order companies and so-called private mints (which are in no way connected with the U.S. Mint) are doing a land-office business in commemorative coins by pushing them as either valuable keepsakes or solid investments or both. But don't order them thinking you're going to make any money. Even though they're often promoted as gold and silver coins, some contain scant amounts of the precious metals. Some gold coins offered are as little as 10 karats and a reputable coin dealer would probably buy them only at scrap metal prices, if at all. Their historical value is also questionable. Some are gold and are beautifully minted, but that doesn't make them a good investment. Be careful of coins or other commemorative memorabilia sealed in plastic; you should always examine all sides of anything you buy. It's also a good idea to have an established coin dealer in your community inspect any mail-order coin advertisement before you respond.

HERE ARE MY TEN TIPS TO MAIL-ORDER HAPPINESS (BUT THERE ARE NO GUARANTEES)

- Don't buy anything from a post office box. That's often where the fly-by-nighters nest. If you're intrigued, ask for the company's name, address, and phone number. In some states, such as California, a mail-order company is required by law to list a street address.

- Throw away any offer that asks for a deposit before you get the merchandise.

- Never order watches and electronic equipment through the mail unless you know the company making the offer. You may get the goods but what happens when you have to send it back for repairs?

- Remember, there's no such thing as a legally binding guarantee. Buy on reputation of the company. If an ad doesn't mention a guarantee, tear it up and toss it.

- It might be worth an extra dollar to order C.O.D. to make sure you get the product. But then again, if you're that worried, forget it.

- If the product is illustrated and not photographed in the offer, proceed with extreme caution. Look for dimensions or relative size on everything you buy.

- Don't forget to pay the shipping charges or the order may be delayed. And make sure you give the company your complete name, address, and zip code.

- Look for a stated delivery time and a policy on returning merchandise in all ads.

- Keep a record of your order including name, address, and phone number of the company and the date you responded.

- Again, never send cash to anyone. Your cancelled check or money order receipt is a valuable proof of purchase you should hold on to. You may need it.

Okay, I've saved the best for last. It may sound like common sense but it's absolutely crucial that you remember it whenever you read a newspaper, magazine, or direct-mail advertisement that urges you to act now: *Do not be pushed, promised, psychologically pressured, or in any way bamboozled into responding to any "miraculous, amazing, incredible" offer.*

Stay far, far away from any advertisement that purports to share self-improvement "secrets" where you don't have to extend *any* personal effort. Nothing in this world is that easy, and don't you forget it. Cynical as that may sound, folks, it's the truth.

I could fill the entire book with these mail-order "consumer alerts," but there is simply not enough room. Besides, if I were to try and tell you everything about mail order you wanted to know but were afraid to ask, I would be writing another entire book.

Remember, there are two cardinal rules on mail order that you should never violate. First, if it sounds too good to be true, it is— don't touch it. Second, when in doubt, check it out thoroughly before you buy.

FIGHT BACK!

The Professions: Doctors, Lawyers, Dentists, Bureaucrats, and Other Bunglers

10

(I would like to clarify one point before I go on with this chapter. I want all my readers to know that I'm fully aware that doctors, dentists, lawyers and other professionals aren't all men. There are plenty of women in the professions and some of them are probably guilty of the same behavior I'm going to discuss in this chapter. But I have to admit that it's really unwieldy to have every sentence say "he or she" or "him or her." We do need an all purpose pronoun in the English language. Maybe one will be developed, just as "Ms." has served the purpose of indicating a woman without denoting her marital status. I'm all for women's lib but in the interest of convenience, I hope you'll understand if I sometimes use the word "he" as a neutral gender.)

I'm getting to the point where I think the word *professional* should be stricken from the English language. The word has been so abused, misused, and overused that it has become virtually meaningless.

There was a time when the word *professional* comforted us into believing that a person was educated, trained, skilled, qualified, knowledgeable, experienced, and, above all, honest. A member of the learned professions was thought to be a technical expert and

an ethical person. But now, practically every time I pick up the
newspaper or scan the wire services in the newsroom I read that
a lawyer has been jailed on some stock scheme, a doctor has been
busted for ripping off Medicare, an accountant has been sentenced
to the slammer for an audit fraud, or a pharmacist has been caught
illegally peddling huge amounts of drugs.

Now, this isn't a blanket indictment of all professionals—far
from it. The great majority of dedicated practitioners have
pledged themselves to a strict code of conduct where the patient
or client comes first. But there's a growing tidal wave of professional misconduct washing over this nation, and it's not being
stemmed by regulatory or law enforcement agencies.

To put it bluntly, an increasing number of the people we trust
and turn to have sold out for cash. They've become hopeless ad-
dicts supporting very expensive habits: *status* and *greed*. And you
know something, folks, we're feeding their habits every time we
obediently pay for their services without questioning whether we
really get full value for our money.

That's right, many professional people are living high off the hog
on our hard earned dollars because we're simply too intimidated.
We're afraid to confront the "learned person" with questions that
will help us determine whether we're really receiving the best
medical, dental, legal, or other personal service for the money
we're spending.

Worse yet, when we do find we are getting ripped off from the
cradle to the grave, too few of us fight back. Why? Because we
think the professional is an untouchable who is shielded by his
colleagues and other members of the Establishment Club.

The same holds true for government workers. We pay our tax
dollars, but we somehow feel our only recourse is the vote. "Vote
the bums out" is the only way we seem to know to fight back
against bureaucracy and then we have to wait two to four years.
Forget that myth. Any civil servant—career, appointed, or elected
—can be made accountable for his actions or lack of them if you're
willing to be a little tenacious. You can battle the bureaucrats and
professionals and win. Here's how.

Is There a Doctor in the House?

Let's lay it on the line, folks. Some members of the medical profession try to get away with anything they can. From the time you walk into a doctor's office, he or she has the upper hand. If the waiting room is jammed, you wait, and usually you wait way past your appointment time. And there's always a good explanation. Perhaps he had to handle an emergency. But probably he's just a medical corporation trying to cover a large overhead by overscheduling. For these physicians, the waiting room is the beginning of their production line.

How many of you complain when you're packed in and you can't even find a magazine that's newer than a year old because the doctor or his nurses take home the current copy, recycle the old issues into the waiting room, and then take the tax deduction on the subscription? That really galls me. And more than one doctor has confessed to me they do this. While you're waiting and waiting, the nurse won't even give you a hint of when you'll get in, and she gets annoyed when you ask. The only time she really talks to you is when she slides open that window and pushes out a card asking for your insurance carrier, billing address, and who recommended you.

The next time you see her is when she finally ushers you into another room—for another wait—but this time without even an old magazine. It's enough to make smoke pour out of your ears. You can develop hypertension just waiting to see the doctor!

Now let's be honest. It isn't the magazine and it isn't the little card that gets you uptight. It's the way you are processed by many physicians today—in an almost dehumanizing way. But very few people are willing to complain. They just clam up, say aah, hold their breath, or cough twice. But they should speak up from the start. If you haven't asked on the phone, the minute you walk in the door, ask how much an office visit costs. When the nurse hands you that little card, hand her a copy of your health insurance plan (which you should carry with you, along with your ID number) and find out what is and isn't covered. While you're at it, ask if your doctor charges you if he has to fill out a medical insurance claim form so he can get his money. Doctors are doing that now and making a bundle. One busy physician told me his $4-an-hour assistant can fill out 15 medical claims an hour at a charge of $3.00 each. That's $45 an hour extra. If it bothers you—and it should—tell him you won't pay it. Or ask him why he charges you for a form but won't validate your parking. You should find out what your visit costs when you go so you don't get an end-of-the-month surprise —or an end-of-the-visit surprise, since many doctors now ask to be paid on the spot!

If something is bothering you, tell the doctor. I'm not just talking about what ails you, but the way he is treating you. If enough people complain about the wait and threaten to find another doctor, I'll bet you he will schedule fewer patients or tell you to find another doctor, and that's just fine! Then you know where he's coming from—and that's strictly cash flow.

Second, if, after a long wait, your doctor spends just a few minutes with you (and the other seven patients in other little rooms), don't feel that because he's so busy, a quick going over is all you're entitled to. You are his patient and deserve his full attention. Don't settle for anything less.

Next, look interested in what he's doing to you and ask questions every step of the way. The Health Research Group in Washington has found that medical practitioners skim off $1.4 billion from American consumers each year with needless X rays. I'm not advising you to second-guess your doctor, but if you look and sound aware and informed and always ask relevant questions, chances are a physician will be less tempted to run a few extra tests and run up your bill.

Now, I'm not saying that doctors are merely trying to rip you off. Experts claim that 40 percent of those needless X rays are taken as "defensive" precautions against malpractice suits. Sometimes those precautions are justified. Sadly enough, too many consumers today, encouraged by greedy attorneys, sue a doctor for malpractice at the drop of a tongue depressor. (Malpractice suits should only be considered when you suspect there is gross negligence involved.) Nevertheless, watch out for these extra charges that only fatten his bank account but bloat your bill and raise your insurance costs.

Don't be afraid of getting into a dispute with your doctor. If you genuinely feel you didn't get the medical care or expert treatment you paid for, discuss it with him first and ask for an adjustment. Doctors are not infallible and if they unintentionally shortchange you, they should adjust the bill. But if they give you static or threaten to turn you over to a collection agency, tell the collector to sue you in small claims court and let the judge decide.

Another alternative is to contact your local medical society. Almost all of them have a grievance committee staffed by doctors who want to know if their members are hurting the image of the profession. To be frank, some of these committees are kangaroo courts where the patient has little chance of winning. But most are impartial. Some invite members of the public to hear the grievance and arbitrate the complaint.

If you suspect your doctor is committing fraud—overcharging you for costs that an insurance company will pay or pumping up a bill on some government agency—tip off your insurance company and contact your local state attorney general. It's a disgrace to the profession but some doctors (and hospitals) are lining their pockets on state government-paid medical programs. They are billing the state for services not performed, billing more than once for the same procedure, and billing the state for treating entire families when only one member saw the doctor.

If you're eligible for government-paid medical care, here's how to nail a rip-off doctor. Does he collect identification cards or stickers of accompanying family members when only you are being treated? If so, he's claiming he treated you all. If you see only a nurse instead of a medical doctor, the state's being cheated.

Beware, too, if the doctor collects your sticker or your identification card and also asks you for cash. Or, if you are "ping-ponged" between doctors in the same office when the referral was unnecessary, you can bet the state's being taken for a ride; both doctors are billing. Until states wise up and make the doctor send the patient a copy of the bill he submits for payment (so it can be double-checked), the system is going to be abused and tax dollars are going to be wasted.

Still, there's no real safeguard against larcenous doctors. Last year, one East Los Angeles physician found he could make more money selling hearing aids than treating patients. But when he sold $300,000 worth of hearing aids to elderly people who didn't need them, and filed false medical claims, the attorney general heard about the scheme and moved in for a conviction.

Plastic Surgery: Beware of the Dream Merchants

Until 20 years ago, cosmetic plastic surgery was the dark side of medicine, mired in myth and shrouded in shame. Only film stars and celebrities, we thought, could afford to hang on to their youth. But that is changed. Men, women, and children now undergo various cosmetic surgical operations to free themselves of flaws in their appearance that make them feel self-conscious. No matter what you're reshaping or lifting—eyelids, breasts, face—a competent plastic surgeon can give you a fresh outlook on life and buoy up your sagging spirits. But an incompetent butcher can disfigure you.

Sounds harsh but it's true. Any medical doctor can call himself a plastic surgeon and do plastic surgery. Incredible as it may sound, very few patients really check out a plastic surgeon's credentials. The ill-informed and the desperate see him as a savior who can solve all of their problems with a wave of his scalpel.

If you're even remotely thinking about plastic surgery, I want you to read this closely because a false step in here could mar you for life or even kill you. The truly professional plastic surgeon is generally a member of the American Society of Plastic and Reconstructive Surgeons and is board qualified, but preferably certified, by the American Board of Plastic Surgeons. Certification is crucial in plastic surgery because it assures you the doctor has had proper training. There are other plastic surgery societies but the ASPRS is the most stringent. Write the ASPRS, 29 East Madison Street, Suite 800, Chicago, IL 60602 or call (312) 641-0593 to verify a plastic surgeon's membership or to get the address of your state society so they can refer you to one.

A competent plastic surgeon may even refuse to operate. If you get turned down, thank him and go home. Don't look for a doctor who is eager to cut. The competent doctor knows from experience that plastic surgery won't cure deep-seated emotional problems; in fact it often makes them worse. Don't think you'll save a failing marriage with a breast enlargement or a hair transplant. And a face lift won't make you look 20 years younger; a good one though should make you look better.

A fast-buck artist, on the other hand, will try to hustle you onto the operating table. He'll dazzle you with swanky offices, show you slides of his successes but he will often gloss over the risks. Don't be duped into thinking plastic surgery is as trouble-free as a trip to the dentist. Ask plenty of questions. Ask about fees, ask where he plans to operate (some of them even have full operating rooms in their offices), and ask if he is on the staff of a major hospital where you can check him out further. If he claims he can do all plastic surgery operations in his office, walk out. Most "body contouring" operations must be done in the hospital.

Above all, you should beware of plastic surgeons who advertise. Some cosmetic surgery clinics that stalk their prey through newspapers, magazines, radio, and television can be a front for the most despicable kind of rip-off medicine men. Some of the savvier clinics claim they are staffed with board-certified cosmetic surgeons but don't be misled; ask for the doctor's name and check that with the ASPRS.

In California, the Board of Medical Quality Assurance has shut down at least four plastic surgery mills in the last 18 months and yanked the medical licenses of some six self-proclaimed plastic surgeons who drummed up patients through ads in the Yellow Pages or the media. Some even paid kickbacks and commissions to "consultants" who recruited patients off the street. It's that blatant.

Once again, a good plastic surgeon isn't a miracle man or woman —and hopefully that was made clear at the outset. So if surgery didn't turn you into a Farrah Fawcett-Majors or Burt Reynolds— and it won't—don't blame the doc. Your expectations were too high. However, if you sincerely feel he was grossly negligent, consult the chief of plastic surgery at a hospital. You may need corrective surgery. What's more, he can tell you whether you have legitimate grounds for a medical malpractice lawsuit; but do see that second plastic surgeon before you rush out to find an attorney.

Grievances should be taken up, as I suggested earlier, with your local county medical association, though it usually won't handle fee disputes. Don't complain to the ASPRS or other specialist society unless you have a serious complaint about one of its members. And again, don't bother to lodge a protest or a lawsuit if you are just disappointed at the way you look. But if you are disfigured, definitely let them know.

Then you should really fight back. Notify the state board that licenses physicians if you think you've been criminally carved up. Official state medical licensing boards have told me they are looking for complaints about plastic surgeons. And if you can put one of those knife-happy, profit-hungry cosmetic con men out of business, you may literally be saving someone else's skin.

Generic Drugs: Don't Always Play the Brand Name Game

Many doctors don't want the hassle of looking up the non-brand or generic name of a prescription drug. The reason: Major drug companies spend millions to blitz physicians with samples of their branded products, along with calendars, prescription pads, and other advertising gimmicks that remind the doctors constantly that their Brand X is best.

Well folks, the federal Food and Drug Administration tells us there is no difference between the name brand and the generic, although the manufacturers claim brand drugs are made under more exacting quality control standards. But you can rest assured the FDA would not allow the drug to be sold unless it met its own tough requirements. So don't think it's like buying plain wrap groceries at the supermarket where the quality matches the lower price. Some generics cost 50 percent less than the name brand depending on the store in which you buy it. In 41 states the pharmacists can substitute the less expensive generic with the doctor's or patient's permission. But the way you can fight back and save is to insist on having your doctor look up the generic equivalent and specify it on the prescription. Demand it.

If you think the brand name is best you can also save some money by shopping the prescriptions from your telephone at home. In several states the law requires pharmacists to give out prices of the most commonly prescribed drugs. That way, you can easily shop your local drugstores and save while you put them on notice that they will have to compete for your business. In places where there is no law, if a druggist refuses to tell you a price, tell him you'll take your business elsewhere and you'll let your neighbors know about his attitude. I've found no good reason for any pharmacist not to quote a price over the phone.

If other people in your area feel the same way, tell it to your state legislator. Tell them you and your fellow consumers want a law that will require the druggist to give prescription prices over the telephone and post them in the store. In California state law requires pharmacies to list the prices of the most commonly prescribed drugs in a conspicuous place where they can be easily seen. That way, people don't even have to bother the druggist, they can just spot-check neighborhood stores for the best bargain.

How often do you count the number of pills in the bottle? I've been told that a dishonest pharmacist can make a mint by short-counting and then selling his private supply of the prescription drugs illegally at street prices. If you *do* count, and find only 98 pills instead of 100, the pharmacist can simply apologize for the counting "error" and give you the 2 pills. But if it happens regularly, you should report him. You'll never know if you don't take the time to count.

Meantime, you do have recourse if you feel you've been cheated on a prescription either by the pharmacist or the drugstore. A state licensing board has jurisdiction over all pharmacists and has clout with drugstores too. Submit a written documented complaint and your problem will be investigated.

Dentists: Open Wide but Don't Swallow Everything

Dentists are probably the most difficult doctors to communicate with. Most of the time your mouth is propped open and they are doing all the talking. But don't use that as a cop-out if you get ripped off by a dentist. You should always ask plenty of questions; just don't swallow all the answers.

I once did exactly that. A dentist once sweet-talked me into believing that I needed a full-mouth restoration, and because I was a celebrity he said I should have my silver fillings removed and replaced with gold and porcelain. Instead of getting a second opinion, I took his advice. Later, I discovered I never needed that expensive restoration. Meanwhile my dentist got my "autograph" on a fat check.

Fortunately, I didn't fall for the same spiel twice. Another dentist told my wife that she should have a "bite adjustment." I got a second and third opinion. Both of those dentists flatly told me that my wife did not need a "bite adjustment" and both denounced that first opinion as nothing but a rip-off. Had I listened to the first dentist, I would have had a $2000 bite taken out of my wallet.

Sounds callous but you should always shop dentists before getting involved in major dental work. Get estimates and second opinions and have a deep discussion with your dentist before giving him the go-ahead. Get all the facts beforehand. What exactly is he proposing and how much will it cost—for everything? How long will it take before the treatment is completed and what are the risks?

Don't be ashamed to ask the dentist to draw, somehow illustrate or explain exactly what he plans to do. Find out the cost differences and the comfort differences between a partial and a removable bridge. Dentists tell me that too many patients are embarrassed to ask for fear of looking ignorant. That's ridiculous. As I've said before and will say again, you can't ask enough questions and you can't ask a dumb one when it comes to your health and your money. For instance, while some dentists will accept credit cards, they will also offer you interest-free terms if you ask. You're making a major investment in yourself and you better be able to afford it, plus be satisfied.

The competent dentist knows that not everyone is satisfied. So if you have pain, other problems, or a complaint, see the person who did the work; hopefully, he can lick the problem. An irreconcilable beef with your dentist should be taken to the grievance committee of your local dental society. You'll be asked to submit a brief of what happened in your own words. The dentist will be given the chance to offer his side. Members of the grievance committee might examine you and render a decision. A dentist who doesn't go along with the findings of his peer review committee is in for some real trouble. He can be charged with a violation of his dental society's code of ethics and can eventually be tossed out. If you think you got a raw deal from the county society you can appeal the decision to the state dental society.

If you're really convinced, however, that a dentist was grossly negligent in his work, you can lodge a complaint with your state board of medical examiners, the state governmental agency that licenses dentists. This is serious, folks. Just make sure you have good proof to back yourself up.

Meanwhile, some traditions in the dental profession are being shaken right down to their roots. Last year, Oregon's senior citizens, led by a 39-year-old consumer advocate, fought back against high prices and passed a state law allowing denturists (dental lab technicians) to measure and fit false teeth. The jubilant seniors, whose ballot initiative won an overwhelming 77.7 percent approval, claimed millions of older people in America are going without uppers or lowers because of the high cost of dentures. They pounded home the charge that Oregon's dentists pay $120 for a set of false teeth from any of nearly 50 dental labs in Oregon but soak patients an average of $600 a pair.

Opticians Are Making Direct Contact with Consumers

The public is also angry at the high price of eyeglasses today. But a new federal law now makes it easier for you to shop for the best value in eyeglass fitting and frames.

Historically, a prescription was written when your eyes were examined. But rarely would you actually see it. The prescription would be phoned or sent to a dispensing optician while the consumer would be ushered into a room to pick out a pair of frames. What's more, if you did request a copy of your prescription, the ophthalmologist (medical doctor) or optometrist would sometimes tack $10 onto the cost of your eye examination.

But no longer. Under a recent Federal Trade Commission rule, the doctor performing your eye examination must give you a written copy of your prescription. You can either have it filled there or you can shop around for the best buy. And today, it's wise to comparison shop.

Leading eye doctors and opticians have told me there is no mystery to grinding lenses. The optician makes a large initial investment to buy a machine that does all the work. Then, when you bring in a prescription, the optician simply selects a "pattern," reads your prescription, adjusts the pattern, and inserts it into the machine, which grinds the lens. Unless the consumer has some special visual impairment, lens grinding is a relatively uncomplicated process.

But markups here are substantial. One optician confided to me that it costs him about $10 wholesale for a pair of lenses that he can grind and sell to the consumer for $35. Even the latest stylish frames might cost the optician just $12 wholesale when he buys in quantity, but the consumer can pay up to $75. You have to be aware of this. Further, while researching a report on the high cost of eyeglasses for my "Consumer Buyline" show, we found that some opticians use nothing more than ordinary clothing dye to tint lenses. It takes a few quick dips and the consumer pays $15 for the tinting.

I am not saying that ophthalmologists, optometrists, and opticians are not entitled to make a profit, but why let them get fat on your ignorance of what they do? Get that prescription and the model number of the frames you like, and shop around. I found the identical frames at three different optical stores and the lowest price was about 60 percent less than what the trendy optical boutique wanted to charge.

Here are some other useful tips: Ask the eye doctor or optician if he has last year's fashion frames. Usually you can save money but you have to ask. Unless you're an up-to-the-second fashion buff you can't see the difference, so why pay more? Next, find out if your company or union has a referral program with an optical company that can fill your prescription at a savings. Finally, discount eyeglass and contact lens stores owned by maverick opticians are opening across the country. The technicians who filled prescriptions for ophthalmologists and optometrists are making direct contact with the consumer at prices that are a lot lower.

Meanwhile, if you have a dispute with either of these three groups—ophthalmologists, optometrists, or opticians—and you can't settle it, contact their state associations and ask them to step in on your behalf. And if that doesn't work, file a complaint with the state licensing board that examines and regulates these visual care practitioners.

Hospital Bills: Check Them Over After You Check Out

There are more human errors in the hospital accounting office than in the operating rooms, but few people ever really audit their hospital bill. They are convinced computers never make mistakes or it's too much of a hassle. Or the insurance company will pay for it so why bother.

But you would never pay a $30-a-night hotel or motel bill without checking it over to make sure the charges are correct. So what makes you think that a hospital, where the average stay is $350 a day, is less likely to make a billing blunder? Maybe the computers don't make mistakes, but computer operators do. And when you consider the blizzard of billing charges that pour out of a dozen different hospital departments, it's easy to see how you can get stuck for someone else's costs.

It's almost impossible to audit the different drugs; you're paying a lot more for them because overhead costs are packed into every pill they pop into you. But double-check to make sure you were charged the correct room rate (I hope you asked when you were admitted), right number of days, the exact number of physical therapy treatments, and any other costly extras. Don't laugh. I've had countless letters from viewers who claim they were charged for intensive care treatment, even operating room costs, when they were in for overnight stays or weekend checkups.

Hospital bills are almost impossible to decipher. They are usually several pages long and filled with computer entries for bandages, I.V.s, medications, oxygen tanks and tests of every kind. The worst of it is that the bills aren't necessarily posted on the day the service was rendered and if you're really sick, you don't know what treatments you got, much less when. Personally, I think the patients should get a copy of the little ticket that goes down to the computer room. But no matter how overwhelming it may seem to try and make sense out of the bill, you should scan it as carefully as you can to see that you weren't charged for services you never got.

If you find an error, don't pay your share of the hospital bill until it's straightened out. And notify your insurance company that you found a mistake. Too many hospitals say they will make the refund after the entire bill is paid. BALONEY! I've personally handled thousands of cases involving promised hospital refunds that weren't paid back despite numerous requests. They parted with the cash only when they feared the lash of having the problem exposed on a television "consumer action" segment. It's incredible how quickly hospitals find how and where a mistake was made after they get a letter or a phone call from a consumer reporter. And if you can't document your claim, I've seen hospitals give the refund as a so-called goodwill gesture, without admitting that they screwed up.

Meantime, some hospitals are really trying to listen to the patients' gripes. Valley Hospital in Las Vegas, Nevada, and Blanchard Valley Hospital in Findlay, Ohio, last year announced a money-back guarantee for unhappy patients. The two hospitals will refund bucks for such things as cold food, rough handling during blood tests, and being detained in the hospital an extra day. Everything is covered except the medical treatment. The guarantee is designed to keep patients pacified but it's also a way to keep hospital employees on their toes. And here's the hook. At Valley Hospital in Las Vegas, if there's a goof up, the hospital staff has to cough up the patient's refund out of their bonus money. So it doesn't cost the hospital a dime.

Funeral Directors: Don't Get in Over Your Head

Without question the worst time to look for a funeral director is when you need one. Most people are so grief-stricken or guilt-ridden that they spend and spend to comfort their loved ones, and frequently bury themselves financially.

There is no rational reason to be frightened of the funeral director or of discussing death before it happens. If you're not frightened and do discuss the subject, you're less likely to fall for the subtle sales ploys that can run funeral costs into the thousands.

You simply have to realize that funeral directors are not public servants—they're business people. And like any other smart business folks, they want to sell you the merchandise that generates the highest profits for them. Nothing wrong with that unless they try to hoodwink you when you're most vulnerable. And according to a Federal Trade Commission, 526-page report delivered in mid-1977, that's precisely what's happening. Some unscrupulous funeral directors are preying on the public's ignorance and emotions, selling myths along with funeral services. For that reason, I want to clear the air right now. First, no state law says you need a casket for a funeral and only Massachusetts requires one for cremation. No state law says you must be embalmed although a few states require it if the person has died due to a communicable disease or if the person died out of state and the body is shipped in. No state requires burial vaults or grave liners, but some cemeteries *want* liners. And "sealed" caskets do not preserve the body for a long period of time.

You can protect yourself from the soft, subconscious sell if you remind yourself that a funeral home is like a fine restaurant: Everything is à la carte and you only have to buy what you actually need. Among the "extras": the casket (or urn if you're being cremated), embalming (yes, you pay extra), the limousine, flower car, organist, death announcements, newspaper notices, cosmetology (hair styling and makeup), and all pickups and deliveries. Everything is extra.

Some ethical funeral directors will give you a check-off list and will spell out the prices. He'll show you a range of caskets from the satin-lined, fluffy-pillowed, hermetically sealed, 20-gauge steel model that could cost anywhere from $800 to $2000 and up, to a budget box—plywood covered with felt—that is nailed shut. What's more, the concerned funeral director won't make you feel like a cheapskate if you opt for a lower priced funeral. And although funeral directors do not like to be "shopped," compare prices. You're under no obligation to make your arrangements with a given one just because he showed you his wares.

Keep in mind there's nothing wrong with a no-frills funeral, and more people are going that route. You may also want to donate your body or parts of it to medical science or to be cremated and have your ashes scattered at sea. There are a number of low-cost funeral societies that you can join. You should check into them if you are interested in finding out the exact terms of their money-saving arrangements. Some states have powerful groups of funeral directors which try to stop the societies from functioning, but more and more are cropping up. Space doesn't permit a complete discussion, but there are several good books on the subject and it's definitely worth a trip to the library. There are plenty of choices, so check them out before you check out.

The important thing is not to get swept away by the funeral director's spiels; listen closely for empty hype. In researching a Buyline show, I found one funeral home that was pitching a steel casket with a 20-year guarantee against leakage. On the surface that sounds quite reassuring. But I wondered who, if anybody, had ever challenged that guarantee. I called the casket manufacturer and he admitted no one had ever complained. Certainly the "loved one" couldn't gripe and no past purchaser had dug one up to check for leaks. One more thing some funeral directors do is to try to sell you different kinds of trust funds or pre-paid funeral arrangements (in addition to pre-selling plots or crypts). Some of these deals are very shady—with either no interest paid to you on the money you put in, or sometimes as little as 2 or 3%. In the old days, the mortuary would guarantee that the amount in your account would cover the whole funeral even if prices later increased. That was sometimes a good deal and many people benefited by it. But nowadays, most of those contracts are just for a specified amount, say $1,000, and it is applied against the actual cost of the funeral. So the family will have to come up with the difference when the time comes. Usually, you'd be better off to put the money into a long term savings account where you could get 8% interest for a number of years and just leave it there until it's needed.

If you have a complaint with a funeral director or a funeral home, there are lots of ways you can fight back. First, contact a local funeral directors' trade association; your mortician may be a member, and they'll lean on him as well as on non-members. You might also try the National Funeral Directors Association of the United States at 135 W. Wells Street, Milwaukee, WI 53203 (414/276-2500) or the International Order of the Golden Rule at 929 S. 2nd Street, Springfield, IL 62704 (217/544-7428). As associations, they too are trying to get rid of the unprofessional funeral director who might bring about more government scrutiny and regulation. If that doesn't work, check your state government directory. States license funeral directors and embalmers and the board hears complaints. If you can prove a mortician ripped you off, the board could yank his license. Finally, if you think you were a victim of outright fraud or if you've dug up some swindle, write your state attorney general and the local office of the Federal Trade Commission.

Defending Yourself Against Rip-Off Lawyers

I'm convinced lawyers are the most intimidating of all professionals. I call them "fine print artists." They are experts in a field that we fear. We don't understand the jargon of law or what *really* goes on behind the scenes. So for most of us, while the law is something we know absolutely nothing about, we *do* know there are times when we need an attorney to save our skins and our wallets.

How do you find a lawyer who's going to be your knight in the courtroom? The field of law itself is so vast and so complex that no one lawyer is a true all-around expert who can defend you in a criminal lawsuit, analyze a franchise contract if you're buying into a fast food venture, represent you in a negligence battle with a hospital, *and* probate your estate when you die.

What's frightening though is that many attorneys, especially younger ones, will claim they can do it or get it done. And it's not surprising. Law schools are pumping out 35,000 new attorneys who are able to pass the bar exam every year. Today there are 490,000 attorneys; ten years ago, there were 245,000, so there is quite a scramble out there for clients.

Sooner or later almost everybody needs an attorney, so why wait until you're in a jam to look for one? Instead, make it a point to locate a lawyer while you have time to "shop." It's a worthwhile investment and can save you a lot of grief later on. You don't want to have a dispute with your attorney midway through some lawsuit. It's like having a row with a surgeon when you're laid out on the operating table.

Assuming you aren't going out and knock off a bank next week, I'll confine this advice to a search for a civil instead of criminal lawyer. And to further focus it, I'll presume you're going to get a divorce. Unfortunately, one out of every three Americans does.

Here's where you should become a private investigator. Don't shop the gossip grapevine looking for an attorney who wrangles the fattest settlements. Talk to at least two or three lawyers who have been recommended by people whose judgment you trust. Or call your local Bar Association's referral service. Some lawyers may not charge a fee for the initial consultation, but get that settled before you sit down. Seasoned pros will probably charge you, usually for an hour of their time, starting at around $50. If you pay and discover he or she is an excellent lawyer, it will be worth the money.

Whether you're paying the fee or getting free advice, ask hard questions. Ask for recent copies of his or her trial briefs and rulings. They will show you what kind of custody and property settlements have been secured for other clients. Don't worry about requesting these. Once the settlements are recorded with the court, they are public record. While you're at it, try to locate some past clients to see if they were satisfied with his or her legal prowess. However, don't expect the attorney to discuss the *details* of other client cases. If a lawyer does violate the client/attorney relationship and boasts about his track record, forget him. You could be the next topic of his conversation.

Ask about the fee structure and do it in a firm, matter-of-fact voice. Put him on notice that you aren't a pushover when it comes to money. You should be quoted a basic or hourly fee plus filing costs and other expenses if the divorce settlement appears to be cut and dried with no prolonged haggling over child custody and property. That costs extra, but have him tell you how much. He should at least be able to quote a ballpark figure. Some attorneys charge a percentage of the estate to be settled. That can be very costly. Decide how and when you'll pay his fee so there are no surprises.

Law, like medicine, is beginning to certify its specialties through rigorous board examinations although few states have established boards of legal specialization. Check it out in your own area, though. As for divorce cases, you probably won't find an attorney board certified in family law (certification was initially limited to criminal law and workers' compensation) but then, to me, it's not as crucial as in plastic surgery. You just don't want to be giving somebody on-the-job training at your expense.

A lawyer who does specialize or who has a number of cases similar to yours under his belt should be able to give you a realistic idea of the various risks you face. Press him on all possible pitfalls. Naturally he can't read the judge's mind, but at the same time he'll realize he doesn't have a naive pollyanna as a client. He might also think twice about the possibility of "overlitigating" your case and running up the bill.

How to Spot the Shysters

Despite the fact that we're a nation overrun with attorneys, I feel the vast majority are ethical, responsible, and competent. Nevertheless, there are still plenty of shysters out there, folks. For starters, check your prospective attorney's credentials with your state bar. Fire off a fast letter to bar headquarters and find out whether that lawyer has ever been reprimanded or suspended.

Be suspicious of any lawyer who claims he has all the answers to your case five minutes after you sit down. A good lawyer has to do some research; he can't just reach into a file and pull out a guaranteed solution. There *are* no guarantees in law. Back off if the lawyer tries to force you into a decision that goes against your gut instinct. It could be a shrewd legal maneuver, but it could also be a shyster's shortcut. Note it and check it with the bar association.

Be superskeptical of the unethical attorney, the suave, silver-tongued charlatan who induces you or conspires with you to bilk an insurance company. Scorned by the rest of the legal profession, these swindlers tend to specialize in personal injury and malpractice cases. They work on a contingency fee basis (the lawyer collects one-third to one-half of your settlement), and although there is nothing wrong with that (you pay him no other fees), he often schemes with a doctor to pump up the bill. If he's egging you on, or vice versa, you should be aware that insurance companies are now fighting trumped-up claims instead of meekly settling, and you could be on the losing end of a court decision.

One sure tip-off to a greedy legal beagle is how he bills. An ethical lawyer will provide the client with a fully itemized statement that includes every item he's charging for, how much time he spent on that procedure and the cost in time, filing fees, telephone calls, letters, and court appearances. If the attorney says he's too busy to prepare such a bill and he has to charge you to itemize it, he's just jacking you around.

Lawyers who squeeze people for every last buck can easily do it with a vague bill that says something like: "Fee for services. ... 12 hours @ $50 ... Total $600." Now, how the heck would you know what he's charging you for? That's like telling an auto mechanic to fix your car and just charge you whatever he wants without itemizing the repair bill. No one would be dumb enough to do that, yet because someone is a law school graduate, we think that person is above taking us. Wrong!

Know Your Rights

Okay, you have a good attorney but you're just not comfortable with him. You're talking but you're not communicating on the same wavelength. You can change attorneys even in the middle of a lawsuit if you really feel it's necessary. And if you are honest and do it tactfully, he won't be that insulted or wounded. You also have the right to get a second opinion without offending your attorney. You can examine your file at any time and check his time records, and you should ask for copies of all correspondence, filings, and pleadings. Above all, make sure you understand every aspect of any settlement you agree to. Sometimes that's worth the expense of getting a second opinion. On the other hand, don't expect your lawyer to explain every step; he's not a law professor. It's up to you to ask the questions and you can never ask too many. There is no such thing as a dumb question when your money is on the line.

A Brief Word About Legal Clinics, Do-It-Yourself Law

Even though some bar association referral services have reduced fees for low-income folks, not everyone can afford a private lawyer. That's why profit and non-profit legal clinics have sprung up across the country specializing in personal legal problems: divorces, homesteads, adoptions, and misdemeanor criminal offenses like shoplifting. Some are "people's law" cooperatives where paralegals do much of the paperwork and the lawyers do the court work. Check the appendix for the name of a private consumer organization near you that should be able to suggest a competent alternative legal service.

Lawyers can now advertise and many legal clinics do. A few sound like supermarkets but don't be sucked in by come-on prices. Don't write them off either. Investigate. You'll be working with younger lawyers and paying smaller fees, but still ask for a cost estimate in writing. Check out the legal clinics the same way you'd background a private attorney.

Finally, there are some good do-it-yourself law books on the market. However, don't even attempt it unless you feel 100 percent confident that you have the time, patience, and perseverance to act as your own lawyer in a simple incorporation, name change, or uncontested divorce. Those mail-order ads may make it sound as though do-it-at-home law is a snap, but you could be treading on quicksand and you may end up paying some lawyer dearly to pull you out.

Don't Be Afraid to Fight Back

Let's face it: Most people who would speak up at a restaurant or argue with an auto salesman are afraid to tangle with an attorney. The doctor might be the ultimate power figure (your life is in his hands), but the lawyer runs a close second. Don't be intimidated. If you sincerely feel you were cheated, conned, or otherwise led astray, you can and must fight back. If you're involved in a lawsuit, you have more than just money at stake; your integrity is on the line. Defend it!

Try and talk to your lawyer to iron out your differences. Why is the case taking so long? What led to the fee dispute? Do you feel that you're being ignored and not getting enough attention? Of course, it's not easy to smooth things out if you feel he was grossly negligent in some aspect of handling your case. For instance, if he didn't act quickly enough and filed after the statute of limitations had run out, you've got good grounds for a malpractice suit against him. But lots of luck in finding an attorney to sue another attorney!

Fee disputes can be slugged out in small claims court if the figure doesn't exceed the maximum limit in your state. And remember, you can be your own attorney in small claims court.

Probably the single most effective way to fight back is to take your complaint to your state bar association. Most state bars are out to rid their profession of the flakes and phonies, so they'll take a hard look at your allegations. There's always a chance of a "whitewash" but it's far less likely to happen today; attorneys are extremely concerned about their public image.

Generally, a review committee made up of other lawyers or some board of overseers will investigate your complaint and make a decision. If the lawyer is deemed guilty by his peers and some formal action is taken, your original fee dispute might be paid or refunded by a "client protection fund." The whole procedure may take time but it won't cost you a dime.

Battling the Bureaucrats

Whoever coined that defeatist phrase "You can't fight city hall"
probably never tried. Never has there been a better time to battle
the bureaucrats when you feel ignored, shortchanged, or just plain
pushed around. Whether it's a city, county, state, or federal
worker who's giving you the runaround, you can fight back and
get results.

Today, elected officials are listening to the little guy. And folks
back home, down on the farm, out in the suburbs, in the cities are
speaking out and being heard. As the 1970s come to a close, voters
are putting politicians on notice: "We're sick and tired of waste
and we want a government that's really *for* the people."

Californians showed the nation and the world just how much
muscle taxpayers have when they pushed through Proposition 13
and slashed skyrocketing property taxes. Before that hard-fought
1978 election, doomsayers statewide predicted government
offices would be boarded up and vital services shut down if Prop.
13 passed; well, it won and at this point the state seems to be
surviving—only time will tell.

Think about that the next time some government employee
gives you a groan and a bored, buzz-off glance when you ask for
help. Think about that the next time you are standing in a long
post office line, breeding bunions, and the supervisor refuses to
open another window for you. And really think about that the next
time you get bounced from office to office, desk to desk, trying to
track down your income tax refund or your social security check.

Most government employees are helpful and concerned; others
just put in a robotlike eight hours. But why should you put up with
shabby service or take guff from them? True, they're plagued with
people problems day in and day out, but so is every bank teller,
department store salesperson, and working man and woman who
meets the public. You are standing up to businesspeople, by now,
aren't you, and if they step on you, you'll shop elsewhere—right?
Well just because there isn't a second National Labor Relations
Board to contact or another Farm Bureau office in your county

doesn't mean you have to shut up or put up with "the system." Not anymore you don't. I want you to dig in your heels and stand your ground.

A homemaker in the Midwest did just that when she and her husband and son went camping at a state swim park last summer. They bought swim tickets but were turned away at the door because her son was wearing tennis shorts instead of a conventional pair of swimming trunks. But the ticket taker wouldn't refund the money. It was only $3.75, but to the woman it was pure principle. They didn't get to swim. Why should they pay? She wrote the director of the state department of conservation's division of parks and recreation and got a "sincere apology" but no refund. He claimed it would cost his department more to process the "small refund claim" than the original $3.75 and politely told her to get lost. Instead, she got mad and wrote to me. To be honest, I too was wondering if we should devote time on my "Consumer Buyline" show to a $3.75 complaint, but when I read her letter, *I* got stirred up.

We called the state parks director, who refused to give the woman her money back. He told us—and get this—that the cash registers in their parks make "absolutely no allowances for over-rings"! And if $3.75 showed up missing from one, it could mean a grand jury investigation. He blamed it all on post-Watergate government witchhunting. But he was also astounded that we'd even fight a "paltry" $3.75 battle. Well, we had to fight hard, and after a flurry of phone calls back and forth, we finally got him to bear the responsibility of a possible complete state senate investigation, and he returned the money.

Now here's the kicker, and a rare insight into how many state governments waste taxpayers' (or, in this case, tourists') money and time. That refund check had to be either approved or signed by six state bureaucrats before the woman could get her bucks back. From the park division director's office, the refund request went to the division fiscal officer, then on to the state department of finance budget officer, to the department of finance accounts division, along to the commissioner of finance and administration who signed the check and *finally* to the state treasurer, who countersigned.

The woman persevered and triumphed in what I now consider to be an important battle. After all, if you owed the state, or any other government agency $3.75, they would hound you to your grave to get it. The message here? Once again, you've got to fight back! If you're getting a genuine hassle, not just an insensitive snub from a government worker having a bad day, calmly ask for the supervisor. The secret here is to remain supercool. None of that "I pay your salary, dammit, so give me your attention" nonsense. Frustrated people explode at bureaucrats all day long. It's an occupational hazard for civil servants. You will get far better results at any level of government if you ask to talk to the supervisor privately, and explain your problem.

Of course, sticky problems bundled up in red tape aren't solved that easily and you may have to climb the chain of command to get a sympathetic ear. But it's well worth the climb so push ahead. At the city and county level, it's better to fight back in person. Ask to see the supervisor or agency director; jot down the name and employee number of anybody who cold shoulders you along the way. If they bar the door and won't let you see Mr. or Ms. Big, write that person and send a copy of your letter to the personnel or chief administrative officer and one to your elected city council member. Spell out your problem in detail and explain how bureaucratic bumbling only aggravated it. Be chronological and concise and make it clear you'll go to the press with your story unless you get satisfaction. Bureaucrats know the press love stories where callous government muzzles the little man. Remember, it's always better to type your letter but the important thing is to get your gripe on paper.

Now here's something that will surprise you. The higher you take your complaint in government, the easier it is to fight back. If your beef is with the state and none of the underlings are willing to take responsibility, write to the governor's appointee heading the department. They are not career civil servants and are sensitive to constituent complaints. When you are doing battle with a commission, write the director and send a copy to all the commissioners.

Don't hesitate to write to your governor. In most states the governor's staff will intercept your letter and forward it to the appropriate department or agency chief for a response. Elected officials today are paying more attention to the people. Your complaint letter won't hit the trash can. The Guv or the Mayor doesn't want to risk possible political embarrassment, but it's up to you to follow through.

Once again, you're probably reading this and saying, "C'mon, David, give us a break. Who's going to fight a war of wits with a faceless bureaucracy?" You are! That's the whole rationale for fighting back. Unless we exercise our rights as voters and as taxpayers, government will never take us seriously. You've got to stand up and be counted when you're being stepped on.

Now, how do you scare a state agency to death and virtually assure yourself of a response from the top honcho? Tell him in your letter that unless you get some attention you'll be there to testify to his department's ineptness the next time his budget comes up for approval. Next to his own job the closest thing to a bureaucrat's heart is his department budget. Political appointees also clutch at that kind of threat.

Be prepared to carry out the threat if your letter goes unanswered or your problem goes unsolved. Contact the legislature and find out when the department's budget appropriation bill comes up for approval. Type out your detailed statement, alert the press, get a pile of photocopies to pass out, and when the legislative committee evaluating the budget request calls for witnesses, take the stand and sound off. The next witness is usually the agency chief who's been rehearsing his budget plea for weeks; he probably never expected you to show up but now he has to backpedal, explain, and grovel. You can be sure of one thing though; the next complaint letters he receives won't go unnoticed.

Don't forget the newspaper, radio, and television consumer reporters or action line editors when you're squaring off against government. Our free press is still the best way to get these guys up out of their chairs. They all know there are legions of reporters out there who are just itching for a chance to barbecue the bureaucrats over the fires of public indignation. And if there's one thing a politician can't stand, it's adverse mass public exposure. They all want to be buddy-buddy with the press, so if they've bungled and won't budge, tell it to the media.

Overall, I think civil servants generally are becoming more responsive to taxpayers now that government is taking a hard look at merit pay hikes instead of issuing automatic raises. Federal workers especially are jumping, thanks to the U.S. Civil Service Reform Act of 1978, which gives managers and supervisors bonuses based on performance. That means the people reporting to them are snapping to it now that they are being evaluated more closely. Civil Service Commission officials in Washington tell me that before the change, 98 percent of the federal work force got a "satisfactory" rating from their superiors who did not want to make waves. Now, with fresh bonus loot on the line, they are kicking some rear ends—you can be sure of that.

What does this mean to you?

It's what I've been saying all along. Today your voice *will* be heard. Just be methodical, not mad dog when you complain. Start with the supervisor and go up the proverbial chain of command. Keep at it and you'll strike the right nerve.

Map out a battle plan. For $6.50, you can get a copy of the U.S. Government Manual (Publication number 022-003-00948-5, U.S. Government Printing Office, Superintendent of Documents, Washington, DC 20242) to find out who you should write and where you can reach them. Don't butt your head against stone walls if the appropriate agency is shirking its responsibility; write your congressman.

But if you want to give the bureaucracy a real consumer karate chop, check out the Congressional Directory (it also costs $6.50, but both books are in your library) and find out who sits on the house and senate committees that oversee the agency you're arguing with. Write not only the staff director of each committee but every committee member, and give 'em hell—then watch it hit the fan.

FIGHT BACK!

Credit and Finance: Fancy Figures That Don't Always Add Up | 11

Casually mention the words *credit* and *insurance* to people and watch their eyes glaze over. Except for "You're dying," I can't think of two other words that plunge more fear into us. Basically, it's fear of the unknown. The average person simply does not understand how credit and insurance work. And until Uncle Sam cracked down, especially on the credit industry, there was no way consumers could have known what was going on behind the scenes. We were shut out.

But that's all changed. The dark ages of credit have ended. The credit business is tightly regulated by federal laws that form a valuable new bill of rights for the consumer. In fact, some of the smarter credit companies are becoming more consumer-minded to help make people more credit-minded. It makes good business sense for them. They figure the more you know about credit, the more you'll use and the more interest you'll pay.

Meanwhile, the insurance industry, which saw how the Federal Trade Commission shook up and then reorganized the credit industry, is also listening more to the consumer these days. I think we've penetrated those granite fortresses (insurance company home offices), because we're finally getting information that we need to help us make better buying decisions. Still, the insurance industry has a long way to go.

Today there is no need to feel like a lamb among the wolves when you're shopping for credit or insurance. You've got new rights, powers, and facts at your fingertips. Use them. I know it takes time, patience, and gumption to be an aware consumer. But let me say it again: You have to work awfully hard for your money today. You can't afford to dribble it away.

Credit—Getting It and Keeping It

Let's get one thing straight right at the beginning. There is no federal or state law that says a bank or department store or anyone else has to grant you credit just because you ask for it. Although there are many relatively new credit laws and regulations, not one of them gives you the power to go in and demand a credit card or a bank loan to buy a car. Credit is still a privilege you earn by proving you can and will repay a debt on time as you promised.

Believe me, I'm not just lecturing you on the obvious. Viewers around the country constantly write to me to complain that a company has denied them credit when they assumed it was granted automatically. False assumption. You don't have the right to "put it on the cuff." But at the same time, you don't have to grovel, hat in hand, to establish credit either.

Before you apply, ask yourself if you are creditworthy. Young people without a credit history probably won't get an American Express card. But they can apply and will probably receive a gasoline credit card or a charge account with a small limit at a nearby department store. If you don't have any credit history, start building one now. Borrow or charge a manageable amount and pay it off like clockwork. Every credit manager looks at your *willingness* to pay back on time, not just your ability to repay.

I know of plenty of wealthy people who cannot get credit today because they were cavalier about their credit in the past. They made late, erratic payments and often waited until they got three "reminder" notes before they sent off a check. They never skipped out on the debt, but the credit grantor was still ripped off and reported the late payments, which now appear on their credit history. You see, you don't have to be rich to have good credit, just responsible. A clean credit slate or even a once-blemished credit history that has been wiped clean is a priceless asset in today's credit-conscious world.

Your Credit File—Check It for Errors

Your credit history is actually a file that is either stored in a computer or in a file folder in a credit bureau near your home. Every time you open a charge account, take out a loan, buy a refrigerator on time, or get a new credit card, your credit file can get the word. And everytime you want to borrow money or open another charge account, the lender orders a credit report on you—which is almost always a computer printout of your credit file. It literally tells the lender how you pay your bills.

But even the best credit bureaus make mistakes. And with a blizzard of credit data swirling around those bureaus, it's entirely possible that some "derogs" (credit industry lingo for derogatory or negative information about you) have fallen into your file by mistake. A couple of black marks are all it takes to shoot you down on a credit application. That can be embarrassing and frustrating if it's not your fault.

Before 1971, back in the dark age of credit, you could be refused a loan with no explanation. You were literally at the mercy of loan officers and credit managers at banks, savings and loan associations, department stores, or credit card companies. What's more, your credit file was top secret and *you* couldn't even see it. If the credit bureau goofed, you were stuck.

But the Fair Credit Reporting Act (FCRA) changed the rules. Now, if you're denied credit by anyone, they have to give you the reason and the name and address of the credit bureau that provided the data. Then you have 30 days to get a free review of your credit file. Now, here is where the system breaks down, and it's not the fault of the credit bureau. I've found that a consumer who is refused credit is often either too embarrassed or too lazy to inspect his or her credit file and check it for errors. That really gets me angry. Plenty of dedicated people worked hard to get the FCRA passed, but to make their work meaningful you must use that law when the need arises.

It's not that difficult. You make an appointment to personally inspect your file at the credit bureau's office. Or, if you properly identify yourself, the bureau might send you a copy of your file to review at home. But ask for help in deciphering the credit file codes. Challenge any information you think is wrong. Under the Fair Credit Reporting Act, the credit bureau is required to look into any potential error at no cost to you. If the bureau investigates and finds they are indeed wrong or if the derogatory information can't be verified, that entry has to be stricken from your file. Even if the bureau reinvestigates and insists the "derog" is justified, you have the right to put your side of the dispute in writing and have it placed in your file. Now that's one heckuva consumer protection law. Use it.

Even if you haven't applied for credit recently, I think it's wise to check your credit file for goofs. Why wait for a problem to surface, then fight back when you're flustered? Save yourself the anxiety. Although you haven't been turned down, you can still inspect your file. You just have to pay the credit bureau a $3 to $5 fee to cover their time in pulling the file and discussing it with you. Now I should warn you that credit bureaus don't like to review your file if you haven't been turned down for credit. It's not that they're hiding anything—it's just that they'd rather concentrate on problem cases and do their primary job: provide information to their customers so more credit can be granted. But if you are concerned with your credit file, take a look.

And don't just look for blemishes. You want to make sure all positive credit information is reported to your file. Not all credit grantors report their customers' bill-paying practices. That's great if you're a sluff. But if you pay, say, your Master Charge bill, promptly, you want to make sure that that favorable fact gets recorded in your credit file. Ask when you apply for a bank credit card if that financial institution reports regularly to a credit bureau. And if it doesn't, find one that will. Remember, paying cash for everything does not enhance your creditworthiness. You can build your credit history only by using credit.

How do you know who has your credit file? Look in the Yellow Pages under "credit bureaus" and make a few phone calls. If a local credit bureau doesn't have a file on you, chances are one of the big computerized credit bureaus does. There are five that blanket the nation geographically. The largest is TRW Credit Data, 505 City Parkway West, Orange, CA 92668 (714/991-5100). It has credit files on about 70 million people and offices around the country. Others are Trans Union Systems, Chilton, Credit Bureau International, and Pinger.

But you can't just order it over the phone. At TRW Credit Data, for example, they want a letter from you with your name and address, naturally, plus your social security number, your spouse's name and your home addresses for the last six years. You have to enclose $4 if you just want to review your file and haven't been denied credit in the last 30 days. Why do you get the third degree? The executives at TRW Credit Data tell me it's for your own protection and theirs. You wouldn't want strangers poking into your finances. The detailed request is a safeguard against snoopers.

Generally, most credit bureaus are ethical and law abiding. The name of the game in credit is to make loans, not deny them; mostly they're just reporting credit facts that are reported to them. However, if you're getting the runaround from a credit reporting agency (a credit bureau), you can fight back. Write to the bureau president or manager and let him know you think he's violating the Fair Credit Reporting Act. That should jolt him. Find out if the bureau is a member of the Associated Credit Bureaus Inc. and, if so, contact the association at 6767 Southwest Freeway, Houston, TX 77074 (713/774-8701). This trade association keeps a tight rein on its members, and I know for a fact they move fast to get strays back in line.

Still no luck in settling your problem? Then contact a local consumer action reporter and, more importantly, the local office of the Federal Trade Commission. The FTC is the chief federal watchdog for unfair credit practices. If you are convinced the credit bureau knowingly and willfully violated the Fair Credit Reporting Act in dealing with you, you can file a lawsuit and collect damages and lawyers' fees if you win.

Women: Are You Getting the Credit You Deserve?

For generations, credit-granting financial institutions were ripping off women and getting away with it. Historically, they saw women only as mothers and housewives who just hung on to the shirttails of their husbands and didn't really make a financial contribution at home even though they may have had a job. Few women had their own credit files because men were considered the breadwinners. And a single or divorced woman really got the old shafteroo. It was uniformly agreed within the credit field that unless a woman had a man to support her, she could never repay a loan. Why grant her one and have to hound her for repayment?

Well, thanks largely to the National Organization for Women and other women's rights groups, the Federal Trade Commission, and some of the more progressive minds within the credit industry, we now have a law that says women are potentially every bit as creditworthy as men. The law is the Equal Credit Opportunity Act of 1975-1977, and it's a milestone in consumer protection. In many ways, it's just as important as women's right to vote. Basically, it's women's right to survive in the marketplace.

I'm not going to reel off all of the rights people have under the Equal Credit Opportunity Act—and for good reason. I want you to get a copy of it either from your local Federal Trade Commission Office or from any financial institution, and I want you to sit down and read it two or three times.

You'll find, for example, that you can't be refused credit because of your sex, age, or marital status. By law credit grantors can't ask for this information on credit applications. This law also helps the elderly. Before it was enacted, a loan officer or credit manager could assume that an older person might be losing his earning power, hence his repayment power, and boom, the credit application was rejected. It happened all the time in the past. But it's against the law today.

What's more, a lender or credit grantor cannot refuse you credit because you are suddenly divorced or widowed. And a married woman cannot be denied a separate charge account if she qualifies. Before the ECOA was passed, a woman couldn't get a credit card in her own name if her husband was a bill-dodging deadbeat; she was penalized for his irresponsibility. But not any more. However, if a husband and wife apply for a joint account, his shabby credit is a factor even if hers is excellent.

There are other important provisions in the Equal Credit Opportunity Act. A creditworthy wife no long needs her husband to cosign her credit application; her signature is enough. And no longer can a nosy loan officer or credit manager ask a woman if she practices birth control. Incredible as it may sound, a lender could ask a woman what birth control technique she was using and whether she and her husband were planning to have children. If the couple didn't level with the loan officer, he could refuse to grant the credit. Some of the provisions (such as the creditor's right to ask your marital status) DO NOT APPLY in community property states. So a creditor may ask you whether you're married and for information about your spouse in Arizona, California, Idaho, Louisiana, Nevada, New Mexico, Texas and Washington. Because there are a few special situations such as this, I can only repeat that you should get a copy of the act or a summary of it from the FTC.

As you can see, you women can now fight back in the credit arena. But before you can take full advantage of your legal rights, you must take a personal vow—that you'll never again let yourself be intimidated by such authoritarian figures as a bank manager or loan officer, credit manager, or any other person you feel can make you or break you as a borrower. In the eyes of the law you're every bit as equal as a man when you apply for credit.

Some financial institutions apparently feel the same way. Commercial Credit Corporation, a nationwide lending institution, surveyed other lenders and collected data showing that women are more creditworthy than ever before. In fact, a spokesperson for Commercial Credit told me that women today are every bit as creditworthy as men.

That's why every woman should have her own credit file in her own name. Single women get theirs set up automatically when they open a charge account or get some form of credit. But a married woman has to ask a credit bureau to do it for her. There is usually no charge. Now I'm sure some husbands are probably thinking I'm trying to disrupt their happy home life. Nonsense. U.S. census figures show that 85 percent of the women who are married today will someday find themselves single again, either divorced or widowed. Suppose the husband is accidentally killed tomorrow—the family credit history would die with him. And the survivors would really be screwed.

Commercial Credit Corporation has a fact-packed free booklet on women's credit rights and responsibilities entitled "Women: To Your Credit." To get a copy write the company at 300 St. Paul Place, Baltimore, MD 21202.

Until now, I've talked about your rights. What happens if someone tries to violate them? Suppose that department store denied your request to open your own charge account even though you make $1200 a month and have no past credit problems—just because your husband is continually late with his Master Charge payment. Once again you start climbing the ladder of authority, starting with the credit manager and going up to the president of the department store if necessary. If everyone runs for cover, you should take your complaint straight to the Federal Trade Commission. If you catch a lender or credit grantor robbing you of your rights, I'd let a consumer action reporter know about it and tip off the newspapers. Even if the department store advertises with them a strong newspaper might take an interest in your story.

Just don't shove your complaint under the rug because you don't think you'll get anywhere. Federal Trade Commission officials told me they are committed to enforcing the various credit protection laws they worked so hard to get passed. And if a lender who is bending the law a bit to his own advantage suddenly starts seeing colleagues busted for breaking the law, that lender will think twice before he does it again. Actually, though, it's rare for a company to deny a consumer his or her rights—usually it's an employee or a supervisor who hasn't gotten the word. If you fight back hard enough, they *will* eventually get the message.

Credit Cards: How to Curb the Urge to Splurge

Getting credit is relatively simple. But coping with credit is hard. Especially when we're living in a credit card society where it's so easy to spend money that never seems to run out. When your cash is gone you know it. But the computer has to "tilt" before it will cut off your plastic money privileges.

If you're toting around a wallet or purseful of credit cards, think of this: experts say you spend more if you charge it than if you pay for it with cash. With credit you don't mind spending an extra dollar or two for an item because you don't have to physically peel off those two greenbacks right then and there when you may be down to your last five bucks. But you'll quickly put it on a credit card because somehow you won't feel that two dollars at the end of the month. You opt for pleasure and avoid the pain.

But what we forget are those interest rates, usually 1½ percent per month or 18 percent a year on the unpaid balance. So you're getting stiffed twice when you use a credit card instead of cash: You willingly paid more for the item than you might have done otherwise and, if you don't pay your whole bill at the end of the month, you're paying interest. Doesn't look like much, but the next time you figure out your income taxes, add up all the interest you pay and see what it would buy you.

However, credit cards now have some built-in consumer safeguards that few people know about. First, if your credit cards are stolen or lost, you aren't liable for a dime if someone runs up charges after you notify the company. Naturally, you have to act fast. So keep your credit card account numbers and a list of those addresses handy. You might consider a telegram or registered letter with a return receipt as proof you notified them quickly. Some credit card protection services will do all the work for you for a small fee. If someone starts using your cards before you realize they're gone, you're still only responsible for the first $50 of unauthorized charges, no matter how big the total bill is—and sometimes your homeowner's insurance even covers the $50.

Until recently credit card companies and card-issuing concerns had you over a barrel whenever you had a beef with a merchant, whether a hotel, restaurant, or rent-a-car concern. They had your signature on the charge slip, so you were stuck. When a problem arose, you would get mad, subtract the charge from your month-end bill, and pay the statement. But before long you were getting nasty letters from their computer.

The Federal Trade Commission saw too many people getting ripped off this way. So as part of the Fair Credit Billing Act of 1974 (you should read this law too), the commission made it such that the credit card organization has to step in and settle the argument between you and the merchant. Just write a letter—a rational complaint letter—and by law the credit grantor must set aside the amount you're disputing and not charge you interest or late fees. If the problem is resolved and the merchant is at fault, the amount will be wiped off your statement. If you lose, you've got to pay up. It's a brilliantly conceived consumer protection measure and it works.

Meanwhile, just don't sign your name to any blank credit card charge forms. That can be tough. Most hotels and motels and car rental agencies, for example, use your signature as a guarantee you'll pay your bill. But I've been ripped off this way several times when I've cancelled a room and then was charged for it. So be careful.

A final word about credit cards. The merchant who accepts them pays anywhere from 2½ to 7 percent to the credit card company. Usually, the merchant has factored that cost into his prices. Why not ask for a discount when paying cash. You'll be surprised how many restaurants and companies will adjust your bill. That's not being chintzy; that's smart. You're both saving money and it's legal.

Credit Tips of Consuming Interest

You didn't buy this book to get a financial encyclopedia, and I didn't plan to write one. Credit is complex and it takes a commitment on your part to understand it. But there are facts you should be aware of when you buy on time or borrow. Here's a rundown of the more important ones.

- Shop hard for interest rates. The more creditworthy you are, the harder you can bargain for interest rates when you borrow. If you're a good customer at the bank, press your manager for an extra half percent less than the prevailing rate. Credit unions often have the best interest rates—they usually pay the highest on savings and charge the least for loans. But don't take this as gospel. Interest rates vary. You've got to do the digging. It will pay off. A couple of percentage points saved over the life of the loan is worth the effort.

- How much interest are you paying? The federal Truth-In-Lending law now forces the lender to tell you exactly how much interest you're getting soaked for. The amount should be clearly specified on every sales contract, so don't sign until you see it and understand it. There are dozens of different ways to calculate interest rates, but to end the confusion the Federal Trade Commission ordered lenders to express it as an annual percentage rate (APR). Don't let any lender or merchant weasel out of giving you the APR on everything you finance. And if you're told that only the "add-on" or "discount" interest rate is available, shop elsewhere and report the outfit to the FTC.

- Savings-checking accounts: look before you leap. A word about those new checking accounts that claim to pay you interest on the balance you maintain. It sounds tempting, but is it such a hot deal? It depends. Basically, here is how it works: you open two accounts—a savings account and a checking account. Your money goes into the savings account and your checking account has a zero balance. Every time you write a check, money is automatically transferred from your savings account into your checking, to cover that check. Therefore the 5 percent interest actually paid is paid on money in your savings account, not on money in the checking account, which never has any money in it.

There are some definite consumer advantages. None of your checks can bounce as long as you have money in your savings account. And, of course, you earn interest on the money you would normally keep in your checking account to cover your checks.

But before you rush to the bank, consider this: most banks require a $500 minimum deposit to open the savings account. Next, unless you keep a $2000 balance in the account, you're hit with a service fee plus an additional fee for each check written. In Los Angeles, some banks charge $2.00 a month and 15 cents for every check written.

Privately, bankers tell me that only people who keep a lot of money in their checking accounts should even consider this deal. Unless you keep a couple of thousand dollars in your savings account, service fees will eat up any interest you might earn. It's just another example of being sold the sizzle instead of the steak, which in this case can turn out to be a hamburger.

• Beware of bill consolidation loans. It sounds so easy to take out a loan to pay off all your other loans or debts, but in the long run it will cost you more than it's worth. Debt consolidation loans are generally made by finance companies at the highest interest rates permitted by law. Remember, when it's too easy to borrow, you're going to be paying sky-high interest rates. The worst offenders we've found are the mail-order loan companies.

• Take your credit balance in cash. If you overpay, make sure you never leave a credit balance in any account. Demand the cash back. I've had too many complaints from viewers who say their credit balance mysteriously disappeared into the corporate kitty. If they won't give it back, remind them the law is on your side. If you don't get a check, let the local office of the Federal Trade Commission know about it and tell all your friends to shop elsewhere.

But don't expect a cash refund on merchandise returns. Unless it's stated policy to give a cash refund, a store can give you a credit refund if you bring something back. No law says it has to give you cash. Some states require stores to post refund policies, others don't. But if the store doesn't post its refund policy somewhere in the store or write it on a sales slip, you may have a good case for demanding cash. People have gotten their cash in small claims court. To save yourself the hassle, though, know the store's refund policy *before* you buy or charge.

Help Yourself Get Out of Debt

Credit cards can be tough to get but they're easy to use. Whip out that "plastic money" often enough and you can be eyeball deep in debt before you realize it. If you're one of those people who can't control your spending or hang on to your cash—and don't feel you're alone—you can get help, free. The National Foundation for Consumer Credit sponsors 203 non-profit debt counseling services throughout the nation.

These services are designed to help people dig themselves out of their financial holes or at least prevent them from plunging deeper into debt. Believe me, if you're a creditaholic, they don't coddle you. You quit cold turkey. You usually have to fork over your credit cards the minute you walk in the door. The manager of the Consumer Credit Counselors of Los Angeles even gives you the scissors so you can cut them in half. Then you're put on a strict cash budget.

These people are more than just debt counselors; they will contact your creditors and try to persuade them to accept a reasonable payment on what you owe. Counselors have told me that most creditors are willing to take something small to avoid spending time and money on collection or having to take back the merchandise to resell it.

Under most state laws, there is no charge for debt counseling. However, if you have the agency take over your finances to keep creditors at bay while you work out repayment schedules, there is a monthly fee of $5 to $10. If you're having credit problems and want to get back on your feet contact the National Foundation for Consumer Credit, 1819 H. Street, NW, Washington, DC 20006 (202/223-2040). Ask for the address of the consumer credit counseling service headquarters or branch office nearest you. It's too complicated to go into detail here, but the Federal Bankruptcy Court also offers a fantastic service for people who are in debt over their heads but who still have a steady job and regular income. They can file a "Chapter 13" plan and the court will get all the creditors to hold off on collection efforts and agree to a long term payoff. Then the bankruptcy trustee will collect the monthly payments and distribute them to the creditors over a period of about three years. This service is not free, but it isn't very costly and the great advantage is that a bankruptcy doesn't show on your credit record for 14 years—which can just about ruin some people. If you want more information, call any Federal Bankruptcy Court in your area and ask about it. The initial interview as to whether you qualify or not doesn't cost a cent and all the terms of the Chapter 13 filing will be explained to you. You can fight back against that overwhelming urge to charge.

Bill Collectors Can't Browbeat You Anymore

Debt collectors can no longer use terror tactics to get you to pay up. A federal law that went into effect in 1978 now protects you against unscrupulous collectors who try to intimidate you if you owe money. The law wasn't designed to let deadbeats off the hook; they still have to pay their debts. But it does let you work out your repayment programs in peace without being harassed.

No longer can a debt collector call you in the middle of the night to browbeat you into coughing up the cash. The law prohibits collectors from calling before 8 A.M. or after 9 P.M. If you're contesting the debt and have legal counsel, they must call your attorney and leave you alone.

Debt collectors can't telephone you at work if your boss gets angry. They can't discuss your debt with anyone other than your spouse, parent, or legal advisor unless they have the court's permission. You can put a stop to their dun letters by writing the collector and stating on paper that you are refusing to pay because it is a disputed bill.

In the past some debt collection agencies threatened people with violence, harangued them with profanity, and published their names in a list of people who owed money. But now these thuglike pressure tactics are against the law. Collectors can no longer pose as lawyers, policemen, or FBI agents and threaten to arrest you unless you pay. And they can't threaten you with a lawsuit unless they actually plan to file one.

Why are these collection agencies so hardnosed? They get a big chunk of everything they collect from you. The actual collector also gets a fat piece of the cash he recovers. But now they can't tighten the thumb screws on you anymore. The first time some collector tries to use these illegal ploys, let that person know that he's breaking a federal law and that you're going to turn him in —to his boss and the Federal Trade Commission. If he keeps it up, file a complaint and send a copy to the credit manager of the company who originally turned you over to the collection agency. You may have recourse against him.

Send another copy of your complaint to the American Collectors Association, Inc., Box 35106, Minneapolis, MN 55435 (612/926-6547). This association represents many of the 4500 debt collection agencies in the United States. It supported the new federal law and wants to get rid of the goons in its industry. Finally, check with your state government to see if you have a fair debt collection practices act; find out whom you can complain to if you get harassed. Some state laws are even stronger than the federal law and that's to your advantage to find out.

Getting the Banker to Bet on You

Borrowing money for the first time can be scary, particularly for women and young people, who usually only see a banker when they're depositing money in a savings or checking account or making a withdrawal. Even then, most people only smile or wave. Few folks ever shoot the breeze with their bankers the way they might do with their butcher or dentist. But why don't they? Giant corporations are certainly in daily contact with *their* bankers to keep their credit lines clear and flowing. And it's just as important for you to establish a solid banking relationship, especially if you want to borrow money. Bankers are in business to lend money, not hoard it, and like you and me they would rather do business with a familiar face than with a strange one.

But it takes more than that to get a loan. You have to make a businesslike, creditworthy impression. So if you're borrowing money for the first time, here are ten ways to impress your banker.

Even if you're borrowing for the second or third time, these tips apply.

1. Dress conservatively and tastefully. Wear a business suit or skirt and blouse, but nothing flashy and no jeans. Theoretically what you wear shouldn't affect your creditworthiness, but realistically it does. We're all still hung up on first impressions. And don't "dress down" to look like you need the money; "dress up" so you look like you can pay it back.

2. Call your bank and make an appointment with the manager or the loan officer. Don't just walk in off the street and plop down in the chair. It shows you are serious about borrowing money and it implies you'll be diligent in repaying it. Be straightforward and self-confident. Don't look or act as if you're confused by money and banking and need help. You should have done your homework before you walked in the front door.

3. As a first time borrower, make sure you have a good reason for wanting the money. It's best to borrow to buy something sensible—furniture, specialized tools for your work, an educational course, an automobile. Or you might want to establish or strengthen your credit history by borrowing the funds, putting them in a savings account at that bank or savings and loan, and repaying that obligation on time every month. Just don't be frivolous. Bankers have told me they would rather see you buy a car with their money than jet off to Hong Kong. And be realistic. Don't go for a Porsche if you can only afford a Chevette.

4. Ask intelligent, relevant questions. What are the terms of each loan and the *total* finance charges for each? They vary widely, but it's not always wise to shop other banks unless you have solid credit and can easily get a loan anywhere. This time (as a first timer) it might be smart to stick with the bank that has your checking and savings accounts—to build that relationship. But if one bank or savings and loan offers you a super deal, just move your accounts there.

5. Prepare a financial resumé. Similar to a career resumé, it also lists all your assets (savings, stocks, property, automobiles—paid for or not) and liabilities (what you owe, to whom, and the outstanding balances on each). The resume should also list your credit

cards and charge accounts, including account numbers, addresses, average monthly payments, amounts owed. The more personal information details it contains the better. You will still have to fill out a loan application and your credit will be checked, but the resumé makes the officer's job easier—and that's to your benefit. Even more important, you never have to worry about the officer's overlooking an obscure asset that could weigh in your favor and possibly swing the loan for you.

6. If you've had credit problems in the past, tell your banker about them. Don't try to hide or ignore old sins. They'll probably turn up in your credit file. Give him all the facts, such as, you were off work for seven months because of an injury and fell behind in your bills. Or you were divorced and your ex-husband or wife went hog wild with the credit cards. Explain that you subsequently paid them off but the payments were late.

7. Be calm and sincere in discussing your loan. Don't get anxious, emotional, or look the least bit desperate for the money. Your banker knows that "crisis" loans are forgotten once the crisis has passed.

8. You don't have to complete the loan application on the spot. Take it home with you, study it thoroughly, and read all the fine print. Then fill it out *completely*. Bankers say partially completed applications are a good tip-off to a bad credit risk.

9. Make it clear that you've shopped hard to get the best price and value, whatever you're borrowing the money for. If the banker thinks you were sandbagged by some fast-talking salesperson, you're less likely to get the loan. The banker will figure that you'll soon wake up to the fact you were fleeced. You'll kick yourself and you'll want to forget the whole unpleasant mess. Including timely repayment on the money you're borrowing from that bank.

10. Leave on friendly terms if you are turned down for the loan because you weren't creditworthy enough. But first ask the loan officer to give you the precise reasons you were declined. Then find out what you should do to reapply. Don't get angry though. You're a first timer and you want to build that solid relationship. And, of course, you can always try another bank.

Discriminated Against? Take Action

Discrimination is hard to prove. But as I said earlier the Equal Credit Opportunity Act (ECOA) was designed to stamp out unfair discrimination by lenders. I've already discussed how you can fight back if you think someone has violated an ECOA provision. But if a bank's involved and you can't get the problem settled, there are several state and federal government agencies you can complain to.

The enforcement agency for national banks is the Comptroller of the Currency. Write the agency's Consumer Affairs Division at Washington, DC 20219 and give them all the details. Also, national banks and state chartered banks are regulated by the Federal Deposit Insurance Corporation, and that agency has an Office of Bank Customer Affairs for complaints. Write: Office of Bank Customer Affairs, Federal Deposit Insurance Corporation, Washington, DC 20429 (202/389-4427). The complaint will probably be checked out by a regional office. You can also contact your state banking commission. Or, if the complaint is against a federally chartered savings and loan, you can complain to the Federal Home Loan Bank Board in your area. These enforcement agencies are concerned with far more than just discrimination, which is basically under the Federal Trade Commission's scrutiny. Any unfair or deceptive banking practice used to rip you off should be reported to the appropriate agency via a written complaint.

Life Insurance: Compare Costs and Beware

Welcome to consumers' No Man's Land, probably the only nationwide industry that doesn't have a regulatory watchdog agency in Washington where you can take your complaint if you don't get satisfaction from the company or the state.

So powerful is the insurance industry, it has been able to keep the Federal Trade Commission and the Securities and Exchange Commission out of its hair on most policies it sells. What's more, until now, life insurance companies have fought off any attempts to establish a simple price index where you can compare the actual costs of different policies and different companies. But that's changing. At the end of 1978 some 21 states are forcing insurance companies to tell consumers the cost. And if all 50 states do not play ball, Uncle Sam is sure to step in and impose a federal truth-in-insurance cost law.

But until that happens, you've got to be aware and on your toes when you buy life insurance. You'll have to make some important choices on how you want to protect yourself. But before I plunge into that, let me give you a little pep talk.

Even though we're finally getting some real pressure on insurance companies to reveal those closely guarded life insurance costs, people who need the protection—and we all do—are still scared to buy it. We all cringe at the thought of dying; that's a natural fear. But I think the real reason we put off the purchase until someone persuades us to buy is that we're afraid of the life insurance salesperson. And we don't really understand what he's selling. His wares, designed by actuaries and written by lawyers, practically defy comprehension. The speaker of the California Assembly once surveyed students and found that four of the state's nine best-selling insurance policies were harder to read than Einstein's theory of relativity. He also discovered that it took the reading skill level of a college postgraduate degree holder to actually understand the policies. Yet we depend on an agent to translate the hieroglyphics. And when we suddenly realize he works on commission and doesn't eat unless he sells, we feel helpless and trapped and either sign up just to get him off our backs or we squirm out of the sale. But there's no need to be intimidated. You can be the hunter stalking the best value, not the hunted.

Find a Competent Agent with a Solid Company

You can start by interviewing a life insurance agent as if you were hiring him for a lifetime job. In fact, you're doing just that. An agent handling your life insurance program has to make a lifelong commitment to watch out for you and your family and be there when you need him. That's a tall order—especially since about half of the new life insurance agents drop out of the business within a year. These newcomers sell all of their close friends and family, then run out of prospects. When their commissions dry up, they give up.

I ought to know. I was a life insurance agent with a major midwestern-based carrier for three years and a top producer while I was going to college. But I have to confess I was totally unequipped to advise a client on how he or she should plan their financial future; yet I was one hell of a salesman so I survived.

As a former agent, my advice to you is to avoid new life insurance agents unless they are associated with an established agency staffed with seasoned salespeople who can rescue you if your agent drops out of the business. Besides, why should you be the guinea pig for a new agent who is trying to learn the ropes? Sounds cruel but life insurance is complex enough, and the last thing you need is some novice dispensing advice that he's memorized from a canned sales pitch. I would also avoid part-timers and relatives who put the arm on you to buy, plus anyone who seems hungry and pushy and who hasn't been in the fiercely competitive life insurance business for at least five years.

Don't be impressed by those Million Dollar Clubbers either. Today a successful agent can sell a million dollars of life insurance to just one wealthy customer; it's not that rare anymore. But more importantly, a hotshot salesperson might be too busy selling to give you the personal attention and thoughtful advice of a skillful counselor when you need it.

You would be wise to ask your prospective agent for a half dozen references and personally talk to his other clients. Check out all credentials. The more dedicated life insurance agents invest four tough years in their career to become a Chartered Life Underwriter (CLU). Still, that's no assurance either that he or she will be the answer to your prayers. Just keep on probing. Finally, to protect yourself, ask your state insurance department if the agent has ever been reprimanded for ripping off a client or a company.

Does your new agent represent a solid company with a reputation to uphold? The Alfred M. Best Company rates the financial strength of insurance companies; ask for proof that his company currently has at least an A, but preferably an A+, financial rating from Best's. Agents with top-rated companies are usually loaded down with copies of the report. Check with a Best's directory at your library or with your state insurance department if the agent doesn't have one with him. And while you're at it, ask the insurance department if the company claims department he represents has any history of hassling policyholders or if it pays claims promptly. You may have to push to get the question answered, but it's worth it.

Finally, be aware that there are two kinds of people who can sell you insurance. One is the agent who works only for his own company, while the other is a broker who handles policies from several different companies. The advantage of the latter is that he can give you some cost comparisons between one company and another, or even among a number of companies for the same coverage. There are also two kinds of insurance companies: stock companies (such as New York Life) and mutual companies (such as Liberty Mutual or Mutual of Omaha). The latter may be able to offer cost savings on certain types of policies, but you may not have your very own agent. You could be assigned to one and he or she could change from time to time. However, if the policy is something like a homeowner's policy or automobile policy and the coverage is excellent, that shouldn't matter.

I know it is a colossal bore to do this detective work, but you're only protecting yourself. As I said earlier, there is no federal agency with powers over the insurance industry, so there's no one to fight for you. Your state insurance department is your only real watchdog, and while some have sharp teeth, others have been defanged by state legislatures where insurance lawyers and prominent insurance agents hold powerful committee posts. Most people don't know it, but state insurance departments aren't supposed to regulate costs to keep them *down*—they're there to see that the company charges *enough* to be able to pay all claims without going bankrupt.

On top of that, there can sometimes be rather cozy relationships between insurance companies and state insurance departments— not surprisingly. Since insurance is so perplexing, insurance commissioners are frequently plucked from insurance company executive suites or from law firms with a raft of insurance company clients. And when the commissioner leaves office, he's often recycled back to the company side as a president. It happens in other industries, but there is usually another layer of regulatory insulation to keep old chums at greater arm's length. And by the way, the commission won't be of any help to you if the company you're insured with isn't licensed to do business in your state!

The crux of all this? Watch out for your own hide.

Does It Just Pay Off When You Kick Off?

Let's get down to the nitty-gritty: How do you get the insurance coverage that suits you best at the best price? As they used to say at the White House, let me make one thing perfectly clear: Although I sold life insurance to help me get through my undergraduate work at Bradley University, I never was nor am I now an expert insurance planner and adviser. Besides, this chapter can't be a primer on life insurance. That's why you need that agent and why you should dig so hard to find one you can depend on and communicate with.

But there are some basics you should know and some legends that should be laid to rest. So even though life insurance is about as exciting as reading a zip code directory, you've got to pay close attention. First you must realize that although there are hundreds of different insurance policies, all are basically variations on two themes: cash value life insurance (sometimes called permanent, ordinary whole, or straight life), which gives you protection and forces you to accumulate cash, and term life insurance, which I call death insurance because it only pays off when you kick off.

Cash value life is obviously more expensive than term life but you get more. The cash builds up and you get paid a low rate of tax-free interest, about 3 to 4 percent, although some companies are considering upping it to 5 percent to keep pace with banks. You can borrow that money with no difficulty but this time you have to pay interest; older policies charge around 5 percent; newly issued policies charge you 2 to 3 percentage points more to lend you your own money. Normally you pay the same, level premium for the life of a cash value policy, but if you buy it and get sick or become uninsurable, the policy can't be cancelled on you as long as the premiums are paid and many policies waive the premiums entirely if you're disabled for more then 6 months. Some cash value coverages, known as participating policies, pay "dividends." But you're only getting your own money back—that is, you're getting back excess premiums left over after expenses are covered and profits are pocketed.

Term life insurance is pure protection with no cash value. It's a great bargain compared to whole life but, as its name implies, you can buy it only for a specific term—one year, five years, ten years, and up to twenty. Then it must be renewed, usually at a higher price because the chances you'll die are greater as you get older. Almost all group life insurance programs provided by employers, unions, and employee or fraternal associations are term. Individual term policies can be converted to costlier whole life insurance but you would only want to do that if you suddenly developed a serious ailment and you wanted to load up on insurance without having to take a medical examination you might flunk or to supply other "evidence of insurability" such as a medical history record from your doctor.

There are some other facts you should beware of:

• Most life insurance agents will try their damnedest to sell you cash value life insurance. The first year commission is fat, often equal to or greater than the amount you pay in premiums. Plus, they collect scaled down renewal commissions for the next nine years. However, if you are disciplined enough to save money elsewhere and you simply want protection while your family is growing, term life insurance is a wiser choice.

• Suppose you're offered a cash value life insurance policy designed to pay for a child's college education. Fine, but when the youngster is 17 or 18 and about to enter school, you'll have to give up your insurance protection when you cash in the policy to pay tuition.

• Don't let an agent convince you that life insurance is a great investment. Prospects are often dazzled by reams of computer printouts showing how cash values and dividends build up to a mountain of money in your golden years. You can almost see yourself cruising the Riviera or lying on a snowy white beach on a remote island in the South Pacific. But let me bring you back to earth. You've seen what inflation has done to your dollar in the last decade. Some cash value policies have inflation-fighting features, but many do not. Think about that when you're counting cash you won't get for 20 or 30 years.

• Never let an agent persuade you to drop an old policy or cash it in and replace it with one of his. This is called "twisting"—it's unethical and illegal and you should tell the agent you're going to report him to the insurance commissioner for even suggesting it. Then do it. Old whole life insurance policies are like fine antiques: You bought them in your youth when prices were lower; now they have value that you can't afford to replace at today's costs. However, if you have paid for a policy and you don't need the protection, you may want to cash it out and put the proceeds in a bank. Discuss it with a qualified agent.

There are two things you should be very wary of: (1) The insurance plans some agents try to sell in which you keep borrowing the cash value of the policy to pay premiums. It's a complicated, sophisticated plan and you should be financially very wise before you go into it. (2) If you are going to put money into an Independent Retirement Account (IRA) tax sheltered plan, you can put that money into a savings and loan or a stock fund—but also into a life insurance policy. That's OK if you are sure that you'll NEVER have to take the money out. But if you should have an emergency and need the cash within 2 or 3 years, you'll only get back a small part of what you put in because the costs for the entire life of the plan are deducted from the first year or so's premiums. It's always a financial loss to cash in an IRA plan since you have to pay heavy penalties in interest losses as well as back taxes to the IRS, but with an insurance plan you have the added loss of having paid the costs up front.

I've thrown a lot at you so let's take a breather. It's important to remember that life insurance can easily boggle your mind if an agent tries to bombard you with a dozen different policies, programs, or plans to choose from. You shouldn't feel inadequate if you can't absorb all those numbers, benefits, and features. Hardly anyone can. You do have one excellent protection. After the policy is mailed to you, you have 10 days to read it over and decide that it fits the bill. If it doesn't, follow the directions and mail it back. Your premium will be fully refunded. That's the law. Just take your time and don't get pushed into making a snap decision. You may make a costly mistake that you'll pay for the rest of your life.

On the other hand, your agent, any agent, is going to press you to take some action. He knows it's only human nature for people to procrastinate over matters of life and death, especially when their life isn't hanging in the balance. But if your life insurance agent really pours on the pressure, and heaps on the guilt, back off.

When I was selling life insurance, my agency director had a favorite closing line reserved for that crucial moment at the kitchen table. There I was, eyeball to eyeball with a young couple, the wife was bouncing a baby on her knee while another child was tugging at her dress. I had the application on the table and was handing him the pen when I'd look into his wife's eyes. "It's your decision," I'd tell him, "but if something happens to you tomorrow do you want your lovely young wife to scrub floors and clean toilets for a living to take care of your kids just because you didn't love her enough to protect her right now when she needs it most?"

Wow! Talk about guilt. Most folks couldn't sign that application fast enough. Everybody needs a little shove when it comes to life insurance, but don't let yourself by stampeded or browbeaten into buying something you don't fully understand. In fact, here's a great comeback if some zealous life insurance salesman or saleswoman tries to drench you in guilt to get your name on the dotted line: Look that turkey square in the eyeballs and calmly say: "I love my wife enough to make sure she and the kids are going to get the best possible insurance protection at the best possible price and I'm going to spend the time and the energy to find it." Now that's fighting back.

Okay, Okay, David, but What About Costs?

As I said at the beginning of this section, life insurance companies are finally starting to tell consumers the facts of life—the actual cost of a life insurance policy—whether it's cash value or term. The premium isn't an accurate yardstick; that's the retail price you are paying for the coverage. To help you figure out if you're getting the best value, state insurance commissioners have settled on the "interest adjusted index" method. It boils everything down to a single number: premiums paid minus the cash values and dividends plus the interest and what that money could have earned elsewhere. The lower the policy's interest adjusted cost for every thousand dollars of coverage, the better the bargain.

Now you can simply go to your library and ask for the National Underwriter's interest adjusted index or for *Best's Flitcraft*, look up their index tables, and "shop" 100 companies in five minutes flat. (Your state insurance department might have an index, too.) Naturally, you have to compare apples with apples, that is, the same size policy issued at the same age. You can't compare cash value with term policies. But since you'll be paying premiums for a lifetime or at least for a long time, you can save a lot of money by shopping.

More people should shop life insurance this way. It might persuade some of the high-priced companies to take a hard look at their costs and give the consumer a break. And you know something, if I were buying life insurance and had narrowed down my decision to two companies, I'd opt in the end for more than just lower premiums. Then I'd write a letter to the president of the other company telling him why I made my choice. It could make a difference by putting him on notice that his company's rates aren't competitive.

You might think it's odd that I would suggest finding an agent before locating the life insurance company with the best buys. Is that putting the proverbial cart before the horse? No way. Your life insurance agent, if you choose him wisely, should be your trusted advisor. Even if his company doesn't have the bargain-priced policy, he might be able to get it for you anyway. Give him a chance.

I can't close this discussion without mentioning "The Consumers Union Report on Life Insurance." I've mentioned *Consumer Reports* magazine several times in this book. It is almost unfailingly a source of outstanding information on every conceivable subject of consumer interest. This book gives you complete information on how to compare policy costs. But that's not all, it gives you a guide to help you decide how much insurance you should have and the kind of policy best suited to your needs.

Later in this chapter I'll discuss automobile insurance. *Consumer Reports* has done several good studies on that too, including the comparisons of various companies on how efficiently and justly claims are handled. You don't have to subscribe—you can get copies of current and old issues at any library and you should. If you do want the book on life insurance, it costs $3 plus 50¢ handling and postage. You can order it from *Consumer Reports,* Orangeburg, N.Y. 10962.

Fighting Back

Your agent should run interference for you at the insurance company if you have hang-ups getting a beneficiary changed, or foul-ups with the premium payments, or some other hassle. But what happens if you have a problem and you discover your agent is now a computer programmer or he took off for Tahiti three months ago? Suddenly you've become what's known as an "orphan policy-holder." Hopefully someone at his old agency will adopt you. But you may have to fight your own battle.

Most life insurance companies have a policyholder service department at the regional office, and that should be your first stop. Write the director and wait ten days or, if it's an emergency, call. Today, most life insurance companies are responsive, but if yours isn't and you get the old runaround, step up the attack. Leapfrog up the organization chart to the executive vice president; he's usually number two or three from the top, gets hardly any complaints, but has plenty of clout. Brief him on your problem, your frustrations at the lower rungs of the ladder. Let him know your next stop is the state insurance department. Usually, that's all it takes.

If you get the shaft from the agent *and* the company, file a complaint with the insurance commissioner. Other consumers could have been victimized in the same manner, and by lodging a protest you may be instrumental in getting the agent's license lifted or the insurance company fined. If you were ripped off by a CLU, one of those who hold themselves to be the industry experts, shoot a copy of your complaint letter to the American College of Life Underwriters at 270 Bryn Mawr Ave., Bryn Mawr, PA

19010 (215/525-9500) and let them know you were duped by the designation into believing you were dealing with a professional.

Finally, God forbid, if the company doesn't pay off on a legitimate death claim, sound a full-scale consumer alarm: Fire off a telegram to the insurance commissioner and the governor, contact the press and active consumer groups, and telegraph the Federal Trade Commission demanding that Washington step in and regulate the insurance industry.

Medical Insurance: Your Financial Health Is at Stake

It's rare to get static from a life insurance company on a legitimate claim. Show them the death certificate and they usually pay off like a slot machine. But you can get hassled aplenty on your health and medical insurance claims.

Judging from my consumer complaint mail, it seems that insurers are constantly trying to find new ways to test the patience of their policyholders.

First, you have the old familiar "computer foul-up." Life and health insurers have mastered that excuse. Or, we're told the doctor or hospital didn't fill out the insurance forms, or they filled them out wrong and that botched up the payment. So you check back and the doc's nurse or the hospital business office swears they mailed it off weeks ago. Or, the insurance company claims your file is "temporarily misplaced." Worse yet, it's lost. But these aren't serious snafus.

What I'm hearing more and more from insurance companies is that the policyholder wasn't ever covered for the claim or that only part of the bill will be paid. The reason: The consumer didn't take the time to read the policy he was buying or didn't understand it and didn't ask the right questions.

It's tragic but true. Insurance companies will pocket your premiums, no questions asked, but if you don't know what you're buying, you're out of luck. And most people don't find out the real facts about their medical insurance, especially the holes in their coverage, until it's too late—when they're ready to check out of the hospital and the credit manager slaps them with the bill or when they file a claim and can't get it paid.

It happens to almost everyone. Just because a person is covered by an employee or union group insurance plan is no real protection if there isn't a reputable firm administering and underwriting the master policy. But it seems to happen most often to self-employeds and elderly people who had to buy their own health insurance as either primary protection or to supplement some government plan. And these are the people who can least afford to be taken advantage of. What can be done?

You've got to know what you're buying. More important, you must be aware of the fact there are some insurance vultures out there just circling around waiting to swoop down and pick your wallet clean.

As I discussed in the life insurance section, a qualified agent and a scrupulous insurance company are your best sources of information. So is the Health Insurance Association of America, 1750 K Street, Washington, DC 20006 (202/331-1336), which can supply you with helpful background material. But there are facts you should know about health insurance.

If you're covered at work, find out if you can convert your group protection to an individual plan if you leave the company for any reason. Will the benefits shrivel? What will the individual plan cost? Probably a lot! Also, ask how many days you'll be covered under your group plan if you leave the company. That's called the "grace period" if there is one, and sometimes there isn't—and it's important to know the precise length. Don't always assume you're going to waltz right into another job and be covered immediately by its own group medical insurance programs. Most group plans have an "elimination period" or waiting period before you're eligible for protection. You may not be covered for 90 days, for example.

Most people wait until they get sick or injured, then they examine their policy. They toss medical insurance policies or employee handbooks into a drawer without studying them. Don't. Know your coverage. A basic hospitalization policy, for instance, should cover all the costs you run up in the hospital: room, meals, nursing care, your doctor's visits, lab tests, medication, anesthesia, and surgical and operating room fees, if necessary. But find out exactly how much is covered. Most insurance companies pay 80 percent and you pick up 20 percent, although some plans will pay the full 100 percent. Know in advance what percentage you're going to pay if you go into a hospital so you don't lapse into a coma when the final bill arrives.

Here's where it gets tricky. Your basic hospitalization plan has a dollar limit to the benefits it will pay. Find out what it is. Then check to see if you have what's called "major medical coverage." If it's not included, ask if you can pay an additional premium and get it. Most people have heard the term "major med" but they really don't know what it means. Well, pay attention. Major medical is designed to keep you out of the poorhouse. It insures you against catastrophes—the serious accident or extended illness that could keep you hospitalized for weeks and months. I hate to sound ghoulish but heart disease, neurological illnesses, cancer, these can run up medical bills today that only a millionaire can afford to pay.

If you're struck down and you drain your basic hospital insurance, you pay a deductible, anywhere from $250 to $1000 or more. Then the insurance company usually pays 80 percent of any medical expense above that, both inside and outside the hospital; you pay the other 20 percent. Usually, once the tab reaches $25,000, the insurance company pays 100 percent up to the maximum amount of coverage. Frankly, the way medical costs are soaring, I wouldn't consider a major med policy with a limit lower than $100,000. But talk it over with that agent. You'll be surprised to find that the cost of major med is generally lower than basic hospitalization insurance. There's less of a risk to the insurance company since catastrophes are not that common; actuarily speaking, few people spend two months in a hospital bed and the higher the deductible, the lower the cost of the coverage.

Watch out for medical and hospital insurance plans that pay on an indemnity basis. The word sounds comforting, as if you're indemnified against all costs. But an indemnity policy will only pay a flat dollar amount per day for the room, doctor's visits, and other costs. And normally, only after a seven-day elimination or waiting period. Most people are usually out of a hospital in four days, so that's no help. Besides, the way hospital and doctor costs are spiraling today, a hospital indemnity policy that pays $65 a day on room cost is hardly comforting. That might have helped ten years ago, but today you'll get stuck with a whopping difference. Still, most hospital indemnity programs are only supplemental coverage but people groping for reasonably priced insurance may buy, thinking they're fully protected for all hospital costs.

Look for Loopholes

If you've had health problems in the past, check out the preexisting condition clause in any medical policy you may be considering. I've had thousands of consumers claim they were ripped off by this "loophole." But actually they did themselves in by not reading the fine print or asking enough questions. The preexisting condition clause is designed to keep the insurance company from getting ripped off by a sick person who takes out a policy (or even takes a job to get into a group) and then checks into the hospital for that long overdue operation.

Some insurance companies have carried this too far, however, and put in a three-year exclusion period for preexisting conditions (such as cancer) or permanently exclude that condition. Frankly, a one-year exclusion is reasonable for certain types of non-terminal diseases, but after that you should be covered for that prior ailment. Look closely for that clause. Note, though, that back ailments are often lifetime exclusions. So if you've had a back problem and you're insured, don't drop that coverage thinking you'll do better elsewhere. Chances are you won't.

If you've had so many medical problems that you're basically uninsurable, you might want to consider the indemnity policies. The reason? They are often written without a request for your health history, but with a long "pre-existing illness" clause. If you think that you could wait out the one to three years before you might need to file a claim, it could be the only way you'd get some added protection. Such offers are often of the mail-order variety (which I'll discuss later) and you should read every word of the fine print, but it might be good for your own needs.

Choosing a medical insurance company is a real crapshoot. You have to look at more than costs. The big mystery is how quickly the company pays off on claims and if you'll have to beat the door down to get a check. Once again, you've got to play private eye. Ask a trusted agent, a consumer action reporter, or your local consumer group if they've had any nightmarish complaints against the company. Has the state insurance department had to take any action against the company or is it planning to take any? Press them for an answer.

A clue to a slow pay or no-pay insurer is its loss/benefit ratio. This tells you the percentage of premium dollars that come back to the policyholder as benefits. One hundred percent is a good return for the consumer but a financial "break-even" for the insurance company. Non-profit Blue Cross and Blue Shield average about 90 to 96 percent return. When the loss/benefit ratio drops to around 50 percent, however, look out. The insurance company is either making hefty profits or incurring heavy expenses and not much of the money is getting paid back in claims.

Your state insurance department can give you the company's loss/benefit ratio on its group or individual health insurance. Or ask the agent for proof. But don't let him snow you with an annual report or some sales brochure that brags about how many millions of claims dollars are paid annually. That figure is totally meaningless to you.

Mail-Order Health Insurance: Beware of What You Buy

Mail-order insurance was once the cesspool of the industry, but a nationwide crackdown by state insurance commissioners a decade ago chased out many of the rip-off artists and convinced others to toe the line. Today about $1.5 billion worth of life and health insurance is sold through the mails. The Direct Mail Insurance Council insists that two out of every three people they reach by mail never hear from an agent. They say agents aren't out peddling supplemental hospitalization insurance, accident insurance, or small life insurance policies simply because the commissions are so small.

But if agents aren't out hustling these coverages, huge corporations are. Giant outfits like J.C. Penney Co., Montgomery Ward, Gulf Oil, Household Finance Corporation, plus big banks, department stores, and virtually any other company with a large computerized list of charge account or credit customers are hawking insurance. They're pitching more than protection; they're selling convenience—just "charge it to your account and you automatically pay your premiums when you pay your statement." Painless, eh? Once they program your insurance premiums on the monthly credit billing cycle, they know you are less likely to drop the coverage. Still, some mail-order insurance companies sell direct through mailing lists or via various associations. For example, most of the mail I get from the American Association of Retired People (AARP) is trying to sell me health insurance underwritten by Colonial Penn Insurance Company—which is closely connected to AARP organizationally—quite an arrangement!

Take a very close look at any mail-order insurance before you buy. That alone may take self-restraint. Since the mailer has to do the selling, the advertising copy is usually hyping the "total benefits," the "peace of mind," and "financial security." Naturally, it's urging you to "act now." Simply explaining the cold facts of the policy isn't very appetizing and doesn't push any of your emotional fear buttons. Read the headline but study the fine print.

Read the Ad Copy Between the Lines

Remember, you're up against some persuasive promoters. Insurance advertising copywriters are probably the cleverest of all mail-order pitchmen. They have to walk a fine line: The advertisement must be legal but still compelling enough to get you to "act now" and sign that application. Don't start feeling guilty and buy what you don't fully understand.

• Most hospital insurance you'll buy through the mail is supplementary coverage, not basic hospitalization protection, which, as I said before, pays 80 percent of most hospital costs. These supplementary coverages are indemnity policies and pay a flat rate ostensibly to cover that other 20 percent.

• Never buy "accident only" hospitalization insurance. Chances are remote you'll be hospitalized by an accident; most people wind up in the hospital because of an illness. Make sure any supplemental hospitalization policy covers you for sickness *and* accident.

• Watch out for the long elimination period. The average hospital stay is about four days. If the supplemental policy doesn't start paying until after the seventh day, it's no bargain. Look for a policy offering first day benefits.

• Don't get sucked in by ludicrous headlines. The mail-order policy that claims it "pays $100 a week every week for as long as you live even if you're hospitalized for life" is pure rip-off. First, $100 a week is about twelve bucks a day and that barely pays for one breakfast in bed in a hospital today. Other insurance copywriters will multiply the weekly dollar benefit by the maximum number of weeks so you'll think the policy will pay off like a Las Vegas jackpot. Just ask yourself: How many persons are ever confined to a hospital bed for life?

• Look out for terms like "cash estate policy," where the ad promises to pay you a $100,000 "cash estate" for accidental death. What the policy doesn't tell you is that most people die by natural causes. But the real rip-off is that many older people think they're buying a $100,000 life insurance policy at a bargain price when they're actually only covered for accidental death. I get hundreds of letters a year from the families of policyholders who claim the insurance company didn't pay off when their loved ones died. But in practically all the cases, they bought cheap accident policies, not life insurance.

• Make darned sure the insurance "pays in addition" to all other insurance you have. Many policies do not, but you won't find that fact in the headline. Yet, year after year, people are hoodwinked into believing they're protecting themselves with a handful of smaller policies.

• Does it totally exclude preexisting conditions? It could be worthless to you if a recurring ailment is likely to hospitalize you in a few years.

• If you're a senior citizen trying to plug the gaps in your Medicare coverage, check any Medicare supplement offers you get either through the mail or from an agent with your local Social Security office. Any person over 65 eligible for Medicare should apply for Part A of the government hospital coverage and Part B, which pays toward medical and surgical expense. But if you can't afford Uncle Sam's Part B, don't even consider private insurance coverage.

• Don't be lulled into a false sense of security by mail-order insurance advertising copy that urges you to "show this offer of financial security to your banker, lawyer, accountant, or even your most trusted family financial advisor." One top mail-order copy-writer told me they purposely point you toward every "advisor" except that one you should really see first—a seasoned insurance agent. If you do see an agent, though, make sure he has your best interest at heart, especially if you're buying Medicare supplement insurance.

The Elderly: Unwitting Targets

There has recently been a rash of agents preying on the fears of the elderly to get them to load up on protection. Last year, for instance, an insurance agent wearing a ski mask so he couldn't be identified testified before a House Select Committee on Aging that insurance companies were coaching their salespeople in the "art of scaring senior citizens into buying coverage they do not need or duplicating coverage they already had." I discussed in an earlier chapter that many of these medi-gap policies are virtually worthless.

The hearings told how a 76-year-old Illinois widow bought 71 policies for health, life, and accident coverage over nine years and once bought five policies in a single day. She bought 21 separate policies over the years from a single agent. As a result of these purchases, the woman, who had been in good health all her life, was forced to remortgage the family farm, which had been practi-cally paid off.

Now, this is an extreme case, but it points up how vulnerable we all are when we fall into the hands of a fast-talking con man who razzle-dazzles us on a subject we know little about. So if you're approached by someone claiming he's connected with the federal Medicare program or who threatens that you might lose your Medicare benefits if you don't "sign up," tell him politely (or not so politely) to get lost. Or, if you carry private health insurance to supplement Medicare, don't let any sharpie talk you into dropping that coverage and buying the policy he's selling. Remember: when you drop that old policy for a new one, all the waiting periods for pre-existing illness will start over again and you'll lose *all* your protection. Confused? The Health Insurance Institute, 1850 K Street, NW, Washington, DC 20006 (202/862-4000), publishes a free booklet entitled "What You Should Know About Health Insurance When You Retire." It's worthwhile reading for anyone concerned with Medicare.

Fighting Back

As you can see, it's easy to be fleeced on your health insurance. But it's just as easy to fight back. First stop: the insurance company that actually underwrote the policy you bought. Health insurance companies, like life insurance companies, have a policyholder service department, so write to the director and tell him your story, all facts included. Since people are constantly getting sick and filing claims, this department is usually tuned into your troubles and can act fast. No help? Then climb that corporate ladder as if you were fighting with a life insurance company and go straight to the top.

With health insurance, though, you have some tough allies outside of the insurance company. One is a law allowing you to cancel any mail-order insurance policy within ten days of receiving the policy and getting back any premium payment you made. All states require this "10-day free look" on mail-order insurance.

Another ally? The bank, department store, oil company, or credit card concern that lets an insurance company send advertisements to its charge account customers. While these companies are getting an "administrative fee" from the insurance company, they don't want their prized credit customers ripped off. Their public reputation is at stake. So if you are being stalled on a claim payment or somehow harassed by the insurer, send a copy of your complaint to the president of the company that has your charge account. Let him know you hold him and his company personally responsible for the trouble you're having with the insurer and indicate that you're going to name them in any action you may have to take with the insurance department. Get on their backs like that with your fangs bared and you'll get your problem solved fast.

The same strategy usually works for any association-sanctioned mail-order insurance offer. Write to the association president, or the executive director if you get static from the insurance company, and tell him you don't appreciate having a scam insurer soliciting from you and your fellow members. If they don't contact the insurer on your behalf, let the association brass know you'll drop out and will tell other members and friends why. Insurance is an association membership benefit. So don't get pushed around.

Your voice can also be heard if you think your employer is shortchanging you on your company's group health insurance. Some companies overcharge employees for their portion of the group hospitalization or they trim back the benefits to keep their own costs down. One solution to this problem is to have an insurance broker look at your group policy. He may sniff a possible sale and approach your boss with a more comprehensive policy. But I wouldn't let your company executives know you pointed an insurance broker in their direction. They just might see you as a troublemaker.

Another alternative is a prepaid program known as a health maintenance organization (HMO). Strictly speaking, it's not insurance. For one monthly fee (and it's not that cheap), 100 percent of your medical and hospital costs are paid for—doctor visits, hospital costs, eye care, prescription, you name it. It's sort of one-stop medical care of which the most well-known example is the Kaiser Plan. Under the federal HMO Act of 1973, any company that currently employs 25 or more people must offer their employees an HMO as a second choice to group insurance if approached to do so and if the plan is federally qualified. A trade group favorably disposed toward HMOs, the National Association of Employers on Health Maintenance Organization, insists that 92 percent of the Fortune 500 corporations are offering or considering a prepaid group health program. At the end of 1978, some 7.3 million people were enrolled in HMOs nationwide.

Now I'm not praising or damning HMOs. They're not a surefire remedy to an aching wallet plagued by high health care costs. And, based on my mail, they have their share of paperwork snafus. They vary greatly; some are much better then others. But you should be aware of HMOs and understand their strengths and weaknesses. For more information, write Group Health Association of America, 1717 Massachusetts Avenue, NW, Washington, D.C. 20036 (202/483-4012).

The best way to get your health insurance grievance resolved is to file a complaint with the state insurance department. Most departments move superfast on medical insurance complaints. They know you're likely to be laid up, squeezed for cash, and beset by bills. Your easiest approach is to contact the department's policyholder service staff. A policyholder service supervisor in the Ohio Department of Insurance told me he gets 400 health insurance complaints a week and each one is scrutinized. If your complaint merits investigation, you'll get a postcard telling you they're hot on the trail. The Ohio insurance department, at least, notifies the insurance company's home office; they don't waste time with the agent. The insurer has to write the insurance department and explain what's going on or come in and explain it in person. The supervisor, who insists the health insurance field is "riddled with trickery and overselling," will tell a company to get rid of an agent if more than a couple of people complain that he's ripped them off. Then his name is fed into a computer and programmed to pop up if any other insurer in the state tries to hire him as a salesman.

Few people realize the state insurance department can pull a crooked agent's license and put him out of business. It can also order a company to issue an instant check to any policyholder who's been gypped. But while a good insurance department can crack the whip, you have to give them the ammunition first—so file a complaint.

Now, here's a fight-back tip for some of the bureaucrats who might be reading this book. You should be giving the people in your state the kind of protection and service the people in Ohio are getting. It will pay you plenty of political dividends and it might keep the feds off your front porch.

Automobile Insurance: Shop Around and Save Hundreds

Many Americans today claim their auto insurance costs are driving them to the poorhouse. They tell me they are being overcharged, discriminated against, and just generally ripped off by automobile insurance companies who realize that coverage is compulsory in most states.

But only a very few of these same people really take the time to shop for their automobile insurance. They wouldn't buy the first gleaming car or camper off the showroom floor. They wouldn't buy the first home at the first price they were quoted. Yet they don't compare prices on an intangible like auto insurance.

Small wonder. For decades we've been brainwashed into believing we're lucky to get auto insurance at any price. Especially if we're an "unusual risk"—single male under 25, parents with teenage drivers, or a two-car or more family, or if we live in the "wrong neighborhood" or have a ticket or two. It seems as though the auto insurance industry is just one giant Catch-22 and we're somehow bound to be snagged.

Now there's a defeatist attitude. When it comes to your money, you can't be a quitter. And you don't have to quake with fear everytime your auto insurance premium comes due.

Just never accept the first quote. Instead of swallowing the same old pap that all insurance companies had a bad year and they're tightening up and everyone is raising rates, ask a general insurance broker to get you at least three quotes—in writing. He'll try and smooth your ruffled feathers but don't be pacified. Put him on notice that if he expects to handle all your property and casualty insurance, you expect him to earn his commissions. You'll have to get your own quotes from the companies which sell only through their own agents, such as Allstate, Farmers and the like.

Insurance agents have admitted to me they don't really have to sell automobile insurance. They just sit back take orders and process renewals. What's more, they tell me if an agent handles your homeowners and personal property coverages and thinks your account is secure with his agency, he generally won't get out and scramble for the lowest auto insurance rate. Unless, that is, you raise a real fuss. So raise one. It's worth it.

In car-happy California, the state insurance department took a survey of 11 insurance companies and found that a wise motorist who shops could save as much as $400 on his yearly auto insurance bill! That's right, an average driver with a good record in the

Florence Firestone neighborhood in South Central Los Angeles could pay $712 a year full coverage with one company. Or he could pay $330 a year for the same protection from a smaller, little known auto insurance company. The savings were less dramatic in the suburbs, but the same principle applies no matter where you live in the country. Compare prices before you commit to the coverage.

You're probably aware that automobile insurance is still a smoldering political football although the situation differs drastically from state to state. That's why I'm not going to touch the sensitive subject of no-fault insurance or compare one state system against another. I would rather you be aware of how to prune the price of your own auto insurance costs. Here are some questions you should ask any agent or company before you buy.

• Are you in the correct rating category? Depending on the insurance company's underwriting guidelines, a couple of tickets for moving violations in a 12-month stretch can knock a good driver out of the "preferred" category into the "standard" or even the "substandard" class. And, of course, that can cost you plenty in premiums. Most states penalize you for only three years, but for a moving violation few people keep tabs on when these misdemeanors are supposed to fall off their records. Ask your agent for a Department of Motor Vehicle printout on your driving record and double-check your classification. It could whack 15 to 30 percent a year off the price of your auto insurance.

• Ask for a higher deductible. Big corporations are lowering their insurance costs by assuming more of the risk. It's called "risk management" and the theory is if they assume a little more of the risk, the insurance company will give them a better break on the total cost. Well, there's no reason you can't use those same money-saving techniques. You know that an insurance policy where you pay the first $100 or $100 deductible is much lower than one where you pay the first $50 or the $50 deductible. But why not ask your insurance agent or company if he'll give you a rock-bottom rate with a $500 or a $1000 deductible? Tell him you're willing to accept more of the risk but you want your premiums dropped sharply. I think any smart insurance company would leap at that offer. They know you'll be a more careful driver because now your bucks are on the line along with theirs. Prominent insurance brokers claim "risk management" is the wave of the future. Instead of paying ever-rising auto premiums, and if you have the cash, why not stash $500 in a bank account, let it collect interest and use it to pay high deductibles if you do get into an accident? Try it for several years and see if the savings are worth it.

• Look for the discounts. Some auto insurance companies charge you less if you don't smoke, if you get good grades, have a super-spotless driving record, hold a particular job (insurers generally like accountants and hate bartenders), or insure more than one car with them. But I've found that you've got to ask for these discounts. Sometimes they're hidden or just plain overlooked. If you find a company with a much lower rate, wait until your current policy expires. Never cancel mid-year or you'll end up with a "short-rate" refund for the balance and won't save any money at all.

• Avoid premium financing. Some insurance agents will arrange to have a bank finance your auto premiums especially when you buy a new car. That way the insurance company gets its premiums paid promptly in one lump sum. You repay the bank usually on a monthly basis but at a whopping interest rate. And worst of all, your insurance can be cancelled if you miss one payment! Any greedy agent who tries to foist this scheme onto you isn't doing you any favors. First, he pockets his normal commission for placing your auto insurance coverage. Then he gets a kickback from the bank for steering you there to finance your premiums. My advice: Don't buy the car if you can't afford to insure it without strapping yourself.

You Can Help Drive Down Auto Insurance Costs

I've got a story you're going to love about how the little guy fought back against the giant insurance industry and the entire state of California and won. It all began in the Mexican-American barrio of East Los Angeles where working folks have to stretch every dollar they make. There, a confederation of Roman Catholic and Protestant churches known as the United Neighborhoods Organization (UNO) finally started complaining that motorists could no longer afford to pay auto insurance premiums. They claimed East Los Angeles had been lumped into the same "rating territory" as posh Beverly Hills and was being financially persecuted. While the areas had about the same accident statistics, Beverly Hills motorists drove more expensive cars and were quick to hire a lawyer who would sue for higher damages. In short, UNO leaders claimed poorer East Los Angeles was subsidizing rich Beverly Hills.

The UNO went to its elected official, Los Angeles County Supervisor Kenneth Hahn, who took up the consumer crusade and went to the press. Hahn and UNO leaders hammered away at the stubborn insurers for almost two years but finally convinced some insurance companies in the state to switch to smaller zip-coded rating territories. The fight paid off and insurance rates started to tumble like tenpins. State Farm, Government Employees Insurance Co., and Mercury Casualty cut rates about 37 percent in East Los Angeles.

Better yet, the California Insurance Department jumped on the bandwagon and ordered all 400 auto insurance companies in the state to justify their steep insurance rates or lower them. And California governor Edmund Brown, Jr., "invited" executives from a dozen insurance companies to meet with him to find ways to cut those auto insurance rates—not just in East Los Angeles but statewide. In truth, though, California's governor didn't act until the UNO threatened to vote against him in a reelection. He had failed to keep a campaign promise to try and reduce insurance costs, but once he was reminded he took action.

That's a long story with a short message: you've got the power to protect yourself and your family against unfair prices no matter who's trying to gouge you, as long as you're willing to fight back.

But Don't Try to Rip Off the Insurance Company

Auto insurance fraud seems to be fashionable these days. Criminal rings are "staging" fake automobile accidents, filing phony claims, and bilking insurers out of hundreds of thousands of dollars nationwide. These fraud rings are rife with crooked doctors, scheming lawyers, and cooperative auto repair people, all of whom pump up the claim before it's filed with the insurance company. Auto insurance fraud is a multi-million-dollar a year swindle, according to the

Insurance Crime Prevention Institute. Is it any wonder that auto insurance rates are high while claims adjusters are leery?

But law enforcement officers are cracking down. Convicted attorneys are being disbarred and jailed. Doctors who participate are being prosecuted and packed off to prison. In Baltimore last year, lawmen bore down on doctor-lawyer fraud rings, and auto insurance bodily injury rates were cut by 42 percent. You can help break these rings and keep insurance costs in check by tipping off your local district attorney to any fraud you come across. Your name will remain a *secret,* and if they return a conviction you will have the satisfaction of having put a swindler in the slammer.

To Fight Back, Know Your Rights

Laws vary from state to state, but generally an auto insurance company has the right to cancel you out or refuse to renew. Motorists who pile up their cars and rack up huge claims can expect to be pink-slipped by insurance companies, and should be as far as I'm concerned. But if a company arbitrarily dumps you (or as they put it—"non-renews"), you've got recourse in many states. In California, for example, an insurance company must explain in writing why you were cancelled out. But you must write the company and ask. Do it. If you sincerely feel you got a raw deal, appeal the decision to your state insurance department. In Massachusetts you can't be cancelled on a whim. State law says all motor vehicle insurance policies are "noncancellable" after 90 days unless the insured fails to pay the premiums, commits fraud, or gets his or her driver's license suspended or revoked. Find out your rights where you live. There are different rules for actual cancellation than for refusing to renew.

Haggling over an auto insurance claim isn't that much different than following up on a health insurance claim. Know the chain of command. Be tenacious. Don't settle too quickly. If you're injured, watch out for the ambulance-chasing attorney who might try and bleed your insurance company and cut himself in for a piece of the action. A lawsuit is a serious step, but you do have rights to legal recovery. Consult a legal service attorney you can trust.

FIGHT BACK!

Moving: A Moving Experience or a Shakedown? | **12**

America is on the move. Experts claim some 40 million Americans pack up and move each year. Let's face it—nothing can kill the thrill of a new home in a new city faster than a messy move.

Is there anything more shattering than to unpack your grandmother's treasured china to discover her century old 12-piece place setting has arrived in 75 pieces? And what about the stomach-wrenching feeling you get when your new white sectional sofa comes off the truck with a strange black stripe that you can't remember being there when you bought it?

Just about the only thing that's worse is to find that a vanload of your personal belongings—all of your worldly posessions—is stranded in a blizzard somewhere in the Rockies and the driver hasn't been heard from in three days. It once happened to me.

Today moving can be a costly, frustrating rip-off. But you can't always blame the moving company. Once again, through ignorance or penny pinching, consumers can cause problems for themselves because they didn't plan ahead, shop around or, quite simply, inform themselves. You don't just call up a van line and give them your new address.

Yet moving is no great mystery. If you do get cheated, or suspect you are about to be bagged, you have at least a half dozen different ways to get even or get your money's worth. The moving industry has had so much bad press that it's driving hard to give customers a fair shake—instead of a shake down—when they move. Remember, unless you do your homework before the truck arrives, don't blame me if you're carted off to the poorhouse.

Beware of Gypsy Movers and Struggling Students

Two strong people with a truck can call themselves a moving company, and being neither licensed nor regulated won't stop them from soliciting jobs. They can run an ad in the newspaper or post a card on a supermarket bulletin board and whammo! they're in business. My advice: steer clear, even if they quote you a rock bottom hourly rate. The reasons are obvious. These people usually are not trained in the fine art of handling and moving furniture. They aren't regulated and, therefore, generally not insured. If they break or lose part of your shipment, you're out of luck.

That's right. These two-guys-and-a-truck moving outfits may sound enticing enough when they quote you a price that undercuts professional movers, but bear in mind that I've received hundreds of letters from viewers who have seen their $700 refrigerators, "priceless" antiques, and $600 television consoles fall out of the backs of pickup trucks or get gouged because they were improperly packed. These people ask me how they can fight back, and all I can tell them is that legally they, like their battered furniture, don't have a leg to stand on.

Assuming you are going to use a professional, licensed moving company, here is a checklist of important points to consider:

- Check out the moving company before you entrust it with your possessions. Ask for references and talk to people who have hired the company in the past. If something went wrong, were they friendly and cooperative in rectifying the problem? Or do they have a reputation for committing consumer atrocities? Contact your State Public Utilities Commission if you're moving intra-

state, or the Interstate Commerce Commission if you're moving
to another state, and check up on the company.

• Every interstate moving company must, by ICC law, give you
a copy of its Performance Record on request. This is like a "report
card" regarding the mover's past performance record. It documents, for instance, how often the company has been late in picking up or delivering loads for other customers. It shows what
percentage of its customers complained about over- or underesti-
mates (more on that later) and what percentage reported losses
greater than $50. It's worth your time to investigate your mover.
If that moving van doesn't show up on the day you're scheduled
to have your furniture delivered to your new home, you'll have to
house your family in a hotel or motel and feed them in a restaurant. Later, you'll have to try to get reimbursed for these "living
expenses." By studying prior performance records, you may be
able to profit by other folks' mistakes.

• Anyone considering an out-of-state move should ask the moving company or the Interstate Commerce Commission for the
booklet, "Summary of Information for Shippers of Household
Goods." It's full of practical advice and helpful hints. Read it and
reread it; it could save you cash and aggravation.

• Get an estimate of what it's going to cost you to move. Remember, on local moves you're charged by the hour. On long
distance or interstate moves, usually anything over 50 miles, your
possessions are weighed and you pay by the pound. Naturally the
moving company can't give you a precise estimate because your
furnishings haven't been weighed at the time the estimate is
given. Besides, you may buy some of the "extras" that will pump
up your final bill. But you're entitled to a reasonable estimate,
which means the mover should come to your home and eyeball
precisely what is going to be moved. Don't settle for a telephone
quote.

• On out-of-state-moves, check to see if the moving company
will honor credit cards instead of having to pay cash at the end of
the line. The Interstate Commerce Commission says that effective
January 1, 1979, movers can accept credit cards to pay for shipment if the moving company offers such terms. This can give you

the customer new leverage in solving complaints with movers. The reason is that now the customer can withhold payment to the credit card company after making a "good faith" effort to settle a dispute. Movers can now also offer discounts if a customer decides to pay cash. So, when shopping for a mover, it is important to ask them how they expect to be paid.

• Make an inventory of everything you ship, and I mean everything. Be exact. List defects or scratches visible on your belongings before they're shipped so you don't have a needless dispute at the other end over what was damaged in transit. Now I realize it's a chore to compile this inventory, but it's an important self-defense strategy.

All of these suggestions take time, but you've got to make the investment even though your life couldn't be more hectic at the time. Most people who move have a thousand things on their minds—a new home or apartment, a new job, new schools and how the youngsters are going to survive the trauma of never seeing their friends and neighbors again. Hey, uprooting your life is an emotional experience and it triggers a lot of anxieties, not least of which is wondering if you're making the right move. As a result, the physical move of your entire household is often chaotic and confusing when it should be conducted with the precision of a well-rehearsed military maneuver.

Before the Van Arrives

Moving companies offer professional packing services for which they charge, increasing the cost by about 10 to 20 percent. The moving companies claim it's a smart investment. But, again, that depends on the mover. Some movers may try to rip you off with "balloon packing"—not filling the packing cartons to capacity. Since you're usually charged by the number of cartons packed, the more cartons, the fatter the bill. Watch out!

On the other hand, if you do your own packing and something arrives broken, you'll probably holler when they deny the claim. The reason? The "PBO" (packed by owner) cartons or crates have to show *external* damage before the claim will be accepted. The moving company has to be convinced its movers dropped, or crushed, the box before they'll accept the liability. Otherwise, you'll be told you didn't pack it correctly and your carton or box didn't withstand "normal handling." But if the movers pack it, they're responsible for what's inside the carton unless you failed to specify it needed special handling or packing.

If you do buy the packing service, don't forget that you're entitled to having the cartons unpacked on arrival, but you pay extra for this service, too. What's more, the moving company must take all empty packing cartons with them unless you want to keep them. Most people, though, don't want 50 to 100 packing cartons strewn around their new home. Some movers will buy back certain sized cartons, so ask about it.

Study That Bill of Lading

When your movers pull up on the big day, they should hand you a bill of lading and a contract spelling out all the particulars—pick up and delivery date, destination address, how many helpers will be on the truck plus the "tare weight." That's how much the van weighs before your furniture and personal possessions are loaded on board. The tare weight is a crucial figure and if it isn't spelled out clearly, question the company representative.

Here is where you also protect your possessions. Contrary to popular belief, you're not "insuring" them (the moving company can't sell you an insurance policy). You're protecting your shipment under the Carrier's Liability on interstate moves. Under ICC law you are covered for a minimum of 60 cents per pound per article. Scant protection, but it's free. However, you have to write in that figure on the bill of lading before the truck pulls out. Even then, if a three pound glass lamp cracks on a cross country move, you get a grand total of $1.80 to replace it.

Extra protection is available. If you don't specify anything on the bill of lading, your shipment is protected at the maximum rate of $1.25 per pound. In other words a thousand pound shipment is protected for $1250 against damage or loss. Or you can write in a lump sum value on the bill of lading, say $20,000. But the extra protection costs extra—50 cents for every $100 of declared or weighed value. If you declare $20,000, for example, you're going to pay $100 to protect it.

Again, have your inventory list handy because the movers are going to make out their own inventory and they'll want you to sign it. Don't be surprised if the movers are overly critical of the conditions of your belongings. They're trying to protect themselves. But if they list the scratch on your coffee table as a gouge, look out. The movers are looking for an out if the table gets scratched in transit. If you disagree with the way they describe the condition of any item on the inventory list, you have the right to make a notation to that effect on the master list before you sign.

What It Weighs Is What You'll Pay

The "bump" was once a popular dance, but in the moving industry it's a way you can be ripped off. "Bumping" means increasing the weight of your load (and your cost) by puttings things on the scale that don't belong to you. Because you pay for the net weight of your shipment, any weight bump can cost you money.

No one knows how often illegal weight bumping occurs. A member of the California Public Utilities Commission Compliance and Enforcement Branch once said that "weights are messed with 95 percent of the time." Spokespersons for national moving companies claim it rarely happens, and since it's a felony they will prosecute any of their agents, drivers or affiliates who engage in it.

You can, however, protect yourself against bumping. Under the law you have the right to find out where the van is weighed before and after it is loaded. Be there and check the scale with your own eyes. And ask questions! Ask whether the van's gas tanks are filled or not. Some movers cheat customers by loading the truck's main gas tanks and saddle tanks to the brim right before the weigh-in. Fuel weighs six or seven pounds a gallon and you could be paying for up to 1000 pounds of gas.

Make sure no one is standing on the scale when the truck is weighed; it happens. Some ICC investigators say concrete blocks, even live horses, have been used to tip the scale in favor of the moving company. However, in all fairness, most moving companies don't use "the bump." Contract drivers, who are paid a commission on the revenues generated often mastermind the weight bump, frequently in cooperation with a weighmaster. And one final point: only the driver can be in the cab when the van is weighed.

But you can fight the bump. First, of course, you should be present at both weigh-ins—before and after the truck is loaded. Inspect the van closely. Second, if you think you're being fleeced, demand a re-weigh and, under federal law, you'll get it. But unless the net weight after reweighing is at least 20 pounds lower than the net weight you were charged for, or at least 25 percent over the estimated net weight, you will have to pay for the reweighing.

Filing the Claim

Moving is not a flawless science, so don't expect it to be perfectly smooth. Trucks do break down. Bad weather does cause delays. Movers are human beings. That's why you should inspect every item when it arrives and keep careful records. If you have any problems, don't hesitate to file a claim.

For instance, if the delivery van is late with your belongings and you have to check into a motel for several days, you can file an "inconvenience claim" for food and lodging. Some people rent a bed and sleep in their new home until their furniture arrives; therefore you can claim the bed rental cost. But if you do have a claim, file it promptly.

The law says you have nine months after delivery to file a loss claim against a moving company. But why drag it out? The moving company has 30 days to respond to your claim. It can either send you a check, deny the claim or make a compromise offer within 120 days. But it must take some action. If it can't settle during that four-month period, it must so inform you within 30 days.

Getting a claim paid can be an exasperating experience. It usually takes about two months. And don't expect full value on anything you lose. Moving companies don't see why they should reimburse you for the cost of a new sofa if the one they damaged was 15 years old. There's some sound logic there. So, unless you can prove an item is brand new, expect it to be depreciated.

Disputes arise when moving companies depreciate items that hold, or even gain, their value, regardless of how old they are. A friend of mine lost half his possessions when his moving van overturned in New York, split open, and was looted by passersby. When he came out of shock and filed his claim, he felt cheated, especially on seven fine hand-woven English sweaters. Granted, they were eight years old, but he felt they shouldn't be appraised as if they were worn out hand-me-downs. He was burned when the moving company only paid him $7 for his $70 sweaters.

If you're shipping genuine antiques, it pays to have them appraised before you move. If there is a claim later, you'll have proof of value. Also, make certain that the antique is specifically listed on the bill of lading along with any other items of special value.

Here's a warning: It is better not to ship items (such as furs, valuable documents, money, jewelry, watches, family heirlooms or other things of extraordinary value) if you can carry them with you.

I've found there are moving companies that will not cover some of these items under any circumstances. Therefore, if your mover says it can be covered, make sure you have it in writing.

When Your Mover Won't Budge, Get Moving

Moving companies can be stubborn and sullen over a complaint, especially if you're dealing with a local affiliate and not a company-owned rig and driving team. If you can't thrash out your problem with the crew that actually moved you, write a detailed, thoughtfully reasoned letter to the president of the moving or van line and mail it to the address where the company's headquarters are located.

No response? No satisfaction? Now it's time for *you* to act. Many giant national moving companies have toll-free WATS lines so you can file a complaint or check on the whereabouts of your prized possessions on your out-of-state move. Among the more consumer-minded moving companies that will let you call free of charge are: Aero Mayflower Transit Co. (800) 428-1200; Allied Van Lines (800) 854-3398; North American Van Lines (800) 348-2111; United Van Lines (800) 325-3870. Check toll free directory assistance—(800) 555-1212—for other moving company WATS lines.

Next, contact the watchdogs. If you're moving from city to city within a state, the State Public Utilities Commission has jurisdiction over the moving company you've hired. It probably issued its operating license, too, and thus has the power to revoke it. Call the PUC first, then follow up with a formal complaint, listing your grievances in great detail and spelling out the remedies you're seeking. Most PUC's move quickly on moving complaints and the quick-buck scamster usually knuckles under. While the PUC in California has no statutory authority to force a settlement, it follows up on every written complaint, contacting the mover and the customer. That pressure is usually all it takes to solve a sticky squabble.

Once your furnishings and belongings cross the state line, the complaint becomes a federal matter and the Interstate Commerce Commission steps in on your behalf. Fortunately for you, the ICC is one of the more responsive and helpful federal agencies. It has regional offices in San Francisco, Fort Worth, Chicago, Atlanta, Philadelphia and Boston, all of which handle complaints. Or you can complain by writing to the ICC's Washington headquarters, 12th and Constitution Avenue, NW, Washington, DC 20243. Or call, toll free, (800) 424-9312. Believe me, when the ICC calls an interstate mover, the mover listens. The agency sets interstate moving rates and has an indirect power to penalize; it can cancel the mover's operating permit and that would put him out of business.

You can also avoid all this bureaucracy by going straight to the moving industry's trade association, the American Movers Conference. This group has always been more sensitive than most to the consumer's plight, but now it's organizing a formal complaint handling procedure. The AMC, part of the American Truckers Association, recently passed a resolution to have a Consumer Appeals Program in place and ready to go by June 1, 1979. An AMC spokesman told me the group will handle all disputes between customers and moving companies which can't be settled to the customer's satisfaction. A member of the trade group will contact, by phone, the president of the moving company, or the person in charge, the day your letter is received. A toll-free WATS line is also slated to be installed, according to the spokesman, and it should be listed with toll-free directory assistance by the time this book is published.

In addition, the American Movers Conference is considering a three-person arbitration panel consisting of a moving industry representative, a public citizen and an impartial attorney who will act as the judge. As envisioned, the panel will hear those disputes that cannot be resolved by the AMC's Consumer Appeals program. As of this writing, the group plans to charge the consumer and the mover $20 apiece to cover arbitration expenses and weed out any crank claims. Still, formation of the actual panel itself has not been finalized. In the meantime, write to the Director of Consumer Appeals, American Movers Conference, 1117 Nineteenth St., Arlington, VA 22209 or telephone (703) 524-5440. Most states also have moving and storage associations, but few are equipped to handle consumer complaints. But if you're in a squeeze, give them a try. The California Moving and Storage Association, for instance, has its own WATS line—(800) 662-9852.

Another smart move is to check with your moving company's insurance carrier. Your mover might be stonewalling on your claim just to protect his insurance rates (a rash of negligence claims can send his insurance premiums rocketing). With a little detective work, you can break the bottleneck. First, check with your state PUC and find out the name of your mover's insurance company. Second, contact the insurance carrier direct (write to the president), and let him know you think you're getting the shaft. Your beef might instantly trigger a check. Moving companies don't like this end run, but it's legal.

These are the most effective ways to solve hassles with your mover. But there are plenty of other options. Tipping off Action Line reporters and consumer organizations, filing a lawsuit in Small Claims Court or relating an exceptionally frustrating moving tale to a sympathetic newspaper reporter are other avenues for redress. Don't be afraid to try them. The majority of moving companies are ethical enterprises, but for some reason this industry has more than its share of scoundrels. The only way to get rid of them is to put on the pressure.

FIGHT BACK!

Fight Back! With CLOUT! 13

The battle lines are drawn, folks, and the time has come for you to make a decision. Will you be a consumer who takes command? Or will you be a consumer who takes it—without a whimper, without a protest? The choice is yours and it's that simple.

In life, the difference between a powerful person and a push-over can be summed up in a single word: *awareness.* Awareness is more important than education, more important than money, more important than social status. If you're *aware* of problems, you can avoid them. If you're *aware* of opportunities, you can seize them. That's power. And if you are aware that someone in the marketplace is trying to give you less than your money's worth, or manipulate you or cheat you, you've got the upperhand. You can ignore the spiel and protect your cash. Or you can go ahead and spend but make every one of your dollars count.

Today, you can't afford not to be aware! Inflation is pushing prices up and up and sucking the buying power out of our pay-checks. We're literally busting our butts to make more money because it takes more money to live. And if we let ourselves be seduced into spending wastefully and not getting full value, we're just kidding ourselves every time we think we're getting ahead.

Hold On to Your Bucks

At the same time companies are desperately searching for new ways to get us to spend. Profit-motivated corporate executives are spurring on vast teams of psychologists, advertising experts, and design engineers to come up with new products or services. That's fine as long as there's a real value and a benefit to the buyer. To me, this is progress in its purest form. But when they start selling us shortcuts that only shortchange us, we owe it to ourselves to let them know we're not going to be conned. And how do we do that? It's easy: Don't buy.

Just consider some of these newest ploys. Supermarkets are toying with the idea of piping delicious aromas into the store to get shoppers hungry while they are roaming. Some food chains are already programming subtle commercial messages into their soothing background music to point people toward high-profit impulse items they might otherwise overlook. Some sales strategies are more blatant. Mail-order companies are now sending a "certificate of authenticity" to anyone who buys that $9.95 "ancient medallion that possesses mysterious good luck powers that could change your life." To seal the sale in your mind, they tell you to store the certificate with your will, insurance policies, stock certificates, and "other valuables" in a safe deposit box at your bank. What bunk!

Just to show you how far some companies will go to get into your wallet, one toy manufacturer recently introduced a doll that breaks out into a diaper rash. Children are instructed to "feed" the doll some orange-colored water and, presto, its bottom turns pink. Naturally, you can buy some replacement disposable diapers—but at $3.15, they cost more than a box of disposable diapers for a real baby.

New products that are long on hype and short on value and those other subliminal merchandising swindles really don't get us mad enough to make a commitment. I lump them into the nuisance category. What burns me up and should get you boiling are the outright rip-offs that are foisted on us, often without our knowledge. For instance, shortcounts and shortweights are becoming commonplace in the all-out push for fatter profits. And even some professional people are succumbing to that scam.

I already told you about the pharmacists who put only 90 to 98 tablets in every prescription for 100 Valiums, tranquilizers, or sleeping pills they fill. A Los Angeles meatpacker was busted for packing bacon by the pound that weighed only 14 ounces. Now these separate mini-swindles may sound insignificant, but just imagine how the shorted pills and ounces can multiply into extra profits. Of course, shortcounts and shortweights could be a legitimate mistake, and I'm not suggesting you count or weigh everything every time you buy. But spotcheck your purchases, and if you find a pattern report the shortages to the appropriate agency —from the Bureau of Weights and Measures to the state pharmacist licensing board.

Record manufacturers and record stores sometimes conspire to rip us off. Record industry insiders admit that as many as 50 percent of the record albums pressed from the master cut are bad reproductions, are warped, or are technically defective. But they're shipped to record stores anyway. Customers often blame the poor sound on their record player if they notice it at all. Those who take back the record get a new one or their money back but the bum record isn't always returned to the manufacturer for credit. Why? Because the record labels will only give return credit on 10 percent of the albums they ship to a store in a given year. What happens to the other 90 percent? You better believe the retailer doesn't eat them. The retailer simply recycles the defective record until he finds a consumer who is either too timid, or who ignores or doesn't hear the obvious defects. The record stores re-shrinkwrap the returned album and put it back on the shelf—so look out.

To save the next consumer from getting cheated, ask the store clerk to write the word *defective* on the record label and the record jacket when you return an album. That way, they can't rewrap it as if it were brand new. But don't you try and rip off the record store. Retailers complain that some customers buy an album, take it home and record it onto a cassette tape, then bring the record back, claiming it was defective, and exchange it for an entirely different recording. Using the record store's refund or exchange policy to build your personal tape library is petty thievery.

It's a great temptation to fill up this chapter with a litany of larcenies just to convince you how easy it is for someone to get control of your cash if you don't care. In my office at NBC in Los Angeles, I have two rooms of file cabinets and a storage basement filled with boxes jammed with enough complaints to fill a 20-volume encyclopedia of consumer injustices. I call it my "Consumer Horror File." They make fascinating reading, all right, and if all of you could sit down and spend a few hours perusing them they'd fire you up. Since you can't, that's the purpose of this book —to show you that you have the power to protect yourself and to get you to use that power every day, every time you're parting with your cash or using your credit. I just don't want you to end up as another folder in my consumer horror files.

You Can Help Change the System

I would much rather give you the Horowitz "Stick It To 'Em Award" for scoring a major consumer victory. A 24-year-old Van Nuys, California, man should be your inspiration because he pulled off what many consider the impossible—he convinced a Los Angeles Superior Court that his 1973 Chevrolet Vega was indeed a "lemon." It was a five-year battle, but he persevered. The saga began when the flywheel shattered the day after he bought his new car. Five weeks later, the Vega needed a new transmission. A few weeks after that, the car was using a quart of oil every 50 miles, and mechanics said the valves had to be replaced. The court finally ordered General Motors to pay him the car's original base sticker price of $3050.

A Pennsylvania woman, bugged by a bad Beetle, fought back for two-and-a-half years and also won a full purchase price refund. Driving her new 1975 Volkswagen home from the showroom, she pushed the horn button and the windshield wipers went on. She switched on the radio and got nothing but static, and she pulled into her driveway just when the engine's power petered out. The dealer fixed those flaws but others surfaced. At 2100 miles the car rattled when in reverse. At 3800 miles, the car rattled when in drive. At 5100 miles, the accelerator stuck, and at 5400 miles the battery went dead. Before the Volkswagen had logged 10,000 miles, the horn wouldn't stop blaring, the engine had sprung an oil leak, all the fuses blew, and the driver's side window stuck and couldn't be moved. Plus, the transmission jumped out of gear. At 11,000 miles, the woman called an attorney and bought a Ford!

That kind of bulldog tenacity paid off in more than just dollars. The victories of these people are landmark triumphs in the battle to change the system. For decades we've been intimidated into believing that everything can be fixed and that once the sale has been made the consumer has to settle for repairs. But now, instead of "Buyer Beware," these court decisions show that we may finally be entering an era that I call "Manufacturer Beware." And it's about time.

Are You Equipped?

In Chapters 7 and 8, I advised you to carry a pocket calculator. A calculator is crucial when you go marketing at the supermarket if you want to doublecheck complex bills and invoices, or compute discounts and unit costs. It is also immensely useful when you examine a restaurant check.

A tape recorder is invaluable if you are about to make a major purchase—just to get the facts straight on the transaction and to make sure there are no misunderstandings later on. Think about it for a minute. Here's an example:

A contractor gives you a written estimate of what it will cost you to enlarge a bedroom. As a rule only costs are spelled out. What would happen if one of the laborers accidentally punched a hole in the wrong wall, broke your antique vase or, halfway into the project, hit a zoning snag because of a code violation? Who would be liable? A tape recording of precisely what was agreed upon and will be done, and who would be responsible if something goes wrong, might save you a lot of grief later on.

Tape recording a transaction does more than get the facts straight. It puts the salesperson on notice that you're no one to fool with. You've got a verbatim record of every statement made and even the smoothest sales type will think twice before trying to pull a fast one on you. Plus, an outright rip-off artist would never want to tangle with you; he knows he's giving you taped evidence in his own words that could be used to prosecute him.

I've found a tape recorder is especially effective with commissioned salespeople who are tempted to exaggerate a bit to close a deal. But it's also smart to tape transactions with private parties. I almost bought a rolltop desk not long ago from a glib lawyer. He told me he found six genuine antique rolltops in the basement of a hospital. The desk he wanted to sell me looked okay, but when I asked him to recount the discovery on tape and write it out on the bill of sale, he clammed up. He knew that misrepresentation of something you're trying to sell, even as a private party, is against the law.

I'm not hawking tape recorders. But an inexpensive one is a wise investment. You might just scare off a potential scamster or two when you flip the switch to get all the facts. They know a voluntary tape recording makes life a lot easier for a prosecuting attorney or an attorney general and is admissible in court. However, the legitimate merchant or honest person will have no qualms about putting promises on record.

Fighting back doesn't have to be a long and lonely battle. Stop and think for a minute how much more effective you would be if you teamed up with another aware and informed person who is also willing to fight back when ripped off. Imagine what would happen, for instance, if two financially qualified women, denied an automobile loan by the same loan officer, wrote the bank president and told their stories. If he didn't budge, suppose they then both complained to the state banking commission, Federal Trade Commission, and local consumer groups, and then asked a newspaper reporter or action-line editor to investigate the possibility of discrimination at the local bank.

One person complaining doesn't always make a dent. But two

people with the same beef will get twice as much attention if they complain in an organized, unemotional way. And if you can find four women who have all been turned down for a personal loan, all the better. You have good cause to believe the loan officer or the lending committee could be in violation of the Equal Credit Opportunity Act.

Strength in numbers is more than a catchphrase. It's the backbone of every solid, successful movement. And the consumer movement is a prime example of how much strength numbers can give you. Remember those Oregon senior citizens in Chapter 10 who were fed up with the high cost of false teeth? People in their 70's and 80's mobilized their muscle and pushed through a new law allowing dispensing denturists to make and sell false teeth at one-fourth the price of dentures designed by a dentist. Of course, the American Dental Association howled that "amateurs" were putting the bite on their profession, but if consumers are satisfied and unaffordable prices are going to be reduced to a reasonable level, then I'm all for it.

And don't forget that consumer-minded coalition of Roman Catholic and Protestant church leaders in East Los Angeles who pressured insurance companies to lower their auto insurance rates. As a result of their fierce determination and refusal to give up, all 400 auto insurance companies in California were ordered to analyze and justify their rate-setting techniques or change them.

You too can make an impact. There are plenty of consumer organizations that are looking for concerned, committed people who aren't afraid to raise hell when they see people getting fleeced. In the back of the book, you'll find the most comprehensive directory of consumer organizations anywhere. Call them, write them, or join them. Or start your own.

CLOUT—How to Form It, How to Use It

CLOUT means power—the kind of energy that is so impressive and awesome that it changes the way we think. CLOUT means the other person is going to listen to you because if he or she doesn't it will spell trouble. CLOUT means organization—banding to-gether with other people who feel the same way you do about being ripped off, even if you're just a few people. CLOUT gets results. It worked for the handful of homemakers who launched a meat boycott a few years ago when meat prices took off like a shot. The housewives raised such a ruckus in Los Angeles that the boycott caught on, spread nationwide, and eventually meat prices came down. Sugar and coffee boycotts have worked in the past, and growers stuck with surplus inventories have cut prices every time.

What I propose is a new kind of CLOUT—an organization you can set up with your friends or concerned neighbors no matter where you live. The kind of CLOUT I am talking about will get the price-gouging gas station to back off, get the rip-off restaurant to treat you fairly, or get the dirty movie theater to clean up its act.

And it will be called CLOUT—"Consumers Looking Out and United Together." Nothing more accurately sums up the essence of fighting back so you don't get ripped off. CLOUT is an informal organization made up of people who will not be pushed around any longer. I visualize CLOUT members wearing buttons saying "I belong to CLOUT, don't rip me off." That will let the world know who you are and who and what you're after.

CLOUT will work because there is no one consumer organiza-tion in this country that represents the concerns of most of us—people who are tired of being intimidated, embarrassed, and nailed to the cash register. What's more, your CLOUT chapter doesn't have to be a separate organization. It can be the part of your neighborhood association that keeps an eye on local mer-chants and politicians. It can be a committee of your union local or employee association, part of your executive club, political ac-tion group, or any service club to which you may belong.

But it has to be responsible, not an angry group of vigilantes trying to lynch the grocer for selling ungraded meat as USDA Choice. If your CLOUT chapter discovered that kind of rip-off, you would visit with the owner of the market first and inform him that you are aware of the deception. Then you would ask him politely to clean up his act and perhaps refund the price difference between the choice and the ungraded meat to all of his customers in the community who were bilked. If he denies cheating anyone and raises a stink, quietly take the evidence to the local district attorney or to the state attorney general's office or the health department and let them investigate. Meanwhile, CLOUT members should tell everyone in the neighborhood to stop patronizing the store until the practice stops. You and other CLOUT members might even picket the store on its busiest day. That will get him where he lives—right in the till.

This same type of unabashed consumer power can work in any situation, but make pretty darn sure that you have adequate evidence that a deception is occurring. Get statements in writing from buyers who were bagged, samples of the product, copies of the law that was violated, any receipts or communiques. Make tape recordings of all related conversations and keep a careful record of all details as though you were taking the case to a hearing or trial.

CLOUT can tackle more than just community rip-offs. Teaming up with other chapters or joining hands with other consumer organizations, CLOUT can shoot a laser beam of public outrage straight at any official or corporation who subtly or flagrantly ignores the best interest of the people who keep them in business or keep them in office.

But you've got to get involved, either as a solo practitioner of consumer power or as part of a group.

At the start of this book, I know you were probably asking yourself where you were going to get the time, energy, and personal resolve it takes to be an effective consumer who battles back with the mind, not just with the mouth. And some of you are probably asking that same question right now. But let me first ask you: How much is your dignity and self-esteem worth? And how hard do you have to work for your money?

You answer those questions honestly and I know you will join me and millions of other aware and informed Americans who are totally committed and always willing to fight back and not get ripped off.

FIGHT BACK!

Appendix
How to Write
a Complaint Letter
That Gets Results

A

Writing an effective complaint letter is an art that's easy to master. You don't have to be either a Hemingway or a Nader to put your point across. Here are ten ways to make sure your complaint letter packs a wallop.

1. *Be Firm and Businesslike*—A complaint letter cannot be angry and accusatory. Never use vulgar language or use 4-letter words. Don't use libelous words like "crook" or "thief" either. Start screaming on paper and those poison pen missives will wind up in the round file. You'll get an answer—smart companies answer every letter they get—but it will probably be a form reply signed by a customer service person who often hides behind a phony name.

2. *Send It to Someone with Power*—Investigate and get the name of the person who has the authority to do something about your problem. Make sure you have his or her name spelled right, the proper title, and an accurate address. Marking a complaint letter "personal and confidential" doesn't speed it and might slow it down.

3. *Get to the Point*—Summarize the problem quickly. Explain chronologically (and include dates) what happened and what you tried to do at the local level to get the problem resolved. This shouldn't take more than two or three paragraphs. Don't ramble or tell your life story. Keep a photocopy of your letter.

4. *Make a Demand*—Tell the person what you feel the company should

do for you, what it would take to satisfy you or to solve your problem. Don't be vague or expect the store or manufacturer to suggest a remedy. You've got to spell out what you want.

5. *Show Them Your Proof*—Send photocopies of cancelled checks, repair orders, purchase receipts, advertisements (if appropriate), correspondence, or any other documentation to support your case. NEVER send the originals. If you lose your evidence, you're out of luck. Also use the information you have compiled on your Fight-Back Fact Form. You will find a copy of the form on page 249 in the appendix.

6. *Set a Time Limit*—Don't give them the impression they can act on your complaint letter at their leisure. You'll get stuck on the bottom of the file or at the end of the computer run. Give the company a time limit for resolving your problem. At least two weeks is fair. However, if it's an emergency, call first to complain, and then follow up with a letter.

7. *Cite a Statute*—Depending on the nature of your complaint, you might be able to cite a law or regulation that they broke, although this is not crucial. For example, if you haven't received merchandise ordered by mail within a month, you should point out in your letter that "according to postal regulations, unless I receive the merchandise within 30 days or a request from you for an extension to fulfill the order, I am under no obligation to accept the merchandise."

8. *Don't Carbon the World*—If a company sees that you are screaming foul to a dozen consumer agencies or government agencies, the company will be instantly turned off. You didn't give it a chance to answer your letter proving that it is a responsible corporate citizen. Meanwhile, a consumer group which might have acted on your complaint may have second thoughts; it sees that you carboned the world and figures another group might act on it so why duplicate the effort? You can try more than one agency, but do it one at a time.

9. *Send It by Certified Mail*—When writing to a company invest the extra postage and request a return receipt, which assures you the letter got into the proper hands. Certified mail shows that you mean business, but it usually isn't necessary when writing to a consumer agency.

10. *Make the Second Letter an Action Letter*—If you don't get a response to your letter or if you get a polite, weasel-worded "bug-off" reply, send an action letter. Let them know you aren't giving up, that you are pursuing the problem with a law enforcement or regulatory agency or a consumer action group. Don't make it an idle threat either; on the other hand, never spray your letter with the names of a dozen different watchdogs. You will only look like you are groping for help when you should be gearing up for a fight.

Appendix
Fight Back
Fact Form

B

This is a sample form that you should have for each and every major item you own. You should set up a separate file folder for cars, appliances, boats, heating and air conditioning systems, cameras, office equipment, power tools and what have you. In it you should also keep the warranty, service slips, receipts, and anything pertaining to the product. Then if a problem pops up you are armed with the facts. A word of caution: Never let the original paperwork out of your possession. Always send or take photocopies with you when you need to Fight Back.

ITEM:		
DEALER: (Address, phone number, salesperson)		SERIAL NUMBER:
DATE PURCHASED:		MODEL NUMBER:
WARRANTY FACTS: (Full, Limited, Implied, Length of Warranty Service, Name of Warranty Service, Phone and address, if other than dealer).		

SERVICE RECORDS				
DATE	WORK DONE	COMPANY AND SERVICE PERSON	COST	WARRANTY
	(Describe parts replaced, etc.)			

Appendix
Directory
of Federal
Consumer Offices

C

Your Uncle Sam Is a Fighter! Write Him! Call Him!

Here is the consumer's roadmap to your nation's capital, where to write or call in Washington, DC, to lodge a complaint or get factual information. I've left out specific names to contact because they change so quickly, and asking for specific people would only slow down the wheels of bureaucracy.

This directory can be pure gold for you. Even if you're dueling with a local retailer or the headquarters office of a manufacturer, it wouldn't hurt and would probably help to send a photocopy of your fight-back correspondence to the appropriate federal consumer office listed below. As I've said over and over again throughout the book, if an enforcement office gets enough complaints about the same rip-off, chances are it will open a file and launch its own investigation.

But don't cry wolf. Tell it to the feds only when you've got a legitimate complaint. Petty gripes will only clog the system and create a bureaucratic logjam for your fellow consumers.

Unfortunately, only a few federal consumer offices have toll-free numbers that you can call. Those that do have an 800 prefix. But quite a few of them have toll-free outgoing lines. So be courteous when you call and ask them to call you back on their WATS line to save you some money. Not all will, but it's worth a try.

ADVERTISING
Director, Bureau of Consumer Protection, Federal Trade Commission, Washington, DC 20580; phone 202-523-3727.

AIR TRAVEL/ROUTES AND SERVICE
Director, Office of Consumer Protection, Civil Aeronautics Board, Washington, DC 20423; phone 202-673-5937.

AIR TRAVEL/SAFETY
For general information contact the Community and Consumer Liaison Division, Federal Aviation Administration, APA-430, Washington, DC 20591; phone 202-426-8058. For specific safety problems contact the above office marking correspondence APA-100; phone 202-426-1960.

ALCOHOL
Chief, Trade and Consumer Affairs Division, Bureau of Alcohol, Tobacco, and Firearms, Department of the Treasury, Washington, DC 20226; phone 202-566-7581.

ALCOHOLISM, DRUG ABUSE AND MENTAL ILLNESS
Office of Public Affairs, Alcohol, Drug Abuse and Mental Health Service, 5600 Fishers Lane, Rockville, MD 20857; phone 301-443-3783.

ANTITRUST
Bureau of Competition, Federal Trade Commission, Washington, DC 20580; phone 202-523-3601.

Consumer Affairs Section, Antitrust Division, Justice Department, Washington, DC 20530; phone 202-739-4173.

AUTO SAFETY AND HIGHWAYS
Director, Office of Public and Consumer Affairs, Transportation Department, Washington, DC 20590; phone 202-426-4518.

National Highway Traffic Safety Administration; toll-free hotline 800-424-9393. In Washington, DC call 426-0123.

Associate Administrator for Planning, Federal Highway Administration, Washington, DC 20590; phone 202-426-0585.

BANKS
Federal Credit Unions

National Credit Union Administration, Washington, DC 20456; phone 202-254-8760.

Federal Reserve Banks

Office of Saver and Consumer Affairs, Federal Reserve System, Washington, DC 20551; phone 202-452-3000.

Federally Insured Savings and Loans

Consumer Division, Office of Community Investment, Federal Home Loan Bank Board, Washington, DC 20552; phone 202-377-6237.

National Banks

Consumer Affairs, Office of the Comptroller of the Currency, Washington, DC 20219; phone 202-447-1600.

State Chartered Banks

Office of Bank Customer Affairs, Federal Deposit Insurance Corporation, Washington, DC 20429; phone 202-389-4427.

BOATING
Chief, Information and Administrative Staff, U.S. Coast Guard, Washington, DC 20590; phone 202-426-1080.

BUS TRAVEL
Consumer Affairs Office, Interstate Commerce Commission, Washington, DC 20423; phone 202-275-7252.

BUSINESS
Office of the Ombudsman, Department of Commerce, Washington, DC 20230; phone 202-377-3176.

Director, Women-in-Business and Consumer Affairs, Small Business Administration, 1441 L Street, NW, Washington, DC 20416; phone 202-653-6074.

CHILD ABUSE
National Center on Child Abuse and Neglect, PO Box 1182, Washington, DC 20013; phone 202-755-0593.

CHILDHOOD IMMUNIZATION
Office of the Assistant Secretary for Health, Office of Public Affairs, Washington, DC 20201; phone 202-472-5663.

CHILDREN AND YOUTH
Director of Public Affairs, Office of Human Development Services, Department of Health, Education, and Welfare, Washington, DC 20201; phone 202-472-7257.

COMMODITY TRADING
Consumer Hotline, Commodity Futures Trading Commission, 2033 K Street, NW, Washington, DC 20581; toll-free hotline in California and states east of the Mississippi, 800-424-9838; states west of the Mississippi except California, 800-227-4428. In Washington, DC call 254-8630.

CONSUMER INFORMATION
For a copy of the free *Consumer Information Catalog*, a listing of more than 200 selected federal consumer publications on such topics as child care, automobiles, health, employment, housing, energy, etc., send a postcard to the Consumer Information Center, Pueblo, CO 81009.

COPYRIGHTS
Copyright Office, Crystal Mall, 1921 Jefferson Davis Highway, Arlington, VA 20559; phone 703-557-8700.

CREDIT
Director, Bureau of Consumer Protection, Federal Trade Commission, Washington, DC 20850; phone 202-523-3727.

CRIME INSURANCE
Federal Crime Insurance, Department of Housing and Urban Development, PO Box 41033, Washington, DC 20014; toll-free hotline 800-638-8780. In Washington, DC call 652-2637.

CUSTOMS
Public Information Division, U.S. Customs, Washington, DC 20229; phone 202-566-8195.

DISCRIMINATION
U.S. Commission on Civil Rights, 1121 Vermont Avenue, Washington, DC 20425; phone 202-254-6697.

Equal Employment Opportunity Commission, 2401 E Street, NW, Washington, DC 20506; phone 202-634-6930.

For complaints about discrimination in lending practices by financial and retail institutions based on race, color, religion, national origin, sex, marital status, age, or receipt of public assistance, contact the Housing and Credit Section, Civil Rights Division, Justice Department, Washington, DC 20530; phone 202-739-4123. (Also see *Housing*)

DRUGS AND COSMETICS
Consumer Inquiry Section, Food and Drug Administration, 5600 Fishers Lane, Rockville, MD 20852; phone 301-443-3170.

EDUCATION GRANTS AND LOANS
Office of Public Affairs, Office of Education, Washington, DC 20202; phone 202-245-7949. Toll-free hotline for Basic Education Opportunity Grants, 800-638-6700. In Maryland, call 800-492-6602.

ELDERLY
Administration on Aging, Washington, DC 20201; phone 202-245-2158.

EMPLOYMENT AND JOB TRAINING
Since nearly all employment and training programs are handled at the state or local levels, check your phone directory under your state government for the Employment Service or under your local government for the mayor's office. If you cannot reach these sources, you can obtain general information by writing to the Employment and Training Administration, Department of Labor, Washington, DC 20213; phone 202-376-6905.

ENERGY
Director, Office of Consumer Affairs, Department of Energy, Washington, DC 20585; phone 202-252-5141.

ENERGY EFFICIENCY
Information Office, National Bureau of Standards, Washington, DC 20234; phone 301-921-3181.

ENVIRONMENT
Office of Public Awareness, Environmental Protection Agency, Washington, DC 20460; phone 202-755-0700.

FEDERAL JOB INFORMATION
Check for the Federal Job Information Center under the U.S. Government in your phone directory. If there is no listing, call toll-free directory assistance at 800-555-1212, and ask for the number of the Federal Job Information Center in your state. In the Washington, DC, metropolitan area contact the Civil Service Commission, 1900 E Street, NW, Washington, DC 20415; phone 202-737-9616.

FEDERAL REGULATIONS
For information on Federal regulations and proposals, the Office of the Federal Register (OFR) is offering, among other services, recorded "Dial-a-Reg" phone messages. Dial-a-Reg gives advance information on significant documents to be published in the *Federal Register* the following workday. The service is currently available in three cities: Washington, DC, telephone 202-523-5022; Chicago, telephone 312-663-0884; and Los Angeles, telephone 212-688-6694.

FIREARMS
(see *Alcohol*)

FISH GRADING
National Marine Fisheries Service, Department of Commerce, Washington, DC 20235; phone 202-634-7458.

FISH AND WILDLIFE
Fish and Wildlife Service, Office of Public Affairs, Washington, DC 20240; phone 202-343-5634.

FLOOD INSURANCE
National Flood Insurance, Department of Housing and Urban Development, Washington DC 20410; toll-free hotline 800-424-8872. In Washington, DC call 755-9096.

FOOD
Assistant Secretary for Food and Consumer Services, U.S. Department of Agriculture, Washington, DC 20250; phone 202-447-4623.

Consumer Inquiry Section, Food and Drug Administration, 5600 Fishers Lane, Rockville, MD 20852; phone 301-443-3170.

FRAUD
Director, Bureau of Consumer Protection, Federal Trade Commission, Washington, DC 20580; phone 202-523-3727.

HANDICAPPED
Director, Division of Public Information, Office of Human Development Services, Department of Health, Education, and Welfare, Washington, DC 20201; phone 202-472-7257.

HOUSING
Department of Housing and Urban Development, Division of Consumer Complaints, Washington, DC 20410; phone 202-755-5353.

For complaints about housing discrimination call the housing discrimination hotline 800-424-8590. In Washington, DC call 755-5490.

IMMIGRATION AND NATURALIZATION
Information Services, Immigration and Naturalization Service, 425 Eye St., NW, Washington, DC 20536; phone 202-376-8449.

INDIAN ARTS AND CRAFTS
Indian Arts and Crafts Board, Washington, DC 20240; phone 202-343-2773.

JOB SAFETY
Office of Information, Occupational Safety and Health Administration, Department of Labor, Washington, DC 20210; phone 202-523-8151.

MAIL
Fraud

Check with your local postal inspector about problems relating to mail fraud and undelivered merchandise, or contact the Chief Postal Inspector, U.S. Postal Inspection Service, Washington, DC 20260; phone 202-245-5445.

Service

Check with your local postmaster or contact the Consumer Advocate, U.S. Postal Service, Room 5920, Washington, DC 20260; phone 202-245-4514.

MAPS
Public Inquiries Office, Geological Survey, National Center, Reston, VA 22092; phone 703-860-6167.

MEDICAID/MEDICARE
Health Care Financing Administration, Department of Health, Education, and Welfare, Washington, DC 20201; phone 202-245-0312.

MEDICAL RESEARCH
Division of Public Information, National Institutes of Health, 9000 Rockville Pike, Bethesda, MD 20014; phone 301-496-5787.

Center for Disease Control, Attention, Public Inquiries, Atlanta, GA 30333; phone 404-653-3311, ext 3534.

MENTAL ILLNESS
(See *Alcoholism, Drug Abuse and Mental Illness*)

METRIC INFORMATION
(See *Energy Efficiency*, National Bureau of Standards)

MOVING
Interstate Commerce Commission; Washington, DC 20423; toll-free moving hotline 800-424-9312. In Florida call 800-432-4537. In Washington, DC call 275-7852.

PARKS AND RECREATION AREAS
National Forests

Forest Service, U.S. Department of Agriculture, Washington, DC 20250; phone 202-447-3760.

National Parks and Historic Sites

National Park Service, Washington, DC 20240; phone 202-343-7394.

Recreation Areas on Army Corps of Engineers Project Sites

Recreation Resource Management Branch (CWO-R), Army Corps of Engineers, Washington, DC 20314; phone 202-693-7177.

Other Recreation Areas

Office of Public Affairs, Department of the Interior, Washington, DC 20240; phone 202-343-3171.

PASSPORTS
For passport information check with your local post office or contact the Passport Office, Department of State, 1425 K Street, NW, Washington, DC 20524; phone 202-783-8200.

PATENTS AND TRADEMARKS
Patents
Commissioner, Patent Office, Department of Commerce, Washington, DC 20231; phone 703-557-3080.

Trademarks
Commissioner, Trademark Office, Department of Commerce, Washington, DC 20231; phone 703-557-3268.

PENSIONS
Office of Communications, Pension Benefit Guaranty Corporation, 2020 K Street, NW, Washington, DC 20006; phone 202-254-4817.

Labor Management Standards Administration, Department of Labor, Washington, DC 20210; phone 202-523-8776.

PHYSICAL FITNESS/SPORTS
President's Council on Physical Fitness and Sports, 400 6th Street, SW, Washington, DC 20201; phone 202-755-8131.

PRODUCT SAFETY
Consumer Product Safety Commission, Consumer Services Branch, Washington, DC 20207; toll-free hotline 800-638-2666. In Maryland call 800-492-2937.

RADIO AND TELEVISION BROADCASTING/INTERFERENCE
Consumer Assistance Office, Federal Communications Commission, Washington, DC 20554; phone 202-632-7000.

RUNAWAY CHILDREN
The National Runaway Hotline; toll-free 800-621-4000. In Illinois call 800-972-6004.

SMOKING
Office on Smoking and Health, 12420 Parklawn Drive, Room 158 Park Building, Rockville, MD 20852; phone 301-443-1575.

SOCIAL SECURITY
Check your local phone directory under U.S. Government. If there is no listing check at your local post office for the schedule of visits by Social Security representatives, or write: Division of Public Inquiries, Social Security Administration, 6401 Security Boulevard, Baltimore, MD 21235; phone 301-594-7705.

SOLAR HEATING
National Solar Heating and Cooling Information Center, PO Box 1607, Rockville, MD 20850; toll-free hotline is 800-523-2929. In Pennsylvania, call 800-462-4983.

STOCKS AND BONDS
Consumer Liaison Office, Securities and Exchange Commission, Washington, DC 20549; phone 202-523-5516.

TAXES
The Internal Revenue Service (IRS) toll-free tax information number is listed in your tax package and is generally listed in your local telephone directory. If you cannot locate the number, call your information operator for the number for your area. If you wish to write, send the letter to your IRS District Director.

Problem Resolution Program (PRP). Offices have been established in each district to solve unique problems and complaints which have not been satisfied through normal channels. Taxpayers may call the toll-free number and ask for the PRP Office.

TRAIN TRAVEL
AMTRAK (National Railroad Passenger Corp.) For consumer problems first try to contact a local AMTRAK consumer relations office listed in your phone directory. If there is not an office near you contact AMTRAK, Office of Consumer Relations, PO Box 2709, Washington, DC 20013; phone 202-383-2121.

TRAVEL INFORMATION
U.S. Travel Service, Department of Commerce, Washington, DC 20230; phone 202-377-4553.

VENEREAL DISEASE
VD toll-free hotline 800-523-1885. In Pennsylvania call 800-462-4966.

VETERANS' INFORMATION
The Veterans Administration has toll-free numbers in all 50 states. Check your local phone directory, or call 800-555-1212 for toll-free directory assistance. For problems that can't be handled through local offices, write Veterans Administration, (271), 810 Vermont Avenue, NW, Washington, DC 20420.

WAGES AND WORKING CONDITIONS
Employment Standards Administration, Department of Labor, Washington, DC 20210; phone 202-523-8743.

WARRANTIES
For a problem involving the failure of a seller to honor a warranty, contact the Division of Special Statutes, Federal Trade Commission, Washington, DC 20580; phone 202-724-1100. Or you may contact the FTC regional office nearest you. They are listed in your telephone directory under U.S. Government.

Source: U.S. Office of Consumer Affairs, 621 Reporters Bldg., Washington, DC 20201, August 1978.

Appendix
Federal Information
Please

D

If you're not sure who to complain to in Washington, the federal government can set you straight. Just dial the Federal Information Center (FIC) nearest you. Staffers will help you find the information you're searching for or direct you to the right agency—federal or even state and local. And it doesn't cost you a dime, not even the phone call. Each city below has an FIC or a tieline, a toll-free local number (printed in italics) connected to an FIC elsewhere. Got a question? Get an answer.

ALABAMA
Birmingham 205-322-8591
Mobile 205-438-1421

ARIZONA
Phoenix 602-261-3313
Tucson 602-622-1511

ARKANSAS
Little Rock 501-378-6177

CALIFORNIA
Los Angeles 213-688-3800
Sacramento 916-440-3344
San Diego 714-293-6030

San Francisco
415-556-6600

San Jose 408-275-7422
Santa Ana 714-836-2386

COLORADO
*Colorado
  Springs 303-471-9491*
Denver 303-837-3602
Pueblo 303-544-9523

CONNECTICUT
Hartford 203-527-2617
New Haven 203-624-4720

DISTRICT OF COLUMBIA
Washington 202-755-8660

FLORIDA
*Fort Lauder-
  dale 305-522-8531*
Jacksonville 904-354-4756
Miami 305-350-4155
Orlando 305-422-1800
St. Peters-
  burg 813-893-3495
Tampa 813-229-7911
*West Palm
  Beach 305-833-7566*

GEORGIA
Atlanta 404-221-6891

HAWAII
Honolulu   808-546-8620

ILLINOIS
Chicago   312-353-4242

INDIANA
Gary/
*   Hammond   219-883-4110*
Indianapolis   317-269-7373

IOWA
Des Moines   515-284-4448

KANSAS
Topeka   913-295-2866
Wichita   316-263-6931

KENTUCKY
Louisville   502-582-6261

LOUISIANA
New Orleans   504-589-6696

MARYLAND
Baltimore   301-962-4980

MASSACHUSETTS
Boston   617-223-7121

MICHIGAN
Detroit   313-226-7016
Grand
*   Rapids   616-451-2628*

MINNESOTA
Minneapolis   612-725-2073

MISSOURI
Kansas City   816-374-2466
St. Joseph   816-233-8206
St. Louis   314-425-4106

NEBRASKA
Omaha   402-221-3353

NEW JERSEY
Newark   201-645-3600
Paterson/
*   Passaic   201-523-0717*
Trenton   609-396-4400

NEW MEXICO
Albuquerque   505-766-3091
Santa Fe   505-983-7743

NEW YORK
Albany   518-463-4421
Buffalo   716-846-4010
New York   212-264-4464
Rochester   716-546-5075
Syracuse   315-476-8545

NORTH CAROLINA
Charlotte   704-376-3600

OHIO
Akron   216-375-5638
Cincinnati   513-684-2801
Cleveland   216-522-4040
Columbus   614-221-1014
Dayton   513-223-7377
Toledo   419-241-3223

OKLAHOMA
Oklahoma
   City   405-231-4868
Tulsa   918-584-4193

OREGON
Portland   503-221-2222

PENNSYLVANIA
Allentown/
*   Bethlehem   215-821-7785*
Philadelphia   215-597-7042
Pittsburgh   412-644-3456
Scranton   717-346-7081

RHODE ISLAND
Providence   401-331-5565

TENNESSEE
Chattanooga   615-265-8231
Memphis   901-521-3285
Nashville   615-242-5056

TEXAS
Austin   512-472-5494
Dallas   214-749-2131
Fort Worth   817-334-3624
Houston   713-226-5711
San Antonio   512-224-4471

UTAH
Ogden   801-399-1347
Salt Lake
   City   801-524-5353

VIRGINIA
Newport
*   News   804-244-0480*
Norfolk   804-441-6723
Richmond   804-643-4928
Roanoke   703-982-8591

WASHINGTON
Seattle   206-442-0570
Tacoma   206-383-5230

WISCONSIN
Milwaukee   414-271-2273

Source: U.S. Office of Consumer Affairs.

Appendix
Action Line
Broadcasters
and Journalists

E

In the relentless battle to hack through red tape, spur foot-dragging companies to action, and get rip-offs remedied, radio and newspaper action lines are powerful allies to the frustrated consumer. Corner merchants and giant corporations hate to have consumer complaints and disputes aired in public. Sometimes it blackens a company's reputation instantly. The threat of bad publicity can be a hot cattle prod and I've wielded it thousands of times on behalf of consumers nationwide. Almost miraculously bureaucratic logjams are broken, letters are answered, and phone calls are returned—often this is enough to rectify the original problem.

This list of action line radio and newspaper reporters was furnished by Corning Glass Works, Corning, New York, which sponsors an annual Consumer Action Line Conference. However, because reporters often shift assignments, check with your newspaper or radio station before complaining to make sure you are directing your beef to the proper person. If you don't find an action reporter listed in the area you live in, call your local radio, TV stations or newspapers to see if they have such a person.

Action Line Broadcasters

ALABAMA

WYDE
Ms. Susan Earle
2112-11th Avenue S.,
Suite 410
Birmingham 35205

ARIZONA

KARK
Ms. Susan Mayes
201 West Third Street
Little Rock 72201

KTAR
Ms. Betsy Buxer
1515 E. Osborn
Phoenix 85014

KTKT
Ms. Hazel Borst
Box 5585
Tucson 85703

CALIFORNIA

KNBC-TV
David Horowitz
3000 W. Alameda Avenue
Burbank 91523

KABC Radio
Nel Benton
4151 Prospect Avenue
Los Angeles 90027

KABC-TV
7 On Your Side
P. O. Box 77
Los Angeles 90027

KFWB
Ms. Bernice Baer
6230 Yucca
Los Angeles 90028

KCRA-TV
Call Three
310 Tenth Street
Sacramento 95814

KCST
Jack Welsh
8330 Engineer Road
San Diego 92111

KGTV
Ms. Dolores Marleau

Box 81047
San Diego 92138

COLORADO

KIZ
Ms. Barbara Hyer
2149 Sout Holly Street
Denver 80222

CONNECTICUT

WELI
Ms. Jeanne Alterman
853 Whitney Avenue
Hamden 06511

WELI
Ms. Patricia Fiege
546 Skiff Street
New Haven 06473

WELI
Ms. Rita Levine
Box 85
New Haven 06501

DISTRICT OF COLUMBIA

WRC-TV
Contact 4
Box 4
Washington 20044

WTOP
Ms. Shirley Rooker
4001 Brandywine Street NW
Washington 20016

FLORIDA

WTLV
Ms. Martha Forbes
Box 1212
Jacksonville 32201

WCIX
Ms. Naomi Chernau
1111 Brickell Avenue
Miami 33131

WDBO
Ms. Mary Kennedy
Box 158
Orlando 32802

GEORGIA

WGST
Ms. Lois Cohen
550 Pharr Road, NE,
Box 11920
Atlanta 30355

ILLINOIS

WIND
Ms. Natalie Allen
625 N. Michigan Avenue
Chicago 60611

WIND
Ms. Barbara Gilbert
625 N. Michigan Avenue
Chicago 60611

WRAU
Ms. Darlene Switzer
500 N. Stewart Street
Creve Coeur 61611

WDZ
Ms. Judy Bear
265 South Park Street
Decatur 62523

KANSAS

KCMO
Ms. Carlyn Hoffman
4500 Johnson Drive
Fairway 66201

MARYLAND

WBAL
Ms. Barbara Halle
3800 Hooper Avenue
Baltimore 21211

MASSACHUSETTS

WBZ
Ms. Pat Lynn
1170 Soldiers Field Road
Boston 02134

WBSM
Ms. Nelda Goggin
PO Box J 4105
New Bedford 02741

MICHIGAN

WJR
Ms. Terry Treiber
Fisher Building
Detroit 48202

MISSOURI

KMOX
Ms. Ellen Conant
One Memorial Drive
St. Louis 63102

NEBRASKA

WOW
Ms. Kay Kathol
11128 John Galt Boulevard
Omaha 68137

NEVADA

Action Reporter
c/o KOLO TV
P.O. Box 10000
Reno 89510
(702) 786-2932

NEW MEXICO

KOB
Ms. Lynn Boyd
Box 1351
Albuquerque 87103

NEW YORK

WROW
Ms. Margaret Blabey
341 Northern Boulevard
Albany 12204

WIVB
Ms. Mary Shields
1612 Gibbard Lane
Alden 14004

WVIG
Ms. Tanny Wells
2077 Elmwood Avenue
Buffalo 14207

WIVB
Ms. Pat Libassi
4990 Pine Ledge Street
Clarence 14031

WGSM
Ms. Bunny Roberts
900 Walt Whitman Road,
Box 740
Long Island 11746

WMCA
Ms. Lucille Merkowitz
888 Seventh Avenue
New York 10019

WNBC-TV
Action 4
Box 4000
Radio City Station
New York 10019

WHEN
Ms. Marian Shaw
620 Old Liverpool Road,
Box 6509
Syracuse 13217

WTLB
Ms. Etta Peabody
Kellogg Road,
Washington Mills
Utica 13479

NORTH CAROLINA

CFA
Ms. Mary L. Smith
115 East Chapel Hill Street
Durham 27701

WRAL
Ms. Jeanette Hicks
Box 12000
Raleigh 27685

OHIO

WAKR
Ms. Eileen Costigan
PO Box 1590
Akron 44309

WERE
Ms. Nora Castle
1500 Chester Avenue
Cleveland 44114

WFMJ
Ms. Ginny Morgan
101 W. Boardman
Youngstown 44503

OKLAHOMA

KWTV
Ms. Margaret Kinser
4421 NW 19
Oklahoma City 73107

KWTV
Ms. Patty Muzny
7401 N. Kelley, Box 14159
Oklahoma City 73114

PENNSYLVANIA

WFIL
Ms. Cynthia Axelrod
4100 City Line Avenue
Philadelphia 19131

KDKA
Ms. Marcy Levin
One Gateway Center
Pittsburgh 15222

RHODE ISLAND

WJAR
Ms. Betty Kingsley
176 Weybosset Street
Providence 02903

TENNESSEE

WDIA
Ms. Carlotta Watson
Box 12045
Memphis 38112

WASHINGTON

KING-TV
Action Reporter
320 Aurora Avenue North
Seattle 98109

WEST VIRGINIA

WWVA
Ms. Ruth Smith
Capital Music Hall
Wheeling 26003

CANADA

CFCF
Ms. Diana Severs
405 Ogilvy Avenue
Montreal, Quebec

CJRN
Ms. Brenda Gibson
Box 710
Niagara Falls

Action Line Journalists

ALABAMA

Post Herald
Ms. Kay Parkhurst
2200 North 4th Avenue
Birmingham 35202

Decatur Daily
Ms. Martha Hill
201 First Ave. SE,
PO Box 1527
Decatur 35601

Tri-City Daily
Ms. Dorla Queen
219 W. Tennessee Street
Florence 35631

Register/Press
Ms. Sherry Nichols
304 Government Street,
PO Box 2488
Mobile 36630

Adv. Alabama Journal
Mr. Robert Hardy
200 Washington Street
Montgomery 36102

Tusc.-Northport News
Mr. Ken Lightsey
2001 6th Street,
PO Drawer 1
Tuscaloosa 35401

ALASKA

Anchorage Times
Action Line
820 Fourth Avenue
Anchorage 99501

Fairbanks News Miner
Ms. Mary Lou Cady
200 N. Cushman
Fairbanks 99701

Ketchikan News
Mr. Lew M. Williams Jr.
501 Dock Street, PO Box 79
Ketchikan 99101

ARIZONA

Courier News
Mr. Larry Binz
PO Box 1108
Blytheville 72316

Douglas Dispatch
Ms. Joyce Smith
530-11th Street
Douglas 85607

Southwest Times Rec.
Ms. Terry Johnson
920 Rogers Avenue
Ft. Smith 72901

Little Rock Gazette
Ms. Julie Baldridge
PO Box 1821
Little Rock 72203

Meza Tribune
Ms. C. L. Witschie
120 W. First Avenue
Meza 85202

Newport Independent
Mr. Mike Masterson
308 Second Street
Newport 72112

Phoenix Gazette
Ms. Bernice F. Jones
120 E. Van Buren Street
Phoenix 85004

Valley News
Mr. Michael Padgett
2210 W. Desert Cove
Phoenix 85029

Commercial
Ms. Eva M. Williamson
300 Beech Street
Pine Bluff 71601

Rogers News
Ms. Terry Johnson
313 S. Second Street
Rogers 72756

Scottsdale Progress
Mr. Bob Snider
7302 E. Earll Drive
Scottsdale 85252

Donrey Media Gram
Ms. Terry Johnson
514 E. Emma Avenue
Springsdale 72764

Tucson Citizen
Mr. Robert McCormick
4850 S. Park Avenue,
PO Box 26887
Tucson 85726

Tucson Star
Mr. John Long
4850 S. Park Avenue,
PO Box 26887
Tucson 85726

ARKANSAS

Little Rock Democrat
Ms. Kathy Flynn
Capitol Avenue & Scott
Little Rock 72203

CALIFORNIA

Bakersfield Californian
Mr. Dean Urnston
1707 "Eye" Bakersfield
Bakersfield 93302

Desert Dispatch
Ms. C. K. Dooley
130 Coolwater Street
Barstow 92313

Brawley News
Ms. Virginia Horn
617 Main Street
Brawley 92227

Burbank Review
Editor
228 Orange Grove
Burbank 91502

Concord Transcript
Ms. La Donna Scanlon
PO Box 308,
1741 Clayton Road
Concord 94522

Corning Observer
Ms. Mary Petty
710 5th Street, PO Box 558
Corning 96021

Valley Times
Mr. Joe Nunes
6909 Village Parkway
Dublin 94566

Imperial Valley Press
Ms. Virginia Horn
205 N. 8th Street
El Centro 92243

Times Advocate
Mr. Richard Phillips
207 E. Pennsylvania Avenue
Escondido 92025

Fresno Bee
Mr. Howard Miller
1559 Van Ness Avenue
Fresno 93786

Glendale News Press
Among Ourselves
111 N. Isabel
Glendale 91209

Hanford Sentinel
Ms. Ruth Gomes
418 W. 8th
Hanford 93230

Indio Daily News
Mr. John Power
45-14 Towne Street,
PO Drawer NNN
Indio 92201

Herald News
Mr. Joe Nunes
325 S "I" Street, PO Box 31
Livermore 94550

Lompoc Record
Mr. Wesley Huffman
115 North H Street
Lompoc 93438

Ind/Press Telegram
Mr. Paul Wallace
604 Pine Avenue
Long Beach 90844

Herald Examiner
Mr. Warren Morrell
1111 S. Broadway
Los Angeles 90051

Los Angeles Times
Mr. Edward C. Gilbert
Times Mirror Square
Los Angeles 90053

Modesto Bee
Ms. Katherine Gearhead
14th & H
Modesto 95352

C Mesa Daily Pilot
Mr. Thomas Keevil
Orange Coast Pilot,
PO Box 1875
Newport Beach 92663

Oakland Tribune
Mr. Clifford Pletschet
401-13th Street
Oakland 94612

Ontario Report
Ms. Marilyn Ware
212 E B Street
Ontario 91764

Mercury-Register
Mr. Don Shaffer
1740 Bird Street
Oroville 95965

Palm Springs Des. Sun
News Carrier
611 S. Palm Canyon Drive,
Box 190
Palm Springs 92262

Palo Alto Times
Mr. Jack Silvey
245 Lytton Avenue
Palo Alto 94302

Wall Street Journal
Mr. Richard Gillespie
1701 Page Mill Road
Palo Alto 94304

Pasadena Star-News
Mr. Harry Bortin Jr.
525 E. Colorado Boulevard
Pasadena 91109

Paso Robles Press
Mr. Blain Roberts
121 Pine Street, PO Box 427
Paso Robles 93446

Progress Bulletin
Ms. Peggy Gonzales
300 S. Thomas Street,
PO Box 2708
Pomona 91766

Red Bluff News
Ms. Tery Johnson
710 Main Street
Red Bluff 96080

Redwood City Tribune
Mr. Otto Tallent
901 Marshall Street
Redwood City 94063

Richmond Independent
Mr. John Adams
164-10th Street
Richmond 94801

Press-Enterprise
Mr. Joseph T. Koehler
3512-14th Street
Riverside 92502

Sacramento Bee
Ms. Katherine Gearhead
21st & Q, PO Box 15779
Sacramento 95813

Sacramento Union
Mr. Gene Keith
301 Capitol Mall
Sacramento 95812

Salinas Californian
Mr. Eric C. Brazel
123 W. Alisal Street
Salinas 93901

Sun/Telegram
Mr. Jan Roddick
399 "D" Street
San Bernardino 92401

Sun-Post
Mr. John Grange
1542 N. El Camino Real,
Box 367
San Clemente 92672

Evening Tribune
Mr. J. D. Thornton
350 Camino De La Reina
San Diego 92108

San Francisco Chronicle
Mr. Lawrence J. Arteseros
901 Mission Street
San Francisco 94103

San Francisco Examiner
Mr. Lawrence J. Arteseros
110 Fifth Street
San Francisco 94103

Chronicle/Exam.
Ms. Judith Weber
625 Mission
San Francisco 94103

Mercury News
Mr. Andy Bruno
750 Ridder Park Drive
San Jose 95190

Times & News Leader
Mr. Bob Foster
1080 S. Amphlett Boulevard
San Mateo 94402

San Pedro News-Pilot
Ms. Donna Mack
362 Seventh Street
San Pedro 90731

San Pedro News-Pilot
Mr. Greg Stevens
PO Box 191
San Pedro 90733

Independent Journal
Ms. Judy Shepardson
1040 B Street
San Rafael 94902

Santa Ana Register
The Trouble Shooter
625 N. Grand Avenue
Santa Ana 92711

Santa Monica Outlook
Ms. Clara McClure
1540 Third Street
Santa Monica 90406

S. Paula Chronicle
Mr. Dale Drake
116 N. Tenth Street
Santa Paula 93060

Stockton Record
Mr. Richard Smith
530 E. Market Street
Stockton 95202

News-Chronicle
Mr. Julius Gius
PO Box 1346
Thousand Oaks 91360

South Bay Breeze
Ms. Donna Mack
5215 Torrance Boulevard
Torrance 90503

Times-Herald
Ms. Terry Johnson
500 Maryland Street
Vallejo 94590

News & Green Sheet
Ms. Barbara Houndt
14539 Sylvan Street,
PO Box 310
Van Nuys 91408

Star Free Press
Mr. Julius Gius
567 E. Santa Clara Street,
Box 171
Ventura 93001

Times-Delta
Mr. Roger P. Beer
330 N. West Street
Visalia 93277

Contra Costa Times
Mr. Gerry McClaughry
2640 Shadelands Drive
Walnut Creek 94598

Contra Costa Times
Mr. Yar Petry
2640 Shadelands Drive
Walnut Creek 94598

Register-Pajaronian
Mr. Bill Reed
1000 Main Street
Watsonville 95076

Whittier News
Scoop
7037 S. Comstock Avenue
Whittier 90608

COLORADO

Colorado Springs Sun
Ms. Joyce Trent
103 W. Colorado Avenue
Colorado Springs 80902

Denver Post
Mr. Bob Burns
650-15th Street
Denver 80202

Daily Sentinel
Tupper Hall
730 S. 7th Street,
PO Box 668
Grand Junction 81501

Longmont Times-Call
Mr. Bruce Hotchkiss
717 Fourth Avenue
Longmont 80501

Reporter-Herald
Mr. John Pfeiffenberger
450 Cleveland
Loveland 80537

CONNECTICUT

Danbury News-Times
Mr. Steve Collins
333 Main Street
Danbury 06810

Rock. Jrnl-Inquirer
Ms. Cynthia S. Bercowetz
Ten Prospect Street
Hartford 06101

Record/Journal
Mr. Jonathan R. Bass
11-19 Crown Street
Meriden 06450

New Haven Register
Ms. Jane Sullivan
367 Orange Street
New Haven 06503

DISTRICT OF COLUMBIA

Consumer News (Help Mate)
Mr. Merill Rose
813 National Press Bldg.
Washington 20045

Washington Star-News
Mr. Dan Poole
225 Virginia Avenue SE
Washington 20061

DELAWARE

Delaware State Times
Ms. Karen Walters
PO Box 737
Dover 19901

FLORIDA

Boca Raton News
Ms. Dorothy Sutton
34 SE Second Street
Boca Raton 33432

Bradenton Herald
Ms. Julie Ross
90 Bradenton Herald
Bradenton 33406

Bradenton Herald
Mr. Alvin Bench
401-13th Street W.
Brandenton 33505

Clearwater Sun
Mr. Dennis Limbach
301 S. Myrtle
Clearwater 33517

Cocoa Today
Ms. Nancy A. Nugent
PO Box 1330
Cocoa 32922

Ft. Myers News Press
Ms. Ann Adams
Box 10
Fort Myers 33902

Gainesville Sun
Ms. Doris Chandler
101 SE Second Place
Gainesville 32602

News-Leader
Mr. Paul Brookshire
15-17 NE First Street
Homestead 33030

Jacksonville Journal
Ms. Helen Bates
One Riverside Avenue
Jacksonville 32202

Jacksonville Journal
Mr. Hugh White
One Riverside Avenue
Jacksonville 32202

Lakeland Ledger
Mr. Bobbie Rossiter
PO Box 408
Lakeland 33802

Marianna Jackson City
Floridan
Mr. Henry Cabbage
104 E. Layfayette Street
Marianna 32446

Miami Herald/News
Ms. Anne Baumgartner
Herald Plaza
Miami 33101

Naples News
For Your Information
1075 Central Avenue
Naples 33940

Herald Tribune-Journal
Mrs. Chandler
801 S. Tamiami Trail
Sarasota 33578

Herald-Tribune/Journal
Ms. Sharon Tucker
801 S. Tamiami Trail
Sarasota 33578

Independent
Ms. Pat C. Fenner
PO Box 1121
St. Petersburg 33731

Tallahassee Democrat
Mr. Collins Conner
277 N. Magnolia Drive
Tallahassee 32302

Tampa Tribune/Times
Ms. Martha Marth
507 East J. F. Kennedy
Boulevard
Tampa 33602

GEORGIA

Athens Banner-Herald
Mr. Rick Parham
One/Press Place
Athens 30601

Ledger/Enquirer
Ms. Judy Fields
17 W. 12th Street
Columbus 31902

Gainesville Times
Ms. Rebecca Schreoder
345 Green Street, Box 838
Gainesville 30501

Macon News
Ms. Madeleine Hirsiger
120 Broadway
Macon 31201

HAWAII

Honolulu Advertiser
"Scoops" Kreger
605 Kapiolani Boulevard
Honolulu 96801

Star-Bulletin
Ms. Joanne Imig
605 Kapiolani Boulevard
Honolulu 96801

IDAHO

Statesman
Ms. Karen Bossick
1200 N. Curtis Road
Boise 83707

Burley S. Idaho Press
Mr. John Eberline
230 East Main Street
Burley 83318

News-Tribune
Mr. Larry Gardner
819 Main Street
Caldwell 83605

Lewiston Tribune
Mr. Charles P. Boren
505 C. State
Lewiston 83501

Nampa Free Press
Mr. Arnold Ruse
316-10th Avenue
S. Nampa 83651

ILLINOIS

Alton Eve. Telegram
Mr. Robert Black
111 E. Broadway
Alton 62002

Cham.-Urb. Courier
Mr. Dedrich G. Schumacher
110 W. University
Champaign 61820

Chicago Sun-Times
Mr. Thomas Sheridan
401 N. Wabash Avenue
Chicago 60611

Chicago Tribune
Mr. Kenan Heise
435 N. Michigan Avenue
Chicago 60611

Commercial News
Mr. Dale Foster
17 W. North
Danville 61832

Elgin Courier-News
Mr. Leroy S. Clemens
300 Lake Street
Elgin 60120

Register-Mail
"Penny"
140 S. Prairie
Galesburg 61401

Lawrence Record
Mr. C. L. Reynolds
1209 State Street
Lawrence 62439

Ottawa Times
Ms. Joan Hustis
110 W. Jefferson Street
Ottawa 61350

Star/Reg. Republic
Ms. C. Mirgain
99 E. State Street
Rockford 61105

State Jour/Register
Mr. Jeff Trewhitt
313 South 6th Street
Springfield 62705

Iroquois County Journal
Mr. Cloyce K. Nichols
313 E. Walnut Street
Watseka 60970

INDIANA

Bloomington Courier-Tribune
Answer Man Staff
Bloomington 47401

Herald-Telephone
Mr. Bill Schrader
1900 S. Walnut Street
Bloomington 47401

Brazil Times
Mr. Daniel T. Smith
119-121 E. National Avenue
Brazil 47834

Elkhart Truth
Mr. John J. Gillaspy
Communicana Building
Elkhart 46514

Herald-Press
Monday Mini's Staff
Seven No. Jefferson
Huntington 46750

Indianapolis News
Mr. Bob Basler
307 N. Pennsylvania Street
Indianapolis 46206

Kokomo Tribune
Ms. Joanne Lake
300 N. Union
Kokomo 46901

Herald-Argus
Mr. Mark Johnson
701 State Street
La Porte 46350

Journal & Courier
Ms. Annalee Firestone
217 N. 6th Street
Lafayette 47901

Lebanon Reporter
Ms. Jane Cassell
117 E. Washington
Lebanon 46052

Pharos-Tribune Press
Ms. Margo Coffman
517 E. Broadway
Logansport 46947

Chronicle-Tribune
Mr. James Mitchell
610 S. Adams
Marion 46952

News-Dispatch
Ms. Karen Wilke
121 W. Michigan Boulevard
Michigan City 46360

South Bend Tribune
Ms. Gayle Zubler
225 W. Colfax
South Bend 46626

IOWA

Telegram-Herald
Mr. Joe Mattes
W. 8th Bluft Street
Dubuque 52001

Sioux City Journal
Ms. Dianne Rose
6th and Pavonia
Sioux City 51105

KANSAS

Kansas City Kansan
Ms. Marilyn Petterson
901 N. 8th Street
Kansas City 66101

Leavenworth Times
Ms. Mary Combs
416-22 Seneca
Leavenworth 66048

Manhattan Mercury
Mr. Robbie Fidle
Fifth at Osage
Manhattan 66503

Topeka Capital/Journal
Ms. Gay Kalbfleisch
6th & Jefferson
Topeka 66607

Eagle and Beacon
Mr. Marvin Barnes
825 E. Douglas Avenue
Wichita 67202

KENTUCKY

Park City News
Mr. Don Stringer
813 College Street
Bowling Green 42101

Messenger
Mr. Ernest Vaughn
221 S. Main Street
Madisonville 42431

LOUISIANA

Alex. Town Talk
Mr. Jim Butler
Main at Washington Street,
Box 7558
Alexandria 71301

Advocate/State Times
Ms. Donna Lynch
525 Lafayette Street
Baton Rouge 70821

Bogalusa News
Mr. Low Major Jr.
525 Avenue V
Bogalusa 70427

Crowley Signal
Mr. Bob Dailey
602 N. Parkerson Avenue
Crowley 70526

Hammond Star
Mr. Stewart Applin
200 SW Railroad Avenue
Hammond 70401

Layfayette Advertiser
Mr. Vince Marino
219 Jefferson Street
Lafayette 70501

States-Item
Mr. A. Labas
3800 Howard Avenue
New Orleans 70140

Opelousas World
Mr. Paul Sandau
127 N. Market Street,
PO Box 1179
Opelousas 70570

Shreveport Journal
Ms. Ann Matthews
222 Lake Street
Shreveport 71130

MAINE

Press Herald/Express
Mr. Emery W. Stevens
390 Congress Street
Portland 04111

MARYLAND

Baltimore Sun
Mr. David F. Woods
Calvert and Centre Streets
Baltimore 21203

News-American
Mr. Donald Otenasek
Lombard and South Streets
Baltimore 21203

Cumb. News-Times
Action Line
7-9 S Mechanic Street
Cumberland 21502

Herald and Mail
Ms. Nellie Umbaugh
25-31 Summit Avenue
Hagerstown 21740

MASSACHUSETTS

Boston Globe
Mr. Alfred J. Monahan
135 Morrissey Boulevard
Boston 02107

Herald American
Mr. Joe McLaughlin Jr.
300 Harrison Avenue
Boston 02106

Cape Cod Times
Write to Know
319 Main Street
Hyannis 02601

Hyde Park Tribune
Mr. Charles A. Radin
Hyde Park 02136

Standard Times
Mr. Avis Roberts
555 Pleasant Street
New Bedford 02742

Quincy Massachusetts Patriot
Mr. Clyde Davis
13-19 Temple Street
Quincy 02169

Southbridge News
Mr. Fred Welch
25 Elm Street
Southbridge 01550

Springfield Daily News
Ms. Jeanne Pueschel
1860 Main Street
Springfield 01129

Springfield News
Mr. George R. Delistle
1850 Main Street
Springfield 01101

Worcester Gazette
Contact
200 Franklin Street
Worcester 01613

MICHIGAN

Ann Arbor News
Ms. Mary Jo Rank
340 E. Huron Street
Ann Arbor 48106

Enquirer & News
Mr. Edward Z. Boles
155 W. Van Buren Street
Battle Creek 49016

Detroit Free Press
Mr. John Castine
321 W. Lafayette Boulevard
Detroit 48231

Fenton Independent
Hot Stuff Staff
112 South Ellen
Fenton 48430

Grand Rapids Press
Mr. A. J. Cruzan
Press Plaza-
Vandenberg Center
Grand Rapids 49502

Greenville News
Ms. Adele Jaehnig
109 N. Lafayette Street
Greenville 48838

Citizen Patriot
Ms. Martha Cotton
214 S. Jackson Street
Jackson 49204

Oakland Press
Ms. Corrinne Aldrich
48 W. Huron Street
Pontiac 48056

Times Herald
Ms. Jan Mitchell
907 Sixth Street
Port Huron 48060

Ypsilanti Press
Ms. Dorothy Zack
20 E. Michigan Avenue
Ypsilanti 48197

MINNESOTA

Duluth Budgeteer
Mr. Dick Palmer
424 W. First
Duluth 55801

Minneapolis Star
Mr. Steve Poulter
425 Portland Avenue
Minneapolis 55415

Pioneer Press/Disp.
Mr. Owen Berg
55 E. 4th Street
St. Paul 55101

MISSISSIPPI

Press Register
Mr. Albert Edwards
123 2nd Street
Clarksdale 38614

Commonwealth
Mr. Frank T. Long
207-09 W. Market
Greenwood 38930

Clarion-Ledger/News
Mr. O. C. McDavid
PO Box 40
Jackson 39205

Vicksburg Post
Mr. Charles Faulk
920 South Street
Vicksburg 39181

MISSOURI

Columbia Missourian
Ms. Manny Paraschos
311 S. 9th Street
Columbia 65201

Columbia Tribune
Mr. Tom Womack
4th and Walnut Streets
Columbia 65201

Flat River Journal
Mr. Joseph Layden
22 E. Main Street
Flat River 63601

Courier-Post
Ms. C. A. Corcoran
200 N. Third
Hannibal 63401

Joplin Globe
Mr. Clair Goodwin
117 E. 4th Street
Joplin 64801

Kansas City Star
Mr. Barry Garron
729 Grand
Kansas City 64108

Daily Dunkin Dem
Ms. Carol Goldsmith
212-4 N. Main Street
Kennett 63857

Mexico Ledger
Mr. Max Thomson
Love & Washington Streets
Mexico 65265

Neosho News
Mr. Bill Ball
1006 W. Harmony Street
Neosho 64850

Rolla News
Mr. Steve Sowers
101 W. 7th
Rolla 65401

Capital/Democrat
Mr. Douglas Kneilbert
7th St &
Massachusetts Avenue
Sedalia 65301

News/Leader & Press
Ms. Peggy Soric
651 Boonville
Springfield 65801

NEBRASKA

Fremont Tribune
Mr. Kevin Parrish
PO Box 9
Fremont 68025

No. Platte Telegraph
Ms. Sharron Hollen
315 E. 5th
North Platte 69101

Omaha World-Herald
Mr. Hub Ogden
14th & Dodge Streets
Omaha 68102

York News-Times
Gripe Pipe
327 Platte Avenue
York 68467

NEW JERSEY

Evening Press
Mr. Jack Hastings
Press Plaza
Asbury Park 07712

Atlantic City Press
Mr. Herbert Brown
1900 Atlantic Avenue
Atlantic City 08401

Courier-Post
Ms. Peggy Morgan
"Trouble Shooter"
Camden 08101

Dover Daily Advance
Ms. Gertrude Z. Lauenstein
87 E. Blackwell Street
Dover 07801

Hunterdon Cnty Dem.
Ms. Carol L. Felder
PO Box 32
Flemington 08822

Bergen County Record
Mr. Stephen Long
150 River Street
Hackensack 07602

Herald News
Ms. Jan Devanna
988 Main Avenue
Passaic 07055

Courier-News
Mr. John S. Brodhead Jr.
1201 Route 22
Somerville 08876

Trenton Eve. Times
Mr. H. Arthur Smith III
500 Perry Street
Trenton 08605

News Tribune
Mrs. Renae Kasper
One Hoover Way
Woodbridge 07095

NEW MEXICO

Albuquerque Journal
Mr. G. Ward Fenley
7th and Silver SW
Albuquerque 87103

Albuquerque Tribune
Ms. Judy Nickell
7th and Silver SW
Albuquerque 87103

La Cruces Sun News
Ms. Beth Franey
256 W. La Cruces Avenue
La Cruces 88001

NEW YORK

Knickerbocker News
Mr. James B. Atkins
645 Albany Road
Albany 12201

News-Time Union
Ms. Irene Keeney
645 Albany-Shaker Road
Albany 12201

Citizen-Advertiser
Ms. Barbara Moody
25 Dill Street
Auburn 13021

Sun Bulletin/Press
Mr. Ed Barrett
Vestal Parkway East
Binghamton 13902

Courier-Express
Mr. Harlan Abbey
787 Main Street
Buffalo 14240

Evening News
Mr. Richard Christian
One News Plaza
Buffalo 14240

Fredonia Observer
Mr. Theodore Lutz
8-10 E. 2nd Street
Dunkirk 14048

Elmira Star Gazette
Ms. Liz Greene
201 Baldwin Street
Elmira 14902

Ithaca Journal
Ms. Monica Glover
123 W. State Street
Ithaca 14850

Long Island Press
Mr. Leo Meindl
92-20 168 Street
Jamaica 11404

Mamaroneck Times
Ms. Regina Smith
126 Library Lane
Mamaroneck 10543

Times Herald Record
Ms. Jean Kaufman
40 Mulberry Street
Middletown 10940

Mount Vernon Argus
Ms. Regina Smith
147 Gramaton Avenue
Mount Vernon 10551

Standard-Star
Ms. Regina Smith
251 North Avenue
New Rochelle 10802

New York News
Mr. Don O'Mally
220 E. 42nd Street
New York 10017

New York World
Ms. Marion Shaw
205 W. 19th Street
New York 10011

Niagara Falls Gazette
Ms. Rebecca Irving
310 Niagara Street
Niagara Falls 14302

Rockland-Journal-News
Ms. Regina Smith
53-55 Hudson Avenue
Nyack 10960

Oneonta Star
Ms. Beth Strong
102 Chestnut Street
Oneonta 13820

Citizen-Register
Ms. Regina Smith
109 Croton Avenue
Ossining 10562

Port Chester Item
Ms. Regina Smith
50 Westchester Avenue
Port Chester 10573

Democrat & Chronicle
Ms. Kay Fish
55 Exchange Street
Rochester 14614

Saratogian-Trico News
Mr. Harold Robillard
20 Lake Avenue
Saratoga Springs 12866

Post-Standard
Ms. Barbara Nappi
Clinton Square
Syracuse 13221

Post-Standard
Mr. Leroy Natanson
Clinton Square
Syracuse 13201

Tarrytown News
Ms. Regina Smith
111 Old White Plains Road
Tarrytown 10591

Troy Times Record
Mr. Vinny Reda
Broadway and 5th Avenue
Troy 12181

Observer Dispatch
Ms. Mary Kendrick
221 Oriskany Plaza
Utica 13503

Westchester Rockland
Newspaper
Ms. Regina Smith
Westchester 10461

Reporter Dispatch
Ms. Regina Smith
One Gannett Drive
White Plains 10604

Herald Statesman
Ms. Regina Smith
Larkin Plaza
Yonkers 10702

NORTH CAROLINA

Charlotte News
Ms. Cathy Chapen
600 S. Tyron Street
Charlotte 28201

Observer/News
Ms. Judy Gaultney
600 S. Tyron Street
Charlotte 28201

Durham Herald/Sun
Mr. Carl Boswell
115-19 Market Street
Durham 27702

Fayetteville Observor
Ms. Jenny Edelman
512 Hay Street
Fayetteville 28301

News/Record
Mr. Rick Stewart
200-04 N. Davie Street
Greensboro 27402

Enterprise
Ms. Posey Gorham
210 Church Avenue
High Point 27261

Robesonian
Ms. Judith Tillman
121 W. 5th Street
Lumberton 28358

Enquirer Journal
Ms. Dolores Lavelle
PO Box 70
Monroe 28110

Raleigh Times
Ms. Sharon Kilby
215 S. McDowell Street
Raleigh 27601

Reidsville Review
Ms. Catherine Shelton
116 N. Scales Street
Reidsville 27320

Rocky Mount Telegram
Mr. Bill Stancil
150 Howard Street
Rocky Mount 27801

Salisbury Post
Mr. Jason Lesley
131 West Innes Street
Salisbury 28144

Concord Tribune
Mr. Trib Staff
125 Union Street
S. Concord 28025

Star-News
Ms. Gwen Hanke
PO Box 840
Wilmington 28401

Wilson Times
Mr. John Scott
117 N. Goldsboro
Wilson 27893

Sentinel
Mr. Bill Williams
416-20 N. Marshall
Winston-Salem 27102

NORTH DAKOTA

Devils Lake Journal
Mr. Jack Zaleski
Third and Fourth Avenues
Devils Lake 58301

Williston Herald
Action Line
14 W. 4th Street
Williston 58801

OHIO

Beacon Journal
Mr. Craig Wilson
44E Exchange Street
Akron 44328

Times Gazette
Mr. Roger Nielsen
40 E. Second Street
Ashland 44805

Enquirer
Ms. Jo-Ann Huff Albers
617 Vine Street
Cincinnati 45201

Plain Dealer
Mr. John Huth
1801 Superior Avenue
Cleveland 44114

Cleveland Press
Mr. Robert McKnight
901 Lakeside Avenue
Cleveland 44114

Journal Herald/News
Mr. James Zofkie
4th and Ludlow Streets
Dayton 45401

Crescent-News
Ms. Teri Hageman
Perry & Second Streets
Defiance 43512

Journal-Times
Mr. Ron Reed
Court & Journal Square
Hamilton 45012

Kenton Times
Mr. John Kauffman
201 E. Columbus Street
Kenton 43326

Lorain Journal
Ms. Joanne Scrivo
1657 Broadway
Lorain 44052

News Journal
Ms. Anne Miller
70 W. Fourth Street
Mansfield 44901

Times-Reporter
Ms. Anna Lee Brendza
629 Wabash Avenue
New Philadelphia 44663

Niles Times
Mr. Bob Miller
35 W. State Street
Niles 44446

Toldeo Blade
Mr. Ken Reiger
541 Superior Street
Toledo 43660

Troy News
Ms. Michele Orzano
224 S. Market Street
Troy 45373

News Herald
Ms. Arlene McClarran
38879 Mentor Avenue
Willoughby 44094

OKLAHOMA

Claremore Progress
Ms. Pat Reeder
315 W. Will Rogers
  Boulevard
Claremore 74017

Oklahoma City Times
Action Line
500 N. Broadway,
PO Box 25125
Oklahoma City 73125

Tulsa Daily World
Mr. David V. MacKenzie
315 S. Boulder Avenue
Tulsa 74102

Vinita Journal
Ms. Sue Cronford
138-140 S. Wilson
Vinita 74301

OREGON

Grants Pass Courier
Mr. Harry L. Elliott
409 SE Seventh
Grants Pass 97526

Mail Tribune
Mr. Earl H. Adams
33 No. First Street
(PO Box 1108)
Medford 97501

PENNSYLVANIA

News-Tribune
Mr. James H. March, Sr.
715 13th Street
Beaver Falls 15010

Globe-Times
Ms. Dolores Caskey
202 W. Fourth Street
Bethlehem 18106

Bradford Era
Round the Square
43 Main Street
Bradford 16701

Columbia News
Mr. Cletus Aston
341 Chestnut Street
Columbia 17512

Courier-Express
Mr. M. L. Bloom
Courier Express Bldg.
Du Bois 15801

Easton Express
Mr. Sidney Watt
30 N. Fourth
Easton 18042

Ellwood City Ledger
Mr. C. R. Moser
835 Lawrence Avenue
Ellwood City 16117

Tribune-Review
Ms. Tracy Krause
Cabin Hill Drive
Greensburg 15601

Lancaster News
The Public Eye
Eight W. King Street
Lancaster 17604

Inquirer
Ms. Connie Lanyland
400 No. Broad Street
Philadelphia 19001

Republican
Ms. Catharine Bright
11-113 Mahantongo Street
Pottsville 17901

Shamokin News-Item
Mr. Thomas D. Brennan
701-709 N. Rock
Shamokin 17872

St. Coll. Pa. Mirror
Mr. Paul W. Houck
PO Box P-10-Benner Pike
State College 16801

Sunbury Daily Item
Mr. Robert E. Lauf
Second and Market Streets
Sunbury 17801

Observer-Reporter
Mr. John L. Northrup
122 S. Main Street
Washington 15301

Wyoming Vly. Obv.
Mr. Paul W. Warnaqiris
Wilkes Barre 18703

PUERTO RICO

San Juan El Mundo
Ms. Doris Coroo
San Juan

RHODE ISLAND

Journal/Bulletin
Mr. Don Sockol
75 Fountain Street
Providence 02902

SOUTH CAROLINA

Greenville-Piedmont
Ms. R. G. Sargent
305 S. Main Street
Greenville 29602

Sumter Item
Mr. Gerry Ingram
20 N. Magnolia Street
Sumter 29150

Rapid City Journal
Mr. Lauren Davis
507 Main
Rapid City 57701

Public Opinion
Mr. Gordon Garnos
120 Third Avenue NW
Watertown 57201

TENNESSEE

Athens-Post Athenian
Mr. Neil Emsminger
320 S. Jackson Street
Athens 37303

Greenville Sun
Mr. John M. Jones Jr.
200 S. Main Street
Greenville 37743

Jackson Sun
Ms. Virginia Yadamec
245 W. Lafayette
Jackson 38301

Kingsport Times-News
Mr. Ginsey Gurney
701 Lynn Garden Dr.
(Box 479)
Kingsport 37662

Alcoa Daily Times
Mrs. Nancy Cain
307 E. Harper
Maryville 37801

Coml Appeal/Press SC
Mr. Mark Hanna
495 Union Avenue
Memphis 38101

Oak Ridger
Ms. Mary Smyser
101 E. Tyrone Road
Oak Ridge 37830

TEXAS

Reporter News
Ms. Judy Bargainer
100 Block Cypress Street
Abilene 79604

Enterprise/Journal
Ms. Virginia Galloway
380 Walnut Street
(PO Box 3071)
Beaumont 77704

Times-Review
Ms. Beth Bradbury
108 S. Anglin
Cleburne 76031

Corpus Christi Times
Ms. Lynn Pentony
820 Lower Broadway
Corpus Christi 78401

Consicana Sun
Mr. Richard Cole
405 E. Collin
Corsicana 75110

Dallas Times-Herald
Mr. Lew Harris
1101 Pacific
Dallas 75202

Record-Chronicle
Ms. Peggy Berg
314 E. Hickory
Denton 75201

Fort Worth Press
Mr. Marvin Garrett
507 Jones
Fort Worth 76102

Star-Telegram
Mr. Ed Brice
PO Box 1870
Fort Worth, 76101

Register & Messenger
Mrs. Betty Stephenson
306 E. California
Gainesville 76240

Herald Banner
Mr. Jerry Crenshaw
2305 King Street
Greenville 75401

Houston Chronicle
Mr. Dave Flowers
801 Texas Street
Houston 77002

Houston Post
Mr. John Boudreaux
4747 SW Freeway
Houston 77001

Laredo Times
Mr. Fernando Pinon
PO Box 29
Laredo 78040

Port Arthur News
Mr. Gerald Gaulding
549 Fourth Street
Port Arthur 77640

Standard Times
Ms. Shirley Alford
34 W. Harris
San Angelo 76901

San Antonio Express
Action
Avenue E and Third Street
San Antonio 78205

San Antonio Light
Mr. Joe P. Faulkner
McCullough and Broadway
San Antonio 78206

San Antonio News
Hotline
Avenue E and Third Street
San Antonio 78205

San Marcos Record
Mr. Rowe Ray
San Marcos 78660

Texas City Sun
Ms. Barbara Lowe
624 4th Avenue,
PO Box 2249
Texas City 77590

VERMONT

Bennington Banner
Mr. Geoffrey Chapman
425 Main Street
Bennington 05201

VIRGINIA

Dumfries Potomac News
Mr. Tommy Burton
Dumfries 22026

Free Lance-Star
Mr. Earle M. Copp Jr.
616 Amelia Street
(PO Box 617)
Fredericksburg 22401

Newport News
Mr. Brown Carpenter
7505 Warwick Boulevard
Newport News 23607

Norfolk Ledger-Star
Mr. Lloyd Lewis
150 W. Brambleton Avenue
Norfolk 23508

Roanoke World News
Mr. Guy Sterling
201-09 W. Campbell Avenue
Roanoke 24010

Williamsburg Virginia Gazette
Ms. Janet McMahon
PO Box 419
Williamsburg 23185

Pulaski SW Times
Mr. Howard Gebeax
223 N. Washington Avenue
(Box 391)
Pulaski 24301

WASHINGTON

Port Angeles News
Mr. Donald V. Paxon
305 W. 1st Street
Port Angeles 98362

Seattle Times
Mr. Dick Moody
Fairview Avenue N & John
(Box 70)
Seattle 98111

Spokesman-Rev Chron.
Mr. Royce P. Gorseth
W. 926 Sprague
Spokane 99253

WEST VIRGINIA

Charleston Mail
Mr. Rex Woodford
1001 Virginia Street E
Charleston 25301

Welch News
Ridge Runner
125 Wyoming Street
Welch 24801

WISCONSIN

Reporter
Mr. John Green
18 W. 1st Street
Fond Du Lac 54935

Merrill Daily Record
Speak Up Staff
Merrill

Milwaukee Journal
Mr. Maurice Wozniak
333 W. State Street
Milwaukee 53201

Wausau Record-Herald
Speak Up
800 Scott Street
Wausau 54401

WYOMING

Riverton Ranger
Mr. Robert A. Peck
Box 993
Riverton 82501

CANADA

London Free Press
Mr. Gordon Sanderson
PO Box 2280
London, Ontario

Niagara Falls Review
Mr. Don Mullen
4801 Valley Way
Niagara Falls, Ontario

Ottawa Citizen
Mr. Roger Appleton
1101 Baxter Road,
PO Box 5020
Ottawa, Ontario

Ottawa Journal
Ms. Helen Turcotte
365 Laurier Avenue W
Ottawa, Ontario

St. Thomas Times Journal
Ms. S. Gowsill
16-18 Hincks Street
St. Thomas, Ontario

Toronto Star
Mr. Rod Goodman
One Yonge Street
Toronto, Ontario

Toronto Sun
Ms. Olive Collins
322 King Street W
Toronto, Ontario

Vancouver Prov.
Ms. R. G. Chatelin
2250 Granville
Vancouver, BC

Winnipeg Tribune
Ms. Marjorie Gillies
257 Smith Street
Winnipeg, Manitoba

Appendix
State-by-State List
of Private
Consumer Agencies

F

Private Consumer Groups: A Helping Hand in Your Hometown

Government consumer organizations can be effective because they wield official clout, but private consumer groups are passionate and persuasive because they believe in the cause of defending your rights. Naturally they are looking for your support, but you don't have to be a member to avail yourself of their help. Just tip them off to a scam and watch them go to work.

Here is a comprehensive list of private consumer groups active in the U.S. at time of publication. The name, address and phone number of each group was checked late in 1978, and while groups form and disband periodically, the list should be especially helpful to you.

ALABAMA

Alabama Council on Human Relations
Lee County Head Start
P.O. Box 1632
Auburn 36830
Nancy Spears
(205) 821-8336

Alabama League of Aging Citizens, Inc.
837 S. Hull Street
Montgomery 36104
(205) 264-0229

Elinore Community Action Committee
P.O. Drawer H
Wetumpka 36092
(205) 567-4361

Federation of Southern Cooperatives
P.O. Box 95
Epes 35460
(205) 652-9676

Minority Peoples Council on the Tennessee-Tombigbee Waterway
P.O. Box 5
Gainesville 35464
(205) 652-9676

Mobile Area Community Action Committee
850 Marion Street
Mobile 36603
(205) 432-3641

North Ana Environmental Coalition
c/o June Allen
412 Owens Drive
Huntsville 35801
(205) 536-0678

ALASKA

Alaska Public Interest Research Group, Inc.
Box 1093
Anchorage 99510
(907) 278-3661

Coalition for Economic Justice
513 W. 7th Avenue, Suite 3
Anchorage 99501
(907) 272-6732

Cooperative Extension Service
Sportsmen's Mall
1514 S. Cushman, Room 303
Fairbanks 99701
Emma Widmark
(907) 452-1548

Department of Law Consumer Protection Agency
604 Barnett Street, Room 228
Fairbanks 99701
(907) 456-8588

Kenai Peninsular Consumer Council
P.O. Box 2940
Kenai 99611
Johnston Jeffries
(907) 283-7838

ARIZONA

Arizona Consumer's Council
1674 N. Countryclub
Tucson 85719
(602) 327-2661

Chandler Community Services
100 W. Boston, Suites 2 & 3
Chandler 85224
(602) 963-4321

Consumer Relations Board University of Arizona
Student Union 107-C
Tucson 85719
(602) 626-3252

National Consumers Affairs Internship Program
P.O. Box 40445
Tucson 85717
(602) 327-2661

Pinal County Legal Aid Society
115 S. Main Street
Coolidge 85228
James Flenner
(602) 723-5410

ARKANSAS

ACORN (Arkansas Community Organizations for Reform Now)
523 W. 15th Street
Little Rock 72202
(501) 376-7151

Arkansas Consumer Research
1852 Cross Street
Little Rock 72206
(501) 374-2394

Ark-Tex Chapter, American Association of Retired Persons
Route 4, Box 325
Texarkana 75501
(501) 772-2136

N.E. Arkansas Citizens Committee
1145 Hearn
Blytheville 72315
James Deal
(501) 762-2769

Urban League of Greater Little Rock, Inc.
2200 Main Street
P.O. Box 6368
Little Rock 72206
(501) 372-3037

CALIFORNIA

Accountants for the Public Interest (API)
Fort Mason Center, Bldg. 310
San Francisco 94123
(415) 885-3306

American Consumers Council
P.O. Box 24206
Los Angeles 90024
(213) 476-2888

California Citizen Action Group
909-12th Street
Sacramento 95814
(916) 446-4931

California Consumer Club
523 W. 6th Street, Suite 642
Los Angeles 90014
(213) 624-3961

The California Council Against Health Fraud, Inc.
Loma Linda School of Dentistry
Box 1276
Loma Linda 92354
(714) 796-0141, ex. 411

California Food Policy
1535 Mission Street
San Francisco 94103
(415) 863-7480

California Public Interest Research Group
2490 Channing, Room 218
Berkeley 94704
(415) 642-9952

California Public Interest Research Group
334 Kalmia Street
San Diego 92101
(714) 236-1508

California Public Interest Research Group of the L.A. Region
University of California at Los Angeles
321A Kerckhoff Hall
308 Westwood Plaza
Los Angeles 90024
(213) 825-8461

California Public Interest
Research Group/San Diego
University
3000 "E" Street
San Diego 92102
(714) 236-1508

California Public Policy
Center
304 S. Broadway
Los Angeles 90013
(213) 628-8888

Campaign Against Utility
Service Exploitation
(CAUSE)
c/o Burt Wilson or Tim
Brick
130 S. Commonwealth
Avenue
Los Angeles 90004
(213) 383-9863

Church Service Bureau
3720 Folsom Boulevard
Sacramento 95816
(916) 456-3815

Citizens Action League
1250 Wilshire Boulevard,
#404E
Los Angeles 90057
(213) 481-2840

Citizens Action League
814 Mission Street
San Francisco 94103
(415) 543-4101

Coalition for Economic
Survival (CES)
5520 W. Pico Boulevard
Los Angeles 90019
(213) 938-6241

Community Economics
6529 Telegraph Avenue
Oakland 94609
Ed Kirschner
(415) 653-6555

Consumer Action
26-7th Street
San Francisco 94103
(415) 626-4030

Consumer and Community
Action Center
1020 N. Fair Oaks
Pasadena 91104
(213) 794-7194

Consumer Panel of America
1424 Windsor Drive
San Bernardino 92404
(714) 885-5393

Consumer Protection Project
Office of Environmental and
Consumer Affairs
308 Westwood Plaza
University of California at
Los Angeles
Los Angeles 90024
(213) 825-2820

Consumers Cooperative of
Berkeley, Inc.
4805 Central Avenue
Richmond 94804
(415) 526-0440

Consumer's Union
1535 Mission Street
San Francisco 94103
(415) 431-6747

Consumers United of Palo
Alto, Inc.
P.O. Box 311
Palo Alto 94302
(415) 494-1858

Davis Consumer Affairs
Bureau
364 Memorial Union
Room 358
University of California at
Davis
Davis 95616
(916) 752-6484

East Bay New American
Movement
6025 Shattuck
Oakland 94609
(415) 652-1723

El Concilio for the Spanish
Speaking
339 I Street
Modesto 95351
(209) 521-2033

Emeryville Neighborhood
Improvement Association
Attention: Nancy DeJong,
Director
4359 Adeline Street
Emeryville 94608
(415) 654-9593

Green Peace
240 Fort Mason
San Francisco 94123
(415) 441-3993

Green Peace
13719 C Ventura Boulevard
Sherman Oaks 91403
(213) 986-2315

"The Group"
457 Haight Street
San Francisco 94115
(415) 861-6840

Long Beach Commission on
Economic Opportunity
Project Head Start
853 Atlantic Avenue
Long Beach 90813
(213) 437-0667

Model Cities Center for Law
and Justice
3421 E. Olympic Boulevard
Los Angeles 90022
(213) 266-2690

New Age Caucus
3900 Grandview
Los Angeles 90066
(213) 391-3731

Northern California Public
Interest Research Group,
Inc.
(NORCALPIRG)
Pat Marrone/Dave Schmidt
P.O. Box 702
Santa Clara 95052

Oakland/Alameda County
Consumer Council
4538 E. 14th Street
Oakland 94601
(415) 261-8440

Oakland Community
Organization
Attention: Scott Reed,
Director
3914 E. 14th Street
Oakland 94601
(415) 261-8440

Ocean Park Projects
203 Hill Street
Santa Monica 90405
(213) 392-8376

Orange County Sponsoring
Committee
614 Bush Street
Santa Ana 92701

Pacific Institute for
Community Organization
(PICO)
3914 E. 14th Street
Oakland 94601
(415) 532-8466

Pasadena Community
Employment Services
2333 N. Lake Avenue
Altadena 91001
(213) 798-0981

Pasadena Community
Services Commission
500 S. Pasadena Avenue
Pasadena 91105

People's Action Research
1206 S. Gramercy Place
Los Angeles 90019
(213) 735-4969

People's Lobby
3456 W. Olympic Boulevard
Los Angeles 90019
(213) 731-8321

Public Media Center
2751 Hyde Street
San Francisco 94109
(415) 885-0200

Sacramento Consumer
Alliance
909-12th Street
Sacramento 95814

St. Paul's Center for Urban
Work and Study
P.O. Box 753
1012-15th Street
Sacramento 95814

San Francisco Consumer
Action
26-7th Street
San Francisco 94103

Self-Help for the Elderly
3 Old Chinatown Lane
San Francisco 94108
(415) 982-9171

Senior Citizens Association
of Los Angeles County, Inc.
427 W. 5th Street
Los Angeles 90013
(213) 624-6467

South East Fresno
Concerned Citizens
430 S. 1st Street
Fresno 93702
(209) 266-7871

South Eastern San Diego
Organization Project
P.O. Box 13664
San Diego 92113
(714) 263-7203

Stanislaus County
Commission on Aging
c/o Gary Morse, Dept. of
Human Services
P.O. Box 42
Modesto 95353
(209) 526-6720

Toward Utility Rate
Normalization (TURN)
693 Mission Street, 8th Floor
San Francisco 94105
(415) 543-1576

Union Neighbors in Action
491-65th Street
Oakland 94609
(415) 654-1797

Watts Labor Community
Action Committee
11401 S. Central Avenue
Los Angeles 90059
(213) 564-5901

COLORADO

Associated Students
Consumer Protection Office
Student Center
Colorado State University
Fort Collins 80521
(303) 491-5931

Associated Students Renter's
Information Office
Student Center
Colorado State University
Fort Collins 80521
(303) 491-5931

Colorado Consumers
Association
P.O. Box 471
Boulder 80302
(303) 441-3700

Colorado League for
Consumer Protection
8230 W. 16th Place
Lakewood 80215
(303) 233-5891

Colorado Public Interest
Research Group
University Memorial Center
#420
University of Colorado
Boulder 80304
(303) 492-5086

Colorado Public Interest
Research Group
1111 W. Colfax, Box 83
Auraria Student Center
#259F
9th and Lawrence
University of Colorado
Denver 80204
(303) 629-3332

Colorado Public Interest
Research Group, Inc.
University Center
Room 221A
University of Northern
Colorado
Greeley 80631

Colorado Utilities Taskforce
(CUT)
P.O. Box 361
Commerce City 80022
(303) 629-0152

Crusade for Justice
1567 Downing
P.O. Box 18347
Denver 80218
(303) 832-1145

East-Side Action Movement
2855 Tremont Place
Room 201
Denver 80205
(303) 534-6228

Environmental Action of
Colorado
2239 E. Colfax Avenue
Denver 80206
(303) 321-1645

Legal Aid Society of
Metropolitan Denver
770 Grant, Suite 5
Denver 80203
(303) 837-1313

Mt. Plains Congress of
Senior Citizens
431 W. Colfax Avenue
Denver 80204
(303) 629-7270

Solar Book Store
2239 E. Colfax Avenue
Denver 80206
(303) 321-1645

CONNECTICUT

Committee on Training and
Employment (CTE)
433 Atlantic Street
Stamford 06901
(203) 327-3260

Community Renewal Team
of Greater Hartford
3580 Main Street
Hartford 06120
(203) 278-9950

Connecticut Citizen Action
Group
130 Washington Street
P.O. Box G
Hartford 06106
(203) 527-7191

Connecticut Citizen Action
Group
246 Church Street
New Haven 06510
(213) 776-2132

Connecticut Citizen Action
Group
64 Wall Street
Norwalk 06850
(203) 866-4410

Connecticut Public Interest
Research Group
Trinity College
Student Government Office
P.O. Box 1388
Vernon Street
Hartford 06106
(203) 247-2735

Connecticut Public Interest
Research Group
248 Farmington Avenue
Hartford 06105
(203) 525-2734

Connecticut Public Interest
Research Group
University of Hartford
Gengras Student Union
200 Bloomfield Avenue
W. Hartford 06117
(203) 243-4460

Connecticut Public Interest
Research Group
University of Connecticut,
Room 302, Student Union
Box U-8
Storrs 06268
(203) 429-1606

Consumer Action Center
Wesleyan University
190 High Street, 2nd Floor
Middletown 06457
(203) 347-9111, ex. 712

Consumer Relations Bureau
One Landmark Square
Suite 100
Stamford 06901
(203) 359-2112

New Opportunities for
Waterbury
232 North Elm
Waterbury 06702
(203) 757-1241

DISTRICT OF COLUMBIA

Auto Owners Action Council
1411 K Street, NW
Suite 800
Washington 20005
(202) 223-4498

Aviation Consumer Action
Project
P.O. Box 19029
Washington 20036
(202) 223-4498

Center for Community
Change (CCC)
1000 Wisconsin Avenue,
NW
Washington 20007
(202) 338-6310

Center for Community
Justice (CCJ)
918-16th Street, Suite 503
Washington 20006
(202) 296-2565

Center for Community
Organization
Attention: Bob Johnson
1214-16th Street, NW
Washington 20063
(202) 467-5560

Citizen's Energy Project
1413 K Street, NW
8th Floor
Washington 20005
(202) 783-0452

Conservation Project
917-15th Street, NW
10th Floor
Washington 20005
(202) 727-3874

Consumer Affairs Committee
of the Americans for
Democratic Action
3005 Audubon Terrace, NW
Washington 20008
(202) 244-4080

Consumer Federation of
America
1012-14th Street, NW
Washington 20036
(202) 737-3732

Consumer Help
National Law Center
George Washington
University
Washington 20052
(202) 785-1001

Contact Four
2000 H Street, NW
Suite 100
Washington 20052
(202) 676-7585

Critical Mass
133 C Street, SW
Washington 20003
(202) 546-4790

D.C. Citywide Housing
Coalition
1346 Connecticut Avenue,
NW, Room 1001
Washington 20036
(202) 737-3703

D.C. Community Research
Foundation
P.O. Box 19542
Washington 20036
(202) 676-6968

D.C. Consumers Association
440 Emerson Street, NW
Washington 20011
(202) 882-2230

D.C. Public Interest
Research Group
P.O. Box 29542
Washington 20036
(202) 676-7388

Environmental Policy Center
317 Pennsylvania Avenue,
SE
Washington 20012
(202) 547-6500

Gray Panthers
711 Eighth Street, NW
Washington 20001
(202) 347-9541

Institute for Local
Self-Reliance
1717-18th Street, NW
Washington 20009
(202) 232-4108

Movement for Economic
Justice
1605 Connecticut Street,
NW
Washington 20009
(202) 462-4200

National Association of
Neighborhoods
1612-20th Street, NW
Washington 20009
(202) 332-7766

National Center for
Consumer Action
1328 New York Avenue,
NW
Washington 20005
(202) 667-8970

National Center for Urban
Ethnic Affairs (NCUEA)
1521-16th Street
Washington 20036
(202) 232-3600

National Women's Political
Caucus
1411 K Street, NW
Washington 20005
(202) 347-4456

Neighborhood Legal
Services
310-6th Street, NW
Washington 20001
(202) 628-9161

People and Energy
1413 K Street, NW
8th Floor
Washington 20005
(202) 393-6700

People's Council
917-15th Street, NW
10th Floor
Washington 20005
(202) 727-3071

Potomac Alliance
Box 9306
Washington 20005
(202) 393-6702

Protection for Elderly
People (P.E.P.)
1806 Adams Mill Road, NW
Washington 20009
(202) 265-4900

Public Interest Research
Group
1346 Connecticut Avenue,
NW, Suite 415
Washington 20036
(202) 833-3935

United Planning
Organization
Consumer Protection Branch
1021-14th Street, NW
Washington 20005
(202) 638-7300

Women's Equity Action
League (WEAL)
805-15 Street, NW
Suite 822
Washington 20005
(202) 638-1951

The Youth Project
1000 Wisconsin Avenue,
NW
Washington 20007
(202) 338-6310

FLORIDA

Consumers Against High
Prices
162 Andover G Century
Village
West Palm Beach 33409
(305) 683-0826

Consumer's Association
University Union, Room 334
Florida State University
Tallahassee 32306
(904) 644-1811

Consumers Committee on
Utility Rates and the
Environment
P.O. Box 10578
St. Petersburg 33733
(813) 393-1106

Consumers Credit Council
4455 W. Roads Drive
W. Palm Beach 33407
(305) 844-1377

Consumers Cure Inc. of
Florida
P.O. Box 10578
St. Petersburg 33733
(813) 393-1106

Environmental Action Group
University Union, Room 334
Florida State University
Tallahassee 32306
(904) 644-1811

Florida ACORN
1616 Silver Street
Jacksonville 32206
(904) 355-1547

Florida Public Interest
Research Group
University Union, Room 334
Florida State University
Tallahassee 32306
(904) 644-1811

Greater Jacksonville
Economic Opportunity, Inc.
P.O. Box 52025
Jacksonville 32201
(904) 355-3651

Jacksonville Community
Council
1045 River Side Avenue
Jacksonville 32204
(904) 356-4136

Leon County CAP, Inc.
P.O. Box 1775
Tallahassee 32304
(904) 222-2043

Orlando People Power
11015 Highgate Street
Orlando 32809
(305) 855-5380

St. Petersburg People Power
c/o Penny Walbren
P.O. Box 10578
St. Petersburg 33733
(813) 393-7917 or 393-1106

Student Consumers Union
University Union, Room 334
Florida State University
Tallahassee 32306
(904) 644-1811

GEORGIA

Federation of Southern
Cooperatives
40 Marietta Street, Room
1710
Atlanta 30303
(404) 524-6882

Georgia Citizens' Coalition
on Hunger, Inc.
201 Washington Street, S.W.
Atlanta 30303
(404) 659-0878

The Georgia Conservancy,
Inc.
3110 Maple Drive, Suite 407
Atlanta 30305
(404) 262-1967

Price Neighborhood Service
Center
1127 Capitol Avenue, S.W.
Atlanta 30315
(404) 522-5792

HAWAII

Citizens Against Noise
1178 Fort Street Mall
Room 9
Honolulu 96813
(808) 537-5229

Kokua Council for Senior
Citizens
Mail: 2535 S. King Street
Honolulu 96826
914 Ala Moana Boulevard,
Suite 206
Honolulu 96813
(808) 521-6464

Life of the Land
404 Piikoi Street, Room 209
Honolulu 96814
(808) 521-1300

IDAHO

Boise Consumer Coop
1350 N. 13th, Hyde Park
Boise 83702

Consumer Credit Counseling
Service
222 N. Latah
Boise 83705

Idaho Consumer Affairs, Inc.
106 N. 6th Street
3 Pioneer, Old Boise
Boise 83702
(208) 343-3554

Idaho Legal Aid,
Administration
P.O. Box 913
Boise 83701

Idaho Legal Aid, Services
P.O. Box 1683
Boise 83701
(208) 345-0106

Idaho Legal Aid Services,
Inc.
P.O. Box 973
Lewiston 83501
(208) 743-1556

Legal Aid
P.O. Box 1439
Coeur d'Alene 83814
(208) 667-9559

Legal Aid
P.O. Box 1136
Idaho Falls 83401
(208) 524-3660

Legal Aid
P.O. Box 2107
Pocatello 83201
(208) 237-6403

Legal Aid
P.O. Box 1296
Twin Falls 83301
(208) 734-7024

Migrant Unit, Legal Aid
P.O. Box 66
Caldwell 83605
(208) 545-2591

ILLINOIS

Aid of McKinley Community
Services
8910 Commercial
Chicago 60617
(312) 768-5115

Business and Professional
People for the Public
Interest
109 N. Dearborn Street,
Suite 1300
Chicago 60602
(312) 641-5570

Chicago NOW
Nancy Shier, Executive
Director
53 W. Jackson
Chicago 60604
(312) 922-0025 or 922-0079

Citizen/Labor/Energy
Coalition
600 W. Fullerton
Chicago 60614
(312) 929-9125

Citizens Economic
Development Coalition
c/o Douglas Lee Thompson
1973 A W. 111th Street
Chicago 60643
(312) 238-8181

Citizens for a Better
Environment
59 E. Van Buren Street,
#2610
Chicago 60605
(312) 939-1984

Community Referral Agency
8910 Commercial
Chicago 60617
(312) 768-5115

Concerned Citizen's Council
1973 A W. 111th Street
Chicago 60643
(312) 779-3079

Consumer Coalition
P.O. Box 913
Highland Park 60035
(312) 564-5624

Consumer Energy Council
2004 3rd Avenue
Rock Island 61201
(309) 793-4845

Consumer Information for
Low Income Consumers
Southern Illinois University
Edwardsville 62026
(618) 692-2420

Housewives for the E.R.A.
Anne Follis
RR #3
Urbana 61801
(217) 684-2422

Illinois Education
Association
1520 North Rock Run Drive
Joliet 60435
(815) 793-4845

Illinois Public Action
Council
59 E. Van Buren, Suite 2600
Chicago 60605
(312) 427-6262

Illinois Public Interest
Research Group
Southern Illinois University,
3rd Fl. Student Center
Carbondale 62901
(618) 536-2140

Illinois Public Interest
Research Group
Southern Illinois U. at
Edwardsville
Student Government Office
Box 67, Student Activities
Edwardsville 62026
(618) 656-3818

Industrial Areas Foundation
12 E. Grand Avenue
Chicago 60611
(312) 329-0430

Jewish Council on Urban
Affairs
116 S. Michigan Avenue
Chicago 60603
(312) 332-6017

Metropolitan Housing
Alliance (MHA)
1123 W. Washington
Boulevard
Chicago 60607
(312) 243-5850

Midwest Academy
600 W. Fullerton
Chicago 60614
(312) 953-6525

National People's Action
(NPA)
1123 W. Washington
Boulevard
Chicago 60607
(312) 243-3038

National Training
Information Center (NTIC)
1123 W. Washington
Boulevard
Chicago 60607
(312) 243-3035

New America Movement
3244 N. Clark
Chicago 60657
(312) 871-7700

Organizing Committee for
the Northwest Side
4957½ W. Diversey
Chicago 60639
(312) 637-3380

Pollution and Environmental
Problems
President, Box 309
Palatine 60067
(312) 381-6695

Proyecto Libre
8910 Commercial
Chicago 60617
(312) 768-5115

PUSH
930 E. 50th Street
Chicago 60615
(312) 373-3366

Self-Help Action of Chicago
1742 W. 87th Street
Chicago 60620
(312) 239-5100

Springfield and Sangamon
County Community Action
Agency
2171 S. 9th Street
Springfield 62703
(217) 525-1117

Women Employed
5 S. Wabash
Chicago 60603
(312) 782-3902

INDIANA

Citizens Action Coalition
3620 N. Meridian
Indianapolis 46208
(317) 923-2494

Community Action Against
Poverty of Greater
Indianapolis, Inc.
611 N. Park Avenue
Suite 516
Indianapolis 46204
(317) 639-9421

Consumer Center
730 E. Washington
Boulevard
Fort Wayne 46802
(219) 422-7630

Indiana Public Interest
Research Group
703 E. 7th Street
Bloomington 47401
(812) 337-7575

New World Center
611 W. Wayne
Fort Wayne 46802
(219) 422-6821

IOWA

Citizens Energy Center
1342-30th Street
Des Moines 50311
(515) 277-0253

Citizens United for
Responsible Energy (CURE)
1342-30th Street
Des Moines 50311
(515) 277-0253

Iowa Consumers League
Box 189
Corydon 50060
(515) 872-2329

Iowa Public Interest
Research Group
Memorial Union, Room 36
Iowa State University
Ames 50010
(515) 294-8094

Iowa Public Interest
Research Group
140 Mauker Union
University of Iowa
Cedar Falls 50613
(319) 277-3368

Iowa Public Interest
Research Group
Box 1297
Grinnell College
Grinnell 50112
(515) 236-6181 x607

Iowa Public Interest
Research Group
Student Activities Center
Iowa Memorial Union
Iowa City 52242
(319) 353-7042

Iowa Public Interest
Research Group
Cornell College
Mary Jane Ruggles
Mt. Vernon 52314
(319) 895-8811

Iowa Women's Political
Caucus
315 E. 5th Street
Des Moines 50309
(515) 282-8191

KANSAS

Area Agency on Aging
217 S. Seth Childs Road
Manhattan 66502
(913) 776-9294

CAN HELP
P.O. Box 1364
Topeka 66601
(913) 295-8499

Community Information
Service
Topeka Public Library,
Bobbi Barber
1515 W. 10th Street
Topeka 66604
(913) 295-8499

Consumer Assistance Center
North Central Kansas
Libraries
Juliette and Poyntz
Manhattan 66502
(913) 776-4741

Consumer Relations Board
Kansas State University
Manhattan 66506
(913) 532-6541

Consumer United Program
8410 West Highway, #54
Wichita 67209
(316) 722-4251

El Centro De Servicios Para
Mexicanos, Inc.
204 N.E. Lime
Topeka 66616
(913) 232-8207

Environmental Action
Committee (E.A.C.)
Kansas State University,
Consumer Relations Board
Student Governing Assoc.,
Kansas State Union
Manhattan 66506
(913) 532-6541

Every Women's Center
c/o YWCA
225 W. 12th
Topeka 66612
(913) 233-1750

Housewives for the E.R.A.
1513 W. 23rd
Topeka 66611
(913) 232-3038

Kansas Home Economics
Association
c/o Family Economics
Department
Justin Hall, Kansas State
University
Manhattan 66502
(913) 532-5515

Kansas Home Economics
Association Consumer
Interest Committee
21 E. Des Moines Avenue
South Hutchinson 67505
(316) 663-5491

Kansas Legal Services
Att: Paul Johnson
112 W. 6th, Suite 202
Topeka 66603
(913) 233-2068

Kansas National Consumer
Information Center
315 N. 20th Street
Kansas City 66102
(913) 342-4574

Manhattan Consumer-
Business Relations Center
c/o KSU Consumer Relations
Board
S.G.A. (Student Governing
Association)
Kansas State Union
Manhattan 66506
(913) 532-6541

Mid-Kansas Community
Action Program, Inc.
(MIDKAP, INC.)
P.O. Box 1034
Eldorado 67042
(316) 321-6373

People's Energy Project
Att: Paul Johnson
112 W. 6th, Suite 202
Topeka 66603
(913) 233-2068

Shawnee County Community
Assistance and Action
603 Topeka Avenue
Topeka 66603
(913) 235-9561

Southeast Kansas Community
Action Program (SEK-KAP)
407 N. 17th
Parsons 65357
(316) 421-2060

Topeka Housing Complaint
Center
East Boro Shopping Mall
3120 E. 6th Street
Topeka 66607
(913) 234-0217

KENTUCKY

American Association of
Retired Persons
R 1 Hilltop Drive
Mt. Washington 40047
(502) 538-4782

Appalachian Research and
Defense Fund of Kentucky,
Inc.
Box 152
Prestonburg 41653
(606) 886-3876

Budget Counseling Club
1730 S. 13th Street
Louisville 40210
(502) 635-2723

Community Incorporated
222 N. 17th Street
Louisville 40203
(502) 583-8385

Concerned Consumers'
P.O. Box 325
747 Liberty Street
Newport 41072
(606) 491-4444

Concerned Consumers of
Electric Energy
Route 2, Box 468
Shepherdsville 40165
(502) 957-3970

Consumer Association of
Kentucky, Inc.
310 W. Liberty, Suite 709
Louisville 40202
(502) 587-0772

Kentucky Public Interest
Research Group
Mark Williams, Student
Government Association
University of Louisville,
BeKnap Campus
Student Center
Louisville 40208

Knott County Citizens for
Social and Economic Justice
Box 473
Hindman 41822
(606) 785-3016 or 785-5749

Louisville and Jefferson
County Community Action
Agency
305 W. Broadway
Louisville 40202
(502) 585-1631

National Retired Teacher
Association (NRTA)
Mrs. Homer Myers
Box 96
Brooks 40109
(502) 957-3815

Senior Citizen's League
Route 2, Box 321
Shepherdsville 40165
(502) 957-4691

LOUISIANA

Cactus Consumer Center
Tulane University
Alcee Fortier, Room 300
New Orleans 70118
(504) 861-1485

Coalition for Action
1742 Terpsichore Street
New Orleans 70113
(504) 588-9973

Consumer Protection Center
P.O. Box 1471
Baton Rouge 70821
(504) 389-3451

Louisiana ACORN
628 Baronne
New Orleans 70113
(504) 523-1691

Louisiana Center for the
Public Interest
Suite 700
Maison Blanche Bldg.
New Orleans 70112
(504) 524-1231 or 8182

Louisiana Consumers'
League, Inc.
P.O. Box 1332
Baton Rouge 70821

Louisiana Consumers'
League, Inc.
P.O. Box 52882
New Orleans 70152
(504) 581-9322

Louisiana Office of
Consumer Protection
P.O. Box 44091
Capitol Station
Baton Rouge 70804
(504) 925-4410

New Orleans Council on
Aging
705 Lafayette Street
Room 100, Gallier Hall
New Orleans 70130
(504) 586-1221

New Orleans Legal
Assistance Corp.
226 Carondelet Street
Suite 605
New Orleans 70130
(504) 523-1297

Opportunities
Industrialization Center
315 N. Broad Street
New Orleans 70119
(504) 821-8222

Public Law Utilities Group
(PLUG)
One American Place
Suite 1601
Baton Rouge 70825
(504) 383-9970

MAINE

Consumer Action Coalition
117 Main Street
Lewiston 04240
(207) 784-9768

Federation of Cooperatives,
Inc. (FEDCO)
Box 107
16 Winthrop
Hallowell 04347

Home Coop or Home
Learning
Box 408
Orland 04472
(207) 469-2026

Northeast Combat
33 Idaho Avenue
Bangor 04401
(207) 947-3331

Pine Tree Legal Assistance
277 Lisbon Street
Lewiston 04240
(207) 784-1558

Pine Tree Legal Assistance
146 Middle Street
Portland 04111
(207) 774-8211

Public Interest Research
Group
68 High Street
Portland 04101
(207) 780-4044

Safe Power for Maine
P.O. Box 774
Camden 04843
(207) 236-3610

Shelter Institute
38 Center Street
Bath 04530
(207) 443-9084

Task Force on Human Needs
12 Park Hill Avenue
Auburn 04210
(207) 786-2481

We Who Care
81 Oak Street
Portland 04101
(207) 772-6395

MARYLAND

Baltimore Urban League
Consumer Services
1150 Mondawmin
Concourse
Baltimore 21215
(301) 523-8150

Betterment of United
Seniors (BUS)
5706 Sergeant Road
Chillum 20782
(301) 853-2400

Dorchester Community
Development Corp.
P.O. Box 549
445 Race Street
Cambridge 21613
(301) 228-3600

Garrett County Community
Action Committee, Inc.
P.O. Box 149
Oakland 21550
(301) 334-9431

The Greater Hampden Task
Force on Youth
3922 Hickory Avenue
Baltimore 21211
(301) 243-5431

Greenbelt Consumer
Services, Inc.
Corridor Industrial Park
8406 Greenwood Place
Savage 20863
(301) 953-2770

Maryland Action Coalition
901 Pershing Drive
Suite 201
Silver Springs 20910
(301) 585-4482

Maryland Action Coalition
Branch Office
5900 York Road
Baltimore 21212
(301) 433-8064

Maryland Association of
Housing Counselors
P.O. Box 549
Cambridge 21613
(301) 228-3600

Maryland Citizens Consumer
Council
P.O. Box 34526
Bethesda 20034
(301) 229-5900

Maryland Public Interest
Group
3110 Main Dining Hall
University of Maryland
College Park 20742

Neighborhoods Uniting
Project, Inc.
3501 Bunker Hill Road
Mt. Rainier 20822
(301) 277-7085

New Directions for Women
2515 N. Charles Street
Baltimore 21218
(301) 366-8570

St. Ambrose Housing Aid
Center, Inc.
321 E. 25th Street
Baltimore 21218
(301) 235-5770

Southeast Community
Organization
10 S. Wolfe Street
Baltimore 21231
(301) 327-1626

Southeast Development, Inc.
(SEDI)
10 S. Wolfe Street
Baltimore 21231
(301) 327-9100

United Communities Against
Poverty, Inc.
3308 Dodge Park Road,
Suite 300
Landover 20785
(301) 322-5255

MASSACHUSETTS

Action for Boston
Community Development
150 Tremont Street
Boston 02111
(617) 357-6000

Association of Massachusetts
Consumers
Boston College Economics
Department
140 Commonwealth Avenue
Chestnut Hill 02167
(617) 969-0100

Berkshire County Consumer
Advocates, Inc.
86 North Street
Pittsfield 01201
(413) 443-9128

Cambridge Economic
Opportunity Center
11 Inman
Cambridge 02139
(617) 868-2900

Consumer Action Center
721 State Street
Springfield 01109
(413) 737-4376

CP-PAX (Citizens for
Participation in Political
Action)
35 Kingston Street
Boston 02111
(617) 426-3040

Emergency Food Service
36 Concord Street
Framingham 01701
(617) 879-4870

Low Income Planning Aid
2 Park Square
Boston 02116
(617) 426-4363

Lynn Economic Opportunity
360 Washington Street
Lynn 01901
(617) 599-2217

Massachusetts Advocacy
Center
2 Park Square
Boston 02116
(617) 357-8431

Massachusetts Community
Center
364 Boyleston Street
2nd Floor
Boston 02116
(617) 266-7505

Massachusetts Consumer
Association
c/o Boston College
140 Commonwealth Avenue
Chestnut Hill 02167
(617) 969-0100

Massachusetts Fair Share
364 Boyleston, 2nd Floor
Boston 02116
(617) 266-7505

Massachusetts Law Reform
Institute
2 Park Square
Boston 02116
(617) 482-0890

Massachusetts Public
Interest Research Group
233 N. Pleasant Street
Amherst 01002
(413) 256-6434

Massachusetts Public
Interest Research Group
120 Boylston Street
Room 320
Boston 02116
(617) 423-1796

National Consumer Law
Center, Inc.
11 Beacon Street
Boston 02108
(617) 523-8010

Nutrition Program for the
Elderly
46 Concord Street
Framingham 01701
(617) 527-5383

MICHIGAN

The Calhoun Community
Action Agency
P.O. Box 1026
Battle Creek 49016
(616) 965-7766

Citizens for Better Care
163 Madison
Detroit 48226
(313) 962-5968

Consumer Affairs Bureau,
Kalamazoo County Chamber
of Commerce
500 W. Crosstown
Kalamazoo 49008
(616) 381-4004

Consumer Research
Advisory
2990 E. Grand Boulevard
Detroit 48202
(313) 873-2600

Environmental Advocacy
Program
School of Natural Resources
Dana Bldg., University of
Michigan
Ann Arbor 48104
(313) 764-1570 or 764-1511

Grand Rapids Urban League
Tenants Union
745 Eastern, S.E.
Grand Rapids 49503
(616) 241-6429

Greater Lansing Area for
Better Care
1514 W. Saginaw
Lansing 48915
(517) 482-1297

Greater Lansing Legal Aid
Bureau
300 N. Washington Avenue
P.O. Box 14171
Lansing 48901
(517) 485-5411

Housing Assistance
Foundation, Consumer
Services Program
935 N. Washington Avenue
Lansing 48906
(517) 487-5488

Kent County Legal Aid
430 Federal Square Bldg.
Grand Rapids 49503
(616) 774-0672

Landlord Tenant Clinic
149 Michigan Avenue
2nd Floor
Detroit 48226
(313) 963-1375

Mediation Services
1011 Student Activities
Bldg.
University of Michigan
Ann Arbor 48109
(313) 764-7455

Memorial Society of Greater
Detroit
4605 Cass
Detroit 48201
(313) TE 3-9107

Michigan Citizens Lobby
24525 Southfield Road
Southfield 48975
(313) 559-9260

Michigan Consumer Council
414 Hollister Bldg.
Lansing 48933
(517) 373-0947

Michigan Consumer
Education Center
217-A University Library
Eastern Michigan University
Ypsilanti 48197
(313) 487-2292

Michigan N.O.W.
22187 Michigan Avenue,
#209
Dearborn 48124
(313) 561-2424

Michigan Women's Equity
Action League (WEAL)
P.O. Box 1043
c/o Virginia O'Toole
Brautigan
Pontiac 48056
(313) 626-4905

The Nature Conservancy
531 N. Clippert
Lansing 48912
(517) 332-1741

Oakland/Livingston Human
Services Agency
196 Oakland Avenue
Pontiac 48058
(313) 858-5134

Public Interest Research
Group in Michigan
590 Hollister Bldg.
Lansing 48933
(517) 487-6001

Tenants Resource Center
855 Grove Street
East Lansing 48823
(517) 337-9795

West Michigan
Environmental Action
Council
1324 Lake Drive, S.E.
Grand Rapids 49506
(616) 451-3051

MINNESOTA

Alphabet Soup Reserve
Center
1401 S. Fifth
Minneapolis 55454
(612) 338-5239

Alternative Sources of
Energy Magazine
Route 2, Box 90A
Milaca 56353
(612) 983-6892

DANCE (Distributing
Alliance of the North
County Cooperatives)
1401 S. Fifth
Minneapolis 55454
(612) 338-5239

Minnesota Public Interest
Research Group
University of Minnesota
Kirby Student Union
Duluth 55812
(218) 726-8157

Minnesota Public Interest
Research Group
3036 University Avenue,
S.E.
Minneapolis 55414
(612) 376-7554

Northeastern Minnesota
Consumer's League
206 W. 4th Street
Duluth 55806
(218) 727-8973 x5

United Handicapped
Federation, Inc.
1951 University Avenue
St. Paul 55104
(612) 645-3417

MISSISSIPPI

Harrison County
Neighborhood Service
Center/Consumer Awareness
and Action Agency
P.O. Box 519
Gulfport 39501
(601) 864-3421

Mid-State Opportunity, Inc.
P.O. Drawer G
Charlestown 38921
(601) 647-2463

Mississippi Consumers
Association
375 Culley Drive
Jackson 39206
(601) 362-6643

Prairie Opportunity
P.O. Box 1526
Starkville 39759
(601) 323-7932

MISSOURI

Center for the Biology of
Natural Systems
c/o Jim Kendell
Washington University
St. Louis 63105
(314) 889-5369

Coalition for the
Environment
6267 Delmar Boulevard
St. Louis 63130
(314) 727-0600

Community Services, Inc.
214 W. Third
Maryville 64468
(816) 582-3114

Housewives Elect Lower
Prices
6942 Waterman
University City 63130
(314) 721-0494

HRC-Education Center
5547 Paseo
Kansas City 64110
(816) 363-8113

Human Resources
Corporation
911 E. Linwood
Kansas City 64109
(816) 756-3712

Legal Aid Society of the
City and County of St. Louis
607 N. Grand
St. Louis 63103
(314) 533-3000

Legal Aid Society of the
County of St. Louis
150 N. Merimac
St. Louis 63105
(314) 727-7791

Legal Aid Society of St.
Louis
5874 Delmar Boulevard
St. Louis 63112
(314) 367-7800

Legal Aid Society of St.
Louis
3684 Lindell Boulevard
St. Louis 63103
(314) 534-4311

Missouri A.C.O.R.N.
3177 S. Grand
St. Louis 63118
(314) 865-3835

Missouri Citizen Action
393 N. Euclid
St. Louis 63108
(314) 361-0777

Missouri Public Interest
Research Group, Inc.
Box 8276
St. Louis 63156
(314) 361-5200

Tax Reform Group
3177 S. Grand
St. Louis 63118
865-3835

Utility Consumers Council of
Missouri, Inc.
393 N. Euclid, Suite 32
St. Louis 63108
(314) 361-5725

MONTANA

Center for Public Interest
P.O. Box 1308
Bozeman 59715
(406) 587-0906

Consumer Affairs
805 N. Main
Helena 59601
(406) 449-4163

Montana Consumer Council
34 W. 6th Avenue
Helena 59601
(406) 449-2771

Montana Legal Services
Association
601 Power Block
Helena 59601
(406) 442-9830

Northern Plains Resource
Council
419 Stapleton
Billings 59101
(406) 248-1154

NEBRASKA

Nebraska Public Interest
Research Group
Nebraska Union #336
University of Nebraska
Lincoln 68508

NEVADA

Citizen Alert
3585 Ormsby Lane
Carson City 89701
(702) 849-0363

Consumer Affairs Division
State Mailroom Complex
Las Vegas 89158
(702) 386-5293

Consumer Protection
Division
Warshoe County District
Attorney's Office
Box 11130,
Reno 89520
(702) 785-5652

Consumers League of
Nevada
2154 Golden Arrow Drive
Las Vegas 89109
(702) 734-1587

Poor People Pulling
Together
1285 W. Miller
Las Vegas 89106
(702) 648-4645

NEW HAMPSHIRE

Clamshell Alliance
62 Congress Street
Portsmith 03801
(603) 436-5414

New England Non-Profit
Housing Development
Corporation
28 S. Main Street
Concord 03301
(603) 224-3363

New Hampshire Social
Welfare Council
20 S. Main Street
Box 1255
Concord 03301
(603) 228-0571

Newmarket Health Center,
Inc.
84 Main Street
Newmarket 03857
(603) 659-3106

Rockingham County Action
Program
50 S. School
Portsmith 03801
(603) 436-3897

SANE (Students Advocating
Natural Energy)
Room 154
Memorial Union Building
University of New
Hampshire
Durham 03824
(603) 862-2257

Senior Citizen Law Project
New Hampshire Legal
Assistance
136 North Main Street
Concord 03301
(603) 224-3333

Total Environmental Action
Churchill
Harrisville 03450
(603) 827-3374

NEW JERSEY

Action Now
City Hall
Plainfield 07061
(201) 753-3229

Community Union Project
389 N. Arlington Avenue
East Orange 07017

Consumers League of New
Jersey
20 Church Street
Montclair 07042
(201) 744-6449

East Orange Taxpayers
Organization
P.O. Box 109
East Orange 07017
(201) 672-5674

Newark Legal Services
Project
449 Central Avenue
Newark 07107
(201) 484-4010

New Jersey Council of
Churches
116 N. Orator Parkway
East Orange 07017
(201) 675-8600

New Jersey Federation of
Senior Citizens
638 Mill Street
Belleville 07109
(201) 759-3705

New Jersey Public Interest
Research Group
Rutgers Law School
5th and Penn Streets
Camden 08102
(609) 757-6175

New Jersey Public Interest
Research Group
Douglass College
College Center, Room 305
New Brunswick 08903
(201) 932-9277

New Jersey Public Interest
Research Group
32 W. Lafayette Street
Trenton 08608
(609) 393-7474

Ocean Community
Economic Action Now, Inc.
40 Washington Street
P.O. Box 1029
Toms River 08753
(201) 244-5337

Office of Economic
Opportunity
525 Penn Street
Camden 08102
(609) 541-7675

NEW MEXICO

All Indian Pueblo Council,
Inc. (A.I.P.C.)
1015 Indian School Road,
N.W.
P.O. Box 6507, Station B
Albuquerque 87197
(505) 247-0371

County Legal Services
420 W. Broadway
Farmington 87401
(503) 325-8886

Energy Consumers of New
Mexico
117 Richmond, N.E.
Albuquerque 87106
(505) 268-6792

Legal Aid Society
505 Marquette, N.W.
17th Floor
Western Bank Bldg.
Albuquerque 87102
(505) 243-3779

Senior Citizens Law Office
505 Marquette, N.W.
17th Floor
Western Bank Bldg.
Albuquerque 87102
(505) 243-3779

Southwest Research and
Information Center (S.R.I.C.)
Box 4524
Albuquerque 87106
(505) 242-4766

The Work Book
Box 5424
Albuquerque 87106
(505) 242-4766

NEW YORK

A.C.C.O.R.D.
264 E. Onondage Street
Syracuse 13202
(315) 422-2331

American Council on
Science and Health
c/o Dr. Elizabeth Whelan
1995 Broadway
New York 10023
(212) 362-7044

Area Four
977 Bedford Avenue
Brooklyn 11205
(212) 857-4521

Citizens Energy Council of
Western New York
P.O. Box 564
Wilson 14172
(716) 751-6227

Concerned Consumers of
Mid-Hudson Area, Inc.
P.O. Box 167
Kerhonkson 12446
(914) 626-7705

Consumer Action
1300 Elmwood Avenue
Claudell Hall, Room 302
Buffalo 14222
(716) 881-6154

Consumer Action Now
355 Lexington Avenue
16th Floor
New York 10017
(212) 682-8915

Consumer Credit
Counselling Service of
Buffalo, Inc.
43 Court Street
Walbridge Building
Buffalo 14202
(716) 854-1710

Council on Environmental
Alternatives
355 Lexington Avenue
16th Floor
New York 10017
(212) 682-8915

Flatbush Tenants' Council
1604 Newkirk Avenue
Brooklyn 11226
(212) 859-4717

Genesee Valley People's
Power Coalition
50 N. Plymouth
Rochester 14614
(716) 325-2560 or 325-2564

Harlem Consumer Education
Council, Inc.
1959 Madison Avenue
New York 10035
(212) 926-5300

Irate Consumers of Ulster
County
Box 149
Saugerties 12477
(914) 246-4021

National Coalition to Fight
Inflation
160 Fifth Avenue
New York 10010
(212) 924-7871

Neighborhood Council
Action Services Economic
Development
105-19 177th Street
Jamaica 11433
(212) 291-8115

New York City Community
Development Agency
349 Broadway
New York 10013
(212) 433-2238

New York Consumers
Assembly
465 Grand Street
New York 10002
(212) 674-5990

New York Public Interest
Research Group, Inc.
1 Columbia Place
Albany 12207
(518) 436-0876

New York Public Interest
Research Group
University Union
SUNY at Binghamton
Binghamton 13901
(607) 798-4971

New York Public Interest
Research Group, Inc.
Brooklyn College Chapter
1479 Flatbush Avenue
Brooklyn 11210
(212) 338-5906

New York Public Interest
Research Group
Queens College
153-11 61st Road
Flushing 11367
(212) 520-8616

New York Public Interest
Research Group, Inc.
5 Beekman Street
New York 10038
(212) 349-6460

New York Public Interest
Research Group
1004 E. Adams Street
Syracuse 13210
(315) 476-8381

Oswego County Consumer
Protection League
Route 8, Box 165
Oswego 13126
(315) 342-3850 or 343-6649
or 343-7852

P.E.A.C.E. INC. (People's
Equal Action Community
Effort)
117-119 Gifford Street
Syracuse 13202
(315) 475-0176

Upstate Community
Resource Institute
Box 732
Ithaca 14850
(607) 277-3505

Women's Resources
133 W. 72nd Street
New York 10023
(212) 724-6670

NORTH CAROLINA

North Carolina Consumers
Council, Inc.
c/o William Winn
RR 6, Box 94
Laurinburg 28352
(919) 276-7099

Operation Breakthrough,
Inc.
200 E. Unstead
P.O. Box 1470
Durham 27702
(919) 688-8111

NORTH DAKOTA

Area Low Income Council
1219 College Drive
Devils Lake 58301
(701) 662-5386

Quad County Consumer
Action
27½ S. Third, 3rd Floor
Grand Forks 58201
(701) 772-8989

OHIO

Cleveland Consumer Action
Foundation
532 Terminal Tower
Cleveland 44113
(216) 687-0525

Community Action
Commission of the
Cincinnati Area
801 Linn Street
Cincinnati 45203
(513) 241-1425

Consumer Conference of
Greater Cincinnati
c/o Mrs. Melba Kistner
6701 Highland Avenue
Cincinnati 45236
(513) 791-6515

Consumer Protection
Agency
420 Madison Avenue
Suite 1025
Toledo 43604
(419) 247-6191

Consumer Protection
Association
3134 Euclid
Cleveland 44115
(216) 881-3434

Consumers League of Ohio
513 Engineers Bldg.
Cleveland 44114
(216) 621-1175

El Centro
Rocky Ortiz, Director
3114 Pearl Avenue
Lorain 44055
(216) 277-8235 or (216)
277-1518

Free Stores, Inc.
2270 Vine Street
Cincinnati 45219
(513) 241-1064

Humanity House
475 W. Market Street
Akron 44303
(216) 253-7151

Lorain County Federation
for Human Services
Bob Groenert, Director
107 Oberlin Road
Elyria 44035
(216) 323-3333

Montgomery County
Community Action Agency
(CAA)
3304 N. Main
Dayton 45405
(513) 276-5011

NAACP
15½ E. Rich Street
Columbus 43215
(614) 221-5187

Neighborhood Home
Association
Lois Bielfelt, Director
1536 E. 39th Street
Lorain 44055
(216) 277-8269

Neighborhood Service
Center
125 S. South Street
Wilmington 45177
(513) 382-4462

Ohio Consumer Association
P.O. Box 52
20 Taylor Avenue
North Bend 45052
(513) 941-4289

Ohio Public Interest
Chester 12th Building
Room 340
Cleveland 44114
(216) 861-5200

Ohio Public Interest
Campaign
16 E. Broad Street
Columbus 43215
(614) 224-4111

Ohio Public Interest
Research Group
Box 25, Wilder Hall
Oberlin 44074
(216) 775-8137

Ohio Public Interest
Research Group
Box 577
University of Dayton
Dayton 45469
(513) 229-2110

Ohioans for Utility Reform
Box 10006
Columbus 43201
(614) 461-0136

People Power
475 W. Market Street
Akron 44303
(216) 434-8943

People's Rights for Benefits
647 Wilson
Columbus 43205
(614) 258-0342

Spanish Speaking
Department
c/o Sylvester Duran
1933 Spielbusch Avenue
Toledo 43624
(419) 248-4091

Spanish Speaking
Information Center
1118 Jackson
Toledo 43624
(419) 248-6261

Student Consumer Union
Bowling Green State
University
405C Student Services Bldg.
Bowling Green 43403
(419) 372-0248

Women Against Rape
P.O. Box 02084
Columbus 43202
(614) 291-9751

Women's Information Center
Ohio State House
Columbus 43215
(614) 466-5580

OKLAHOMA

Delta Community Action
Foundation, Inc.
1024 Main Street
Duncan 73433
(405) 255-3222

Legal Aid Society of
Oklahoma County, Inc.
Colcord Building
15 N. Robinson, 6th Floor
Oklahoma City 73102
(405) 272-9461 or 235-3659

Skyline Urban Ministry
701 N. W. 8th
Oklahoma City 73102
(405) 236-0775

OREGON

Community Care
Association, Inc.
2022 N.E. Alberta Street
Portland 97211
(503) 228-8321

Mid-Columbia Community
Action Council, Inc.
P.O. Box 726
The Dalles 97058
(503) 298-5131

Multnomah County Legal
Aid Service
310 S.W. 4th Avenue
Room 1100
Portland 97204
(503) 224-4086

Neighborhood House, Inc.
3030 S.W. 2nd Avenue
Portland 97201
(503) 226-3251

Nutrition Information Center
239 S.E. 13th Avenue
Portland 97214
(503) 235-9672

Oregon Consumer League
519 S.W. Third
Dekum Bldg, Room 412
Portland 97204
(503) 227-3882

Oregon Student Public
Interest Research Group
918 S.W. Yamhill
Portland 97205
(503) 222-9641

RAIN
2270 N.W. Irving
Portland 97210
(503) 227-5110

Tri-County Community
Council
Community Service Center
718 W. Burnside Street
Portland 97209
(503) 223-1030

PENNSYLVANIA

Action Alliance of Senior
Citizens of Greater
Philadelphia
401 N. Broad, Room 800
Philadelphia 19108
(215) 574-9050

Allegheny County Bureau of
Consumer Affairs
320 Jones Law Annex
311 Ross Street
Pittsburgh 15219
(412) 355-5405

Alliance for Consumer
Protection
1333 Sturdy Oak Drive
Pittsburgh 15220
(412) 279-1333

Areas of Concern
P.O. Box 47
Bryn Mawr 19010
(215) 525-1129

Bucks County Opportunity
Council
Nesshaminy Manor Center,
Route 611
Doylestown 18901
(215) 343-2800 ex. 360

Bureau of Consumer Affairs
35 E. High Street
Cumberland County
Carlisle 17013
(717) 249-1133

Citizens Choice Coalition of
Luzerne County
186 Barney Street
Wilkes Barre 18702
(717) 825-6049

Concerned Citizens of the
Delaware Valley
P.O. 47
Bryn Mawr 19010
(215) LA 5-1129

Consumer Education and
Protective Assn. (CEPA)
6048 Ogontz Avenue
Philadelphia 19141
(215) 424-1411

Consumer Protection
Department of Justice
1405 Locust
Philadelphia 19102
(215) 238-6475

Consumers United Together
(CUT)
1022 Birch Street
Scranton 18505
(717) 346-5642

Council of Spanish
70509 N. Franklin
Philadelphia 19123
(215) 574-3535

Department of Consumer
Protection
Courthouse Annex
Broad and Union Streets
Doylestown 18901
(215) 752-0281

Institute for Community
Services
Edinboro State College
Edinboro 16444
(814) 732-2451

Law Educational and
Participation Program
(LEAP)
Temple University
1719 N. Broad Street
Philadelphia 19122
(215) 787-8953

Lehigh Valley Commission
Box 1602
Allentown 18105
(215) 437-1177

North West Consumer
Council
Box 725
Edinboro 16412
(814) 732-2451

Northwest Tenants
Organization
5622 Germantown Avenue
Philadelphia 19144
(215) 849-7111

PAPIRG
Temple University School of
Law
1719 Broad Street
Philadelphia 19122
(215) 787-8951

Pennsylvania Citizens
Consumers Council
Box 17019
Pittsburgh 15235

Pennsylvania Consumers
Board
Houston Hall
3417 Spruce Street
3rd Floor
Philadelphia 19174
(215) 243-6000

Pennsylvania League for
Consumer Protection
212 Locust
Harrisburg 17108
(717) 233-5704

Philadelphia Consumer
Services Cooperative
3600 Conshohocken Avenue,
#1008
Philadelphia 19131
(215) GR 3-0482

Philadelphia Tenants
Organization
5622 Germantown Avenue
Philadelphia 19144
(215) 849-7111

State Tenants Organization
of Pennsylvania
1516 Peterson
Chester 19013
(215) 874-8421

Students for Penn P.I.R.G.
Pennsylvania University
20 Hetzel Union Bldg.
University Park 16802
(814) 865-6851

Taxpayer's Association
1 North 13th Street
Philadelphia 19107
(215) 567-0224

Tenant Action Group
1411 Walnut, Suite 826
Philadelphia 19102
(215) 563-5402

United Consumers of the
Alleghenies, Inc.
P.O. Box 997
Johnstown 15907
(814) 535-8608

Women's International
League for Peace and
Freedom
1213 Race Street
Philadelphia 19107
(215) 563-7110

PUERTO RICO

Department of Consumer
Affairs
c/o Fredricko Hermandez
Denton, Secy.
P.O. Box 13934
Santurce 00908
(809) 726-6090

RHODE ISLAND

Coalition for Consumer
Justice
410 Broad Street
Central Falls 02863
(401) 723-3147

Rhode Island Consumers'
Council
365 Broadway
Providence 02909
(401) 277-2764

Rhode Island Public Interest
Research Group
University of Rhode Island
Memorial Union, 232
Gorham Hall
Kingston 02881
(401) 792-2585

Rhode Island Public Interest
Research Group
Brown University, Box 2145
Providence 02912
(401) 863-2395

Rhode Island Workers
Association
371 Broadway
Providence 02903
(401) 751-2008

Urban League of Rhode
Island
246 Prairie Avenue
Providence 02905
(401) 351-5000

SOUTH CAROLINA

Chesterfield-Marlboro
Economic Opportunity
Council
71 Second Street
Cheraw 29520
(803) 537-5256

The People Are Coming
c/o Tom Turnipseed
560 Meeting Street
West Columbia, 29169
(803) 794-1512

South Carolina Public
Interest Research Group
Furman University
Greenville 29613
(803) 294-3088

SOUTH DAKOTA

ACORN
611 S. 2nd Avenue
Sioux Falls 57104
(605) 332-2328

Community Action
610 2nd Avenue, East
Sisseton 57262
(605) 698-7654

Consumer Protection
State Capitol Bldg.
Pierre 57501
(605) 773-6691

Consumer Protection
408 W. 34th Street
Sioux Falls 57101
(605) 339-6691

East Dakota Co-op
335 S. Phillips
Sioux Falls 57102
(605) 339-9506

N.E. South Dakota
Community Action Program
610 2nd Avenue, East
Sisseton 57262
(605) 698-7654

Western South Dakota
Community Action, Inc.
5001 Sturges Road
Rapid City 57701
(605) 348-1460

TENNESSEE

Church Women United
c/o Mrs. Richard Bauer
3809 Brighton Road
Nashville 37205
(615) 383-8284

Coal Employment Project
Oakridge Turnpike
Oakridge 37830
(615) 482-3428

Community Services
Administration
444 James Robertson
Parkway
Nashville 37219
(615) 741-2615

Elk and Duck Rivers
Community Association
701 S. Lincoln Avenue
Fayetteville 37334
(615) 433-7182

Environment Center
University of Tennessee
South Stadium Hall
Knoxville 37916
(615) 974-4251

The Highlander Center
Rt. 3, Box 370
New Market 37820
(615) 933-3443

Kingsport Power Users
President: C.E.C. Britton
1010 Wateree
Kingsport 37660
(615) 245-1102

League of Women Voters,
Energy Committee
c/o Rosemary Conrad
406 Chesterfield Avenue
Nashville 37212
(615) 269-9777

Safe Energy in Tennessee
c/o Janine Honiger
362 Brinkley Avenue
Nashville 37211
(615) 832-0392

Save Our Cumberland
Mountains (SOCM)
Jacksboro 37757
(615) 562-6247

Tenn ACORN
2649 Yale
Memphis 38104
(901) 452-8223

TEXAS

Community Action
Resources
1510 Plum Street
Texarkana 75501
(214) 794-3386

Dallas Community Action
Consumer Education Dept.
2208 Main
Dallas 75201
(214) 742-2500, ex. 25

Dallas County Community
Action Center
2208 Main Street
Dallas 75201
(214) 742-2500

Low Income Consumer Club
1510 Plum Street
Texarkana 75701
(214) 794-3386

Public Advocate Review of
Texas
Box 13052
Austin 78711
(512) 441-3148

Senior Citizens Service, Inc.,
of Texarkana
P.O. Box 619
Texarkana 75501
(214) 792-5131

Southwest Utility Watch
Southwest Utility Associates
Box 13052
Austin 78711
(512) 441-3148

Tarrant County Legal
Services
810 Houston, #406
Fort Worth 76102
(817) 334-1435

TCA Education Fund
c/o Ronny Luna
Stuart Title Building
Suite 200
812 San Antonio
Austin 78701
(512) 477-1882

Texas ACORN
4415 San Jacinto
Dallas 75204
(214) 823-4580

Texas Consumer Association
c/o Ronny Luna
Stuart Title Building
Suite 200
812 San Antonio
Austin 78701
(512) 477-1882

Texas Public Interest
Research Group
Rice University
Rice Memorial Center
Houston 77001
(713) 527-4099

Texas Public Interest
Research Group
Box 237-UC
University of Houston
Houston 77004
(713) 749-3130

West Texas Legal Services
810 Houston, #406
Fort Worth 76102
(817) 334-1435

UTAH

Consumer Information
Utah State University
444 S. 300 West
Salt Lake City 84101
(801) 533-7752

Division of Public Utilities
330 East 4th, South
Salt Lake City 84111
(801) 533-5511

League of Utah Consumers
c/o Jane Osborne
147 North, 200 West
Salt Lake City 84103
(801) 533-4124

Ogden Area Community
Action Center
206 24th Street
Ogden 84401
(801) 399-9281

Salt Lake Community Action
Program
28 East, 2100 South
Chapman Plaza, Room 101
Salt Lake City 84115
(801) 582-8181

Utah Consumer Advisory
Committee
c/o Jane Osborne
147 North 200 West
Salt Lake City 84103
(801) 533-4124

Utah Home Economics
Association
c/o Maureen Humphries
5110 Birch Creek Drive
Ogden 84403
(801) 392-7844

Utah Issues and Information
Converse Hall
Westminster College
1840 South 1300 East
Salt Lake City 84105
(801) 467-4825

Utah Nutrition Council
College of Family Life
Utah State University
Logan 84322
(801) 752-4100 ex.7691

Utah State Coalition of
Senior Citizens
306 E. 1st
Salt Lake City 84111
(801) 467-1273 or 359-9705

VERMONT

Bread and Law Task Force
5 State Street
Montpelier 05602
(802) 229-0320

Central Vermont Community
Action Council
15 Ayers Street
Barre 05641
(802) 479-0136

Vermont Alliance
5 State Street
Montpelier 05602
(802) 229-9104

Vermont Public Interest
Research Group, Inc.
26 State Street
Montpelier 05602
(802) 223-5221

Vermont Public Interest
Research and Education
Fund (VPIREF)
26 State Street
Montpelier 05602
(902) 223-5221

Vermont Workers Rights
Project
5 State Street
Montpelier 05602
(802) 229-9104

VIRGINIA

Brumley GAP Concerned
Citizens Association
Secretary: Levonda
McDaniel
Route 7
Abingdon 24210

Citizens Energy Forum
P.O. Box 138
Mc Clain 22101
(703) 528-7703

Citizens for the Preservation
of Floyd County
c/o Bill Blatter
Route 1, Box 176 A
Pilot 24138
(703) 651-8111

The Coalition of
Appalachian Energy
Consumers
c/o Dick Austin
Box 275
Castlewood 24224
(703) 467-2437

Concerned Citizens for
Justice, Inc. (CCJ)
P.O. Box 1409
Wise 24293
(703) 328-9239

Consumer Congress of
Virginia
3122 W. Clay Street
Richmond 23230
(804) 355-6947

Council of the Southern
Mountain
Drawer N
Clintwood 24228
(904) 926-4495 or 926-4489

Land, Air and Water
P.O. Box 238
Clintwood 24228
(703) 762-7985 or 762-7668

New River Coalition
1527 N. Main Street
Attention: Andrew
Campagnola
Blacksburg 24060
(703) 951-2525

New River Community
Action, Inc.
P.O. Box 570
Christiansberg 24073
(703) 382-6186

Office of Appalachian
Ministry
Box 1376
Wise 24293
(703) 328-6800

Old Dominion Chapter, the
Sierra Club
Sue Fulghum, Chairperson
13412 Woodbrian Ridge
Midlothian 23113
(804) 744-1739

Piedmont Alliance
c/o Lindsey Moss
Box 521
Charlottesville 22902
(804) 293-3713

Pittsylvania County
Community Action Agency
P.O. Box 936
Chatham 24531
(804) 432-8250

Retired Senior Citizens
507 Winona Avenue
Peavisburg 24134
(703) 921-2037

Richmond Alternative
Energy Committee
c/o John Sundholm
Box 25007
Richmond 23260
(804) 232-8536

Rockbridge Energy
Information Council
Route 1, Box 35 A
c/o Tom Muckinghaupt
Vesuvius 24483
(804) 377-6397

SAFE Alternatives for Future
Energy of Nelson County
c/o Piper Hollier
Box 89
Covesville 22931
(804) 361-2110

Save Our National Forest
Secretary, Gray Wilson
Route 1, Box 174A
Dungannon 24245

Scott County Sportsmen's
Association
President, Kyle Bishop
Route 1, Box 278
Duffield, 24244
(804) 431-2187

Southwest Virginia Black
Lung Association
P.O. Box 1409
Wise 24293
(703) 328-9239

Stoney Creek Citizens
Committee
Grace Fraysier, Pres.
Route 1, Box 225
Clinchport 24227
(703) 995-2280

The Sunshine Alliance
c/o Piper Hollier
Box 89
Covesville 22931
(804) 361-2110

Total Action Against Poverty
(TAP)
c/o Doug Gordon
P.O. Box 2868
Roanoke 24001
(703) 345-6781

Trout Unlimited, Virginia
Chapter
C. Dixon, Pres.
Route 1, Box 12
Fisherville 22939
(203) 942-0589

Truth in Power
Box 325 c/o John Wills
Virginia Beach 23458
(804) 461-7902

United Citizens Against Fuel
Adjustment
Box 1376
Wise 24293
(703) 328-6800

Virginia Citizens Consumer
Council
823 E. Main, Room 1904
Richmond 23219
(804) 643-2511
Mail: P.O. Box 5462
Richmond 23220

Virginia Citizens Consumer
Council
Box 777
Springfield 22150
(703) 437-4417

Virginia Citizens Consumer
Council
c/o Doug Gordon
R 2, Box 340 A.D.
Troutville 24175
(703) 992-2452

Virginia Citizens Consumer
Council, Roanoke Chapter
702 Shenandoah Avenue,
N.W.
Roanoke 24016
(703) 345-6781

Virginia Citizens for
Reclamation
P.O. Box 390
c/o Frank Kilgore
St. Paul 24283
(703) 762-7985 7668

VIRGIN ISLANDS

Consumer Services
Administration
P.O. Box 599
St. Thomas 00801
(809) 774-3130

WASHINGTON

Blue Mountain Action
Council
19 E. Poplar Street
Walla Walla 99362
(509) 529-4980

Central Area Motivation
Program Consumer Action
105 14th, Suite D
Seattle 98122
(206) 324-1166

Central Seattle Community
Council Federation
4710 University Way, N.E.
Seattle 98105
(206) 522-8507

Citizens Action
P.O. Box 159
Bellingham 98225
(206) 734-5121

Community Action Council
P.O. Box 553
Port Townsend 98368
(206) 385-0776

Environmental Affairs
Commission
204 Q Hub FK-10
University of Washington
Seattle 98195
(206) 543-8700

Hunger Action Center
1063 Capitol Way
Olympia 98501
(206) 352-7980

Hunger Action Center
Alaska Building
2nd and Cherry
Seattle 98104
(206) 682-3326

Hunger Action Center
E 7211-3rd Avenue
Spokane 99206
(509) 924-8118

Seattle Consumer Action
Network
P. O. Box 22455
Seattle, WA 98122
(206) 324-1196

Spokane Office of Legal
Services
N. 14 Howard, Suite 310
Spokane 99201
(509) 838-3671

Washington Public Interest
Research Group
Student Union Building
Fk-10
University of Washington
Seattle 98195
(206) 543-0434

WEST VIRGINIA

Appalachian Research and
Defense Fund
1116 B Kanawha Boulevard,
East
Charleston 25301
(304) 344-9687

Citizens for Environmental
Protection
Pres. David Wooley
1911 Pine Manor Road
Charlestown 25311
(304) 342-5855

Council of the Southern
Mountains West Virginia
Branch
125 McDowell Street
Welch 24801
(304) 436-2185

Multi-County Community
Against Poverty (Multi
C.A.P. Inc.)
P.O. Box 3228
Charleston 25332
(304) 343-4175

North-Central West Virginia
Community Action Assoc.
Inc.
208 Adams Street
Fairmont 26554
(304) 363-2170

Save New River
Pres. William Farley
Box 66
Pipestem 25979
(304) 466-1394

Save Our Mountains
Box 567
Charleston 25322
(304) 344-9687

Stop the Powerline
Steve Hill, Pres.
Box 196
Culloden 25510
(304) 344-9687

West Virginia Citizens
Action Group
1324 Virginia Street, E
Charleston 25301
(304) 346-5891

West Virginia Public Interest
Research Group
S.O.W. Mountainlair
West Virginia University
Morgantown 26506
(304) 293-2108

WISCONSIN

Center for Community
Leadership Development
610 Langdon
Lowell Hall, Room 532
Madison 53703

Center for Consumer Affairs
University of Wisconsin
Extension
929 N. 6th Street
Milwaukee 53203
(414) 224-4177

Center for Public
Representation
520 University Avenue
Madison 53703
(608) 251-4008

Central Wisconsin
Community Action Council,
Inc.
211 Wisconsin Avenue
P.O. Box 448
Wisconsin Dells 53965
(608) 254-8353

Civicom
c/o Norene Goplen
319 Main Street, #112
La Crosse 54601
(608) 782-8142

Citizens for Community
Health
306 N. Brooks Street
Madison 53715
(608) 255-2255

The Concerned Consumers
League, Inc.
614 W. National Avenue
Milwaukee 53204
(414) 645-1808

ESHAC, Inc.
531 E. Burleigh Street
Milwaukee 53212
(414) 372-2473

Inner City Development
Project
2803 N. Teutonia
Milwaukee 53206
(414) 265-7410

Inner City Development
Project
1725 S. 12th Street
Milwaukee 53204
(414) 643-8444

Inner City Development
Project
161 W. Wisconsin
Milwaukee 53203
(414) 272-6256

Inner City Development
Project
2669 N. Holton
Milwaukee 53212
(414) 265-3175

Racine County Community
Action Committee, Inc.
Memorial Hall
72 7th Street, 2nd Floor
Racine 53403
(414) 633-1883

Skilled Jobs for Women
625 W. Washington
2nd Floor
Madison 53703
(608) 257-4373

Wisconsin Consumer's
League
c/o Barbara Hohman
State Arts Board
123 W. Washington Avenue
Madison 53706
(608) 266-0237

Wisconsin N.O.W.
c/o Chris Roerden
Box 422
Elmgrove 53122
(414) 784-1694

WYOMING

Citizens for the Survival of
the Red Desert
c/o Jack Pugh
2135 Mississippi
Green River 82935
(307) 875-6239

Defenders of the Wildlife
c/o Dick Randall
1120 McKinley
Rock Springs 82901
(307) 362-5379

Powder River Basin
Resource Council
48 N. Main
Sheridan 82801
(307) 672-5809

Rawlins Rockbound Gem
and Mineral Club
P.O. Box 1253
c/o Bill Murray
Rawlins 82301
(307) 324-9612

Wilderness Society
c/o Bart Koehler
Box 876
Laramie 82070
(307) 745-5875

Wyoming Consumers United
Program
864 S. Spruce Street
Casper 82601
(307) 234-6060

Wyoming Outdoor Council
P.O. Box 1184
2003 Central Street
Cheyenne 82001
(307) 635-3416

Index